Microsoft® Office Excel 2003

ILLUSTRATED, CourseCard Edition

INTRODUCTORY

Microsoft Office Specialist Program

WHAT DOES THIS LOGO MEAN?

It means this courseware has been approved by the Microsoft® Office Specialist Program to be among the finest available for learning one or more of the applications of the Microsoft Office 2003 Suite. It also means that upon completion of this courseware, you may be prepared to take an exam for Microsoft Office Specialist qualification. If "1 of 2" or "2 of 2" appears below the logo on the cover, this indicates this courseware has been approved as part of a sequence of texts for preparation to become a Microsoft Office Specialist. See the table below for more information.

WHAT IS A MICROSOFT OFFICE SPECIALIST?

A Microsoft Office Specialist is an individual who has passed exams for certifying his or her skills in one or more of the Microsoft Office desktop applications such as Microsoft Word, Microsoft Excel, Microsoft PowerPoint®, Microsoft Outlook®, Microsoft Access, or Microsoft Project. The Microsoft Office Specialist Program is the only program in the world approved by Microsoft for testing proficiency in Microsoft Office desktop applications and Microsoft Project. This testing program can be a valuable asset in any job search or career advancement.

ILLUSTRATED TITLES FOR OFFICE 2003 MICROSOFT OFFICE SPECIALIST CERTIFICATION

The Illustrated Series offers a growing number of Microsoft-approved courseware products that cover the objectives required to pass a Microsoft Office Specialist exam. After studying with any of the books listed below, you should be prepared to take the Microsoft office Specialist Program exam indicated. The following titles have certification approval as courseware for the Microsoft Office Specialist program:

Exam	Course Technology Illustrated Series Textbook
Microsoft Office Access 2003	Microsoft Office Access 2003 – Illustrated Introductory, CourseCard Edition (1-4188-4298-2) or Microsoft Office Access 2003 – Illustrated Complete, CourseCard Edition (1-4188-4299-0)
Microsoft Office Excel 2003	Microsoft Office Excel 2003 – Illustrated Introductory, CourseCard Edition (1-4188-4295-8)
Microsoft Office Excel 2003 Expert	Microsoft Office Excel 2003 – Illustrated Complete, CourseCard Edition (1-4188-4296-6)
Microsoft Office PowerPoint 2003	Microsoft Office PowerPoint 2003 – Illustrated Introductory, CourseCard Edition (1-4188-4304-0)
Microsoft Office Word 2003	Microsoft Office Word 2003 – Illustrated Introductory, CourseCard Edition (1-4188-4301-6)
Microsoft Office Word 2003 Expert	Microsoft Office Word 2003 – Illustrated Complete, CourseCard Edition (1-4188-4302-4)
Microsoft Office 2003 (separate exams for Word, Excel, Access and PowerPoint)	Microsoft Office 2003 – Illustrated Introductory (0-619-05789-0) and Microsoft Office 2003 – Illustrated Second Course (0-619-18826-X) when used in a sequence, meet the requirements for Microsoft Office Specialist for Word, Excel, Access, and PowerPoint.

MORE INFORMATION:

To learn more about becoming a Microsoft Office Specialist, visit www.microsoft.com/officespecialist.

To learn about other Microsoft Office Specialist approved courseware from Course Technology, visit www.course.com.

Microsoft® Office Excel 2003
ILLUSTRATED, CourseCard Edition

INTRODUCTORY

Elizabeth Eisner Reding • Lynn Wermers

THOMSON
COURSE TECHNOLOGY

Australia • Canada • Mexico • Singapore • Spain • United Kingdom • United States

Microsoft® Office Excel 2003—Illustrated Introductory, CourseCard Edition

Elizabeth Eisner Reding, Lynn Wermers

Vice President,
End User Publishing:
Nicole Jones Pinard

Managing Editor:
Marjorie Hunt

Production Editors:
Aimee Poirier, Summer Hughes

QA Manuscript Reviewers:
Alex White, Chris Carvalho

Senior Product Manager:
Christina Kling Garrett

Product Manager:
Jane Hosie-Bounar

Developmental Editors:
Kim Crowley, Barbara Clemens

Text Designer:
Joseph Lee, Black Fish Design

Associate Product Manager:
Emilie Perreault

Editorial Assistant:
Shana Rosenthal

Composition House:
GEX Publishing Services

The Illustrated Series Vision

Teaching and writing about computer applications can be extremely rewarding and challenging. How do we engage students and keep their interest? How do we teach them skills that they can easily apply on the job? As we set out to write this book, our goals were to develop a textbook that:

- works for a beginning student

- provides varied, flexible, and meaningful exercises and projects to reinforce the skills

- serves as a reference tool

- makes your job as an educator easier, by providing resources above and beyond the textbook to help you teach your course

Our popular, streamlined format is based on advice from instructional designers and customers. This flexible design presents each lesson on a two-page spread, with step-by-step instructions on the left, and screen illustrations on the right. This signature style, coupled with high-caliber content, provides a comprehensive yet manageable introduction to Microsoft Office Excel 2003—it is a teaching package for the instructor and a learning experience for the student.

About This Edition

New to this edition is a free, tear-off Excel 2003 CourseCard that provides students with a great way to have Excel skills at their fingertips!

Acknowledgments

Creating a book of this magnitude is a team effort. I would like to thank my husband, Michael, as well as Christina Kling Garrett, the project manager who experienced a true baptism-by-fire, Emilie Perreault, associate product manager, and my development editor, Kim Crowley, for her suggestions and corrections. I would also like to thank the production and editorial staff for all their hard work that made this project a reality.

Elizabeth Eisner Reding

I would like to thank Barbara Clemens for her insightful contributions and guidance. I would also like to thank Christina Kling Garrett for patiently answering and researching my endless questions.

Lynn Wermers

Preface

Welcome to *Microsoft Office® Excel 2003–Illustrated Introductory, CourseCard Edition.* Each lesson in this book contains elements pictured to the right.

How is the book organized?

The book is organized into eight units on Excel, covering creating and editing worksheets, formatting worksheets, and working with charts. Managing workbooks, automating tasks, and using lists are also covered.

What kinds of assignments are included in the book? At what level of difficulty?

The lessons use MediaLoft, a fictional chain of bookstores, as the case study. The assignments on the light purple pages at the end of each unit increase in difficulty. Data Files and case studies, with many international examples, provide a great variety of interesting and relevant business applications. Assignments include:

- **Concepts Reviews** include multiple choice, matching, and screen identification questions.

- **Skills Reviews** provide additional hands-on, step-by-step reinforcement.

- **Independent Challenges** are case projects requiring critical thinking and application of the unit skills. The Independent Challenges increase in difficulty, with the first one in each unit being the easiest (most step-by-step with detailed instructions). Independent Challenges 2 and 3 become increasingly open-ended, requiring more independent problem solving.

- **E-Quest Independent Challenges** are case projects with a Web focus. E-Quests require the use of the World Wide Web to conduct research to complete the project.

- **Advanced Challenge Exercises** set within the Independent Challenges provide optional steps for more advanced students.

- **Visual Workshops** are practical, self-graded capstone projects that require independent problem solving.

Each 2-page spread focuses on a single skill.

Concise text introduces the basic principles in the lesson and integrates a real-world case study.

UNIT
C
Excel 2003

Applying Colors, Patterns, and Borders

You can use colors, patterns, and borders to enhance the overall appearance of a worksheet and to make it easier to read. You can add these enhancements by using the Patterns or Borders tabs in the Format Cells dialog box or by using the Borders and Color buttons on the Formatting toolbar. You can apply color or patterns to the background of a cell, to a range, or to cell contents. You can also apply borders to all the cells in a worksheet or only to selected cells to call attention to individual cells or groups of cells. See Table C-4 for a list of border buttons and their functions. Jim asks you to add a pattern, a border, and color to the title of the worksheet to give the worksheet a more professional appearance.

STEPS

QUICK TIP
Use color sparingly. Too much color can divert the reader's attention from the worksheet data.

1. Press [Ctrl][Home] to select cell A1, then click the Fill Color list arrow on the Formatting toolbar
   The color palette appears.

2. Click the Turquoise color (fourth row, fifth column)
   Cell A1 has a turquoise background, as shown in Figure C-14. Cell A1 spans columns A through I because of the Merge and Center command used for the title.

3. Right-click cell A1, then click Format Cells on the shortcut menu
   The Format Cells dialog box opens.

4. Click the Patterns tab if it is not already displayed
   See Figure C-15. Adding a pattern to cells can add to the visual interest of your worksheet.

5. Click the Pattern list arrow, click the Thin Diagonal Crosshatch pattern (third row, last column), then click OK
   A border also enhances a cell's appearance. Unlike underlining, which is a text-formatting tool, borders extend to the width of the cell.

QUICK TIP
You can also draw cell borders using the mouse pointer. Click the Borders list arrow on the Formatting toolbar, click Draw Borders, then drag to create borders or boxes.

6. Click the Borders list arrow on the Formatting toolbar, then click the Thick Bottom Border (second row, second column) on the Borders palette
   It can be difficult to view a border in a selected cell.

7. Click cell A3
   The border is a nice enhancement. Font color can also help distinguish information in a worksheet.

QUICK TIP
The default color on the Fill Color and Font Color buttons changes to the last color you selected.

8. Select the range A3:I3, click the Font Color list arrow on the Formatting toolbar, then click the Blue color (second row, third column from the right) on the palette
   The text changes color, as shown in Figure C-16.

9. Click the Save button on the Standard toolbar

Clues to Use

Formatting columns or rows
You can save yourself time by formatting an entire column or row using any of the categories that appear in the Format Cells dialog box. You might, for example, want to format all the cells within a column to accept telephone numbers, social security numbers, zip codes, or custom number formats. Click the column or row heading—located at the top of a column or beginning of a row—to select the entire column or row. You can format a selected column or row by clicking Format on the menu bar, clicking Cells, then clicking the appropriate tab in the Format Cells dialog box.

EXCEL C-12 FORMATTING A WORKSHEET

OFFICE-262

Tips, as well as troubleshooting advice, right where you need them—next to the step itself.

Clues to Use boxes provide concise information that either expands on the major lesson skill or describes an independent task that in some way relates to the major lesson skill.

vi

Every lesson features large, full-color representations of what the screen should look like as students complete the numbered steps.

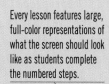

FIGURE C-14: Background color added to cell

Cell A1 with turquoise background

FIGURE C-15: Patterns tab in the Format Cells dialog box

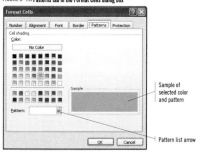

Sample of selected color and pattern

Pattern list arrow

FIGURE C-16: Worksheet with colors, patterns, and border

TABLE C-4: Border buttons

button	function	button	function	button	function
	No Border		Bottom Double Border		Top and Thick Bottom Border
	Bottom Border		Thick Bottom Border		All Borders
	Left Border		Top and Bottom Border		Outside Borders
	Right Border		Top and Double Bottom Border		Thick Box Border

Tables provide quickly accessible summaries of key terms, toolbar buttons, or keyboard alternatives connected with the lesson material. Students can refer easily to this information when working on their own projects at a later time.

The pages are numbered according to application and unit. Excel indicates the application, C indicates the unit, 13 indicates the page.

What online content solutions are available to accompany this book?

Visit www.course.com for more information on our online content for Illustrated titles. Options include:

MyCourse 2.0

Need a quick, simple tool to help you manage your course? Try MyCourse 2.0, the easiest to use, most flexible syllabus and content management tool available. MyCourse 2.0 offers you brand new content, including Topic Reviews, Extra Case Projects, and Quizzes, to accompany this book.

WebCT

Course Technology and WebCT have partnered to provide you with the highest quality online resources and Web-based tools for your class. Course Technology offers content for this book to help you create your WebCT class, such as a suggested Syllabus, Lecture Notes, Practice Test questions, and more.

Blackboard

Course Technology and Blackboard have also partnered to provide you with the highest quality online resources and Web-based tools for your class. Course Technology offers content for this book to help you create your Blackboard class, such as a suggested Syllabus, Lecture Notes, Practice Test questions, and more.

Is this book Microsoft Office Specialist Certified?

Microsoft Office Excel 2003—Illustrated Introductory, CourseCard Edition covers the objectives for Microsoft Office Excel 2003 and has received certification approval as courseware for the Microsoft Office Specialist program. See page ii (the back of the first title page) for more information on other Illustrated titles meeting Microsoft Office Specialist certification.

The first page of each unit indicates which objectives in the unit are Microsoft Office Specialist skills. If an objective is set in red, it meets a Microsoft Office Specialist skill. A document in the Review Pack cross-references the skills with the lessons and exercises.

Excel 2003

Instructor Resources

The Instructor Resources CD is Course Technology's way of putting the resources and information needed to teach and learn effectively into your hands. With an integrated array of teaching and learning tools that offers you and your students a broad range of technology-based instructional options, we believe this CD represents the highest quality and most cutting edge resources available to instructors today. Many of these resources are available at www.course.com. The resources available with this book are:

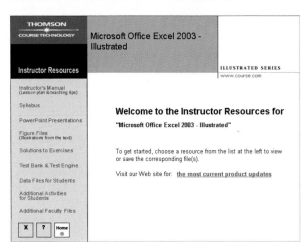

• **Data Files for Students**—To complete most of the units in this book, your students will need **Data Files**. Put them on a file server for students to copy. The Data Files are available on the Instructor Resources CD-ROM, and in the Review Pack, and can also be downloaded from www.course.com.

Instruct students to use the **Data Files List** located in the Review Pack and on the Instructor Resources CD. This list gives instructions on copying and organizing files.

• **Solutions to Exercises**—Solutions to Exercises contains every file students are asked to create or modify in the lessons and End-of-Unit material. A Help file on the Instructor Resources CD includes information for using the Solution Files. There is also a document outlining the solutions for the End-of-Unit Concepts Review, Skills Review, and Independent Challenges.

• **PowerPoint Presentations**—Each unit has a corresponding PowerPoint presentation that you can use in a lecture, distribute to your students, or customize to suit your course.

• **Instructor's Manual**—Available as an electronic file, the Instructor's Manual is quality-assurance tested and includes unit overviews, and detailed lecture topics with teaching tips for each unit.

• **Sample Syllabus**—Prepare and customize your course easily using this sample course outline.

• **Figure Files**—The figures in the text are provided on the Instructor Resources CD to help you illustrate key topics or concepts. You can create traditional overhead transparencies by printing the figure files. Or you can create electronic slide shows by using the figures in a presentation program such as PowerPoint.

• **ExamView**—ExamView is a powerful testing software package that allows you to create and administer printed, computer (LAN-based), and Internet exams. ExamView includes hundreds of questions that correspond to the topics covered in this text, enabling students to generate detailed study guides that include page references for further review. The computer-based and Internet testing components allow students to take exams at their computers, and also saves you time by grading each exam automatically.

SAM 2003 Assessment & Training

SAM 2003 helps you energize your class exams and training assignments by allowing students to learn and test important computer skills in an active, hands-on environment.

With SAM 2003 Assessment, you create powerful interactive exams on critical applications such as Word, Outlook, PowerPoint, Windows, the Internet, and much more. The exams simulate the application environment, allowing your students to demonstrate their knowledge and think through the skills by performing real-world tasks.

Designed to be used with the Illustrated series, SAM 2003 Assessment & Training includes built-in page references so students can create study guides that match the Illustrated textbooks you use in class. Powerful administrative options allow you to schedule exams and assignments, secure your tests, and run reports with almost limitless flexibility.

Brief Contents

Contents

EXCEL 2003	Working with Charts	D-1

| EXCEL 2003 | **Using Lists** | **H-1** |

Read This Before You Begin

Software Information and Required Installation

This book was written and tested using Microsoft Office 2003 - Professional Edition, with a typical installation on Microsoft Windows XP plus installation of the latest Service Pack, and with Internet Explorer 6.0 or higher. Some of the exercises in this book assume that your computer is connected to the Internet. If you are not connected to the Internet, see your instructor for information.

Tips for Students

What are Data Files?

To complete many of the units in this book, you need to use Data Files. A Data File contains a partially completed document, so that you don't have to type in all the information in the document yourself. Your instructor will either provide you with copies of the Data Files or ask you to make your own copies. Your instructor can also give you instructions on how to organize your files, as well as a complete file listing, or you can find the list and the instructions for organizing your files in the Review Pack.

You will also need to create a Unit G folder at the same level as your other unit folders. There are no Data Files supplied for Unit G, but you will need to save the files you create in your Unit G folder.

Why is my screen different from the book?

Your Desktop components and some dialog box options might be different if you are using an operating system other than Windows XP.

Depending on your computer hardware and the display settings on your computer, you may also notice the following differences:

- Your screen may look larger or smaller because of your screen resolution (the height and width of your screen).

- Your title bars and dialog boxes may not display file extensions. To display file extensions, click Start on the taskbar, click Control Panel, click Appearance and Themes, then click Folder Options. Click the View tab if necessary, click Hide extensions for known file types to deselect it, then click OK. Your Office dialog boxes and title bars should now display file extensions.

- The colors of the title bar in your screen may be a solid blue, and the cells in Excel may appear different from the orange and gray because of your color settings

- Depending on your Office settings, your toolbars may be displayed on a single row and your menus may display a shortened list of frequently used commands. Office menus and toolbars can modify themselves to your working style by displaying only the most frequently used buttons and menu commands. To view buttons not currently displayed, click a Toolbar Options button ⌐ at the end of either the Standard or Formatting toolbar. To view the full list of menu commands, click the double arrow at the bottom of the menu.

Toolbars in one row

Toolbars in two rows

In order to have your toolbars displayed in two rows, showing all buttons, and to have the full menus displayed, you must turn off the personalized menus and toolbars feature. Click Tools on the menu bar, click Customize, select the show Standard and Formatting toolbars on two rows and Always show full menus check boxes on the Options tab, and then click Close. This book assumes you are displaying toolbars in two rows and displaying full menus.

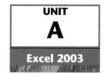

Getting Started with Excel 2003

OBJECTIVES

Define spreadsheet software
Start Excel 2003
View the Excel window
Open and save a workbook
Enter labels and values
Name and move a sheet
Preview and print a worksheet
Get Help
Close a workbook and exit Excel

If you have a SAM user profile, you may have access to hands-on instruction, practice, and assessment of the skills covered in this unit. Log in to your SAM account and go to your assignments page to see what your instructor has assigned.

In this unit, you will learn how to start Microsoft Office Excel 2003 and identify elements in the Excel window. You will also learn how to open and save existing files, enter data in a worksheet, manipulate worksheets, and use the extensive Help system. ▰▰▰ Jim Fernandez is the office manager at MediaLoft, a chain of bookstore cafés founded in 1988. MediaLoft stores offer customers the opportunity to purchase books, music, and movies while enjoying a variety of coffees, teas, and freshly baked desserts. Jim wants you, his assistant, to learn how to use Excel and help him analyze a worksheet summarizing budget information for the MediaLoft café in the New York City location.

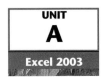

Defining Spreadsheet Software

Microsoft Excel is an electronic spreadsheet program that runs on Windows computers. You use an **electronic spreadsheet** to produce professional-looking documents that perform numeric calculations rapidly and accurately. These calculations are updated automatically so that accurate information is always available. See Table A-1 for common ways spreadsheets are used in business. The electronic spreadsheet that you produce when using Excel is also referred to as a **worksheet**. Individual worksheets are stored within a **workbook**, which is a file with the .xls file extension. Each new workbook automatically contains three worksheets, although you can have up to 255 sheets. ████████ Jim uses Excel extensively to track MediaLoft finances, and as you work with Jim, you will also use Excel to complete many tasks. Figure A-1 shows a budget worksheet that Jim created using pencil and paper, while Figure A-2 shows the same worksheet Jim created using Excel.

DETAILS

When you use Excel you have the ability to:

- **Enter data quickly and accurately**

  With Excel, you can enter information faster and more accurately than with pencil and paper. For example, in the MediaLoft NYC Café Budget, certain expenses, such as rent, cleaning supplies, and products supplied on a yearly contract (coffee, creamers, and sweeteners), remain constant for the year. You can copy the expenses that don't change from quarter to quarter, then use Excel to calculate Total Expenses and Net Income for each quarter by supplying the data and formulas.

- **Recalculate data easily**

  Fixing typing errors or updating data using Excel is easy, and the results of a changed entry are recalculated automatically. For example, if you receive updated expense figures for Quarter 4, you enter the new numbers, and Excel recalculates the worksheet.

- **Perform a what-if analysis**

  The ability in Excel to change data and quickly view the recalculated results makes it a powerful decision-making tool. For instance, if the salary budget per quarter is increased to $17,200, you can enter the new figure into the worksheet and immediately see the impact on the overall budget. Any time you use a worksheet to ask the question "what if?" you are performing a **what-if analysis**.

- **Change the appearance of information**

  Excel provides powerful features for making information visually appealing and easy to understand. For example, you can use boldface type and colored or shaded text headings or numbers to emphasize important worksheet data and trends.

- **Create charts**

  Excel makes it easy to create charts based on worksheet information. Charts are updated automatically as data changes. The worksheet in Figure A-2 includes a 3-D pie chart that shows the distribution of the budget expenses for the MediaLoft NYC Café.

- **Share information with other users**

  Because everyone at MediaLoft is now using Microsoft Office, it's easy for them to share worksheet data. For example, you can complete the MediaLoft budget that Jim started creating in Excel. Simply access the files you need or want to share through the network or from a disk, or through the use of online collaboration tools (such as intranets and the Internet), and make any changes or additions.

- **Create new worksheets from existing ones quickly**

  It's easy to take an existing Excel worksheet and quickly modify it to create a new one. When you are ready to create next year's budget, you can open the file for this year's budget, save it with a new filename, and use the existing data as a starting point. An Excel file can also be created using a special format called a **template**, which lets you open a new file based on an existing workbook's design or content. Excel comes with many prepared templates you can use.

FIGURE A-1: Traditional paper worksheet

MediaLoft NYC Café Budget					
	Qtr 1	Qtr 2	Qtr 3	Qtr 4	Total
Net Sales	56,000	84,000	72,000	79,000	291,000
Expenses					
Salary	17,200	17,200	17,200	17,200	68,800
Rent	4,000	4,000	4,000	4,000	16,000
Advertising	3,750	8,000	3,750	3,750	19,250
Cleansers	2,200	2,200	2,200	2,200	8,800
Pastries	2,500	2,500	2,500	2,500	10,000
Milk/Cream	1,000	1,000	1,000	1,000	4,000
Coffee/Tea	4,700	4,750	4,750	4,750	18,950
Sweeteners	650	650	650	650	2,600
Total Expenses	36,000	40,300	36,050	36,050	148,400
Net Income	20,000	43,700	35,950	42,950	142,600

FIGURE A-2: Excel worksheet

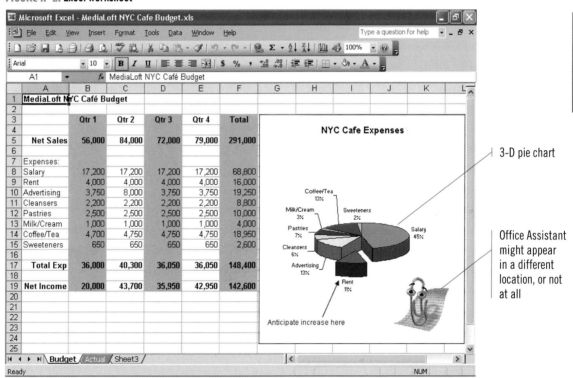

3-D pie chart

Office Assistant might appear in a different location, or not at all

TABLE A-1: Common business uses for electronic spreadsheets

spreadsheets are used to	by
Maintain values	Calculating numbers
Represent values graphically	Creating charts based on worksheet figures
Create reports to summarize data	Creating workbooks containing multiple worksheets of related data, and numbering and printing the worksheets as consecutively numbered pages
Organize data	Sorting data in ascending or descending order
Analyze data	Creating data summaries and short lists using PivotTables or AutoFilters
Create what-if data scenarios	Using variable values to investigate and sample different outcomes

Starting Excel 2003

To start any Windows program, you use the Start button on the taskbar. A slightly different procedure might be required for computers on a network and those that use Windows-enhancing utilities. If you need assistance, ask your instructor or technical support person. ▰▰▱▱ Jim has asked you to work on the budget for the MediaLoft café in New York City, which he created using Excel. You begin by starting Excel.

STEPS

1. **Point to the Start button** **start** **on the taskbar**

   The Start button is on the left side of the taskbar. You use it to start programs on your computer.

QUICK TIP

You might also see Microsoft Office Excel 2003 listed on the left side of the Start menu, which you can also click to start Excel.

2. **Click** **start**

   Microsoft Office Excel is located on the All Programs menu, which is located at the bottom of the Start menu, as shown in Figure A-3.

3. **Point to All Programs**

   The All Programs menu opens. All the programs on your computer, including Microsoft Excel, are listed on this menu. Your All Programs menu might look different, depending on the programs installed on your computer.

4. **Point to Microsoft Office**

   A submenu displays listing all the Microsoft Office programs installed on your computer. See Figure A-4.

TROUBLE

If you don't see the Microsoft Office Excel 2003 icon, see your instructor or technical support person.

5. **Click the Microsoft Office Excel 2003 program icon on the Microsoft Office submenu**

   Excel opens and a blank worksheet is displayed. In the next lesson, you will learn about the elements of the Excel worksheet window.

6. **If necessary, click the Maximize button** 🗖 **on the title bar**

   In the next lesson, you will learn about the elements of the Excel worksheet window.

FIGURE A-3: Start menu

Microsoft Office Excel located on this menu

Click here to open the Start menu

Your list might differ

FIGURE A-4: All Programs menu

Your list might differ

Microsoft Office Excel 2003 program icon

UNIT A
Excel 2003

Viewing the Excel Window

When you start Excel, the worksheet window appears on your screen. The **worksheet window** includes the tools that enable you to create and work with worksheets. ▰▰▰▰ You need to familiarize yourself with the Excel worksheet window and its elements before you start working on the budget worksheet. Compare the descriptions below to the elements shown in Figure A-5.

DETAILS

The elements of the Excel worksheet window include:

QUICK TIP

There are two sets of resizing buttons: one for the program and another for the active workbook. The program's resizing buttons are located on the title bar, while the workbook's resizing buttons appear below the program resizing buttons, on the menu bar (when the workbook is maximized).

- The **title bar** displays the program name (Microsoft Excel) and the filename of the open worksheet (in this case the default filename, Book1). As shown in Figure A-5, the title bar also contains a control menu box, a Close button, and resizing buttons, which are common to all Windows programs. The **control menu box** provides a menu of commands that allow you to move, size, open, or close the program window.

- The **menu bar** contains menus from which you select Excel commands. As with all Windows programs, you can select a menu command by clicking it with the mouse pointer or by pressing [Alt] plus the underlined letter in the menu command name. When you click a menu, only a short list of commonly used commands might appear at first; you can wait or click the double arrows at the bottom of the menu to see expanded menus with a complete list of commands.

- The **Name box** displays the active cell address. In Figure A-5, "A1" appears in the Name box, indicating that A1 is the active cell.

- The **formula bar** allows you to enter or edit data in the worksheet.

- The **toolbars** contain buttons for frequently used Excel commands. The **Standard toolbar** is located just below the menu bar and contains buttons that perform actions within the worksheet. The **Formatting toolbar**—beneath the Standard toolbar—contains buttons that change the worksheet's appearance. Each button contains an image representing its function. For instance, the Print button contains an image of a printer. To select any button, click it with the left mouse button.

QUICK TIP

You can always return to the Getting Started task pane by clicking the Home button 🏠 at the top of any task pane.

- The worksheet window contains a grid of columns and rows. Columns are labeled alphabetically (A, B, C, etc.) and rows are labeled numerically (1, 2, 3, etc.). The worksheet window displays only a small fraction of the whole worksheet, which has a total of 256 columns and 65,536 rows. The intersection of a column and a row is called a **cell**. Cells can contain text, numbers, formulas, or a combination of all three. Every cell has its own unique location or **cell address**, which is identified by the coordinates of the intersecting column and row. For example, the cell address of the cell in the upper-left corner of a worksheet is A1.

- A **task pane** is an organizational tool that allows you to perform routine tasks quickly and easily. The **Getting Started task pane** appears to the right of the worksheet window and lets you quickly open new or existing workbooks. The **Task pane list arrow** lets you choose from 12 different panes.

TROUBLE

If your screen does not display cells in orange and gray as shown in the figure, ask your technical support person to check your Windows color settings.

- The **cell pointer** is a dark rectangle that outlines the cell in which you are working. This cell is called the **active cell**. In Figure A-5, the cell pointer is located at A1, so A1 is the active cell. The column and row headings for the active cell are orange; inactive column and row headings are gray. To activate a different cell, just click any other cell or press the arrow keys on your keyboard to move the cell pointer elsewhere.

- **Sheet tabs** below the worksheet grid let you keep your work in a collection called a workbook. Each workbook contains three worksheets by default and can contain a maximum of 255 sheets. Sheet tabs allow you to name your worksheets with meaningful names. **Sheet tab scrolling buttons** help you display hidden worksheets.

- The **status bar** is located at the bottom of the Excel window. The left side of the status bar provides a brief description of the active command or task in progress. The right side of the status bar shows the status of important keys such as [Caps Lock] and [Num Lock].

FIGURE A-5: Excel worksheet window elements

Title bar
Control menu box
Menu bar
Standard toolbar
Formatting toolbar
Name box
Cell pointer highlights active cell
Formula bar
Sheet tab scrolling buttons

Close button
Resizing buttons
Task pane list arrow
Getting Started task pane lets you open or create a workbook
Worksheet window

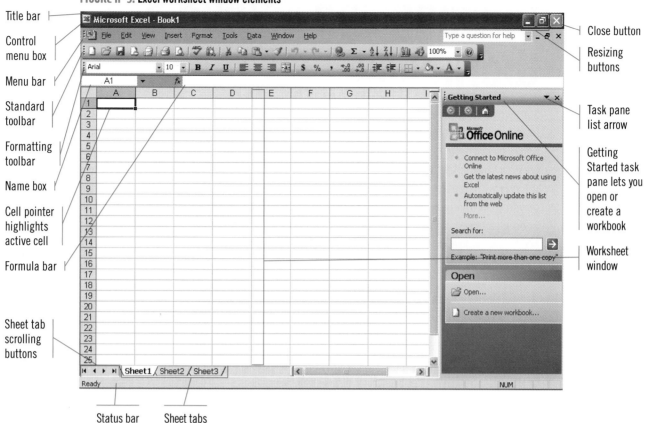

Status bar   Sheet tabs

Excel 2003

Clues to Use

Working with toolbars and menus in Excel 2003

Although you can configure Excel so that your toolbars and menus modify themselves to conform to your working style, the lessons in this book assume you have turned off personalized menus and toolbars and are working with all menu commands and toolbar buttons displayed. When you use personalized toolbars, the Standard and Formatting toolbars appear on the same row and display only the most frequently used buttons, as shown in Figure A-6. To use a button that is not visible on a toolbar, you click the Toolbar Options button  at the end of the toolbar, then click the button on the Toolbar Options list. As you work, Excel adds the buttons you use to the visible toolbars and drops the buttons you don't often use to the Toolbar Options list. Similarly, Excel menus adjust to your work habits, so that

the commands you use most often appear on shortened menus. You can see all the menu commands by clicking the Expand button (double arrows) at the bottom of a menu. It is often easier to work with full toolbars and menus displayed. To turn off personalized toolbars and menus, click Tools on the menu bar, click Customize, then click the Options tab in the Customize dialog box. Select the Show Standard and Formatting toolbars on two rows and Always show full menus check boxes, then click Close. The Standard and Formatting toolbars appear on separate rows and display most of the buttons, and the menus display the complete list of menu commands. (You can also quickly display the toolbars on two rows by clicking a Toolbar Options button, then clicking Show Buttons on Two Rows.)

FIGURE A-6: Toolbars on one row

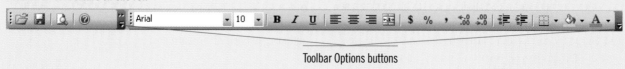

Toolbar Options buttons

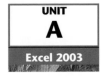

Opening and Saving a Workbook

Sometimes it's more efficient to create a new workbook by modifying one that already exists. This saves you from having to retype information from previous work. Throughout this book, you will create new workbooks by opening a file from the location where your Data Files are stored, using the Save As command to create a copy of the file with a new name, then modifying the new file by following the lesson steps. Saving the files with new names keeps your original Data Files intact, in case you have to start the unit over again or you wish to repeat an exercise. Use the Save command to store changes made to an existing file. It is a good idea to save your work every 10 or 15 minutes and before printing. ▰▰▰▱▱ You want to complete the MediaLoft budget on which Jim has been working.

STEPS

QUICK TIP

If the task pane is not open, click View on the menu bar, then click Task Pane to display the Getting Started task pane.

1. **Click the Open button 📁 in the Getting Started task pane**

   The Open dialog box opens. See Figure A-7. You can also click the Open button 📁 on the Standard toolbar.

2. **Click the Look in list arrow, then click the drive and folder where your Data Files are located**

   The Look in list arrow lets you navigate to folders and disk drives on your computer. A list of your Data Files appears in the Open dialog box.

QUICK TIP

If you don't see the three-letter extension .xls on the file-names in the Open dialog box, don't worry. Windows can be set up to display or not to display the file extensions.

3. **Click the file EX A-1.xls, then click Open**

   The file EX A-1.xls opens. The Getting Started task pane no longer appears on the screen.

4. **Click File on the menu bar, then click Save As**

   The Save As dialog box opens, displaying the drive where your Data Files are stored. You can create a new folder from within the Save As dialog box by clicking 📁 on the dialog box toolbar, typing a name in the Name text box, then clicking OK. To open a file from a folder you create, double-click folders, or use the Look in list arrow in the Open dialog box to open the folder, click the filename, then click Open.

5. **In the File name text box, select the current filename if necessary, type MediaLoft Cafe Budget, as shown in Figure A-8, then click Save**

   Both the Save As dialog box and the file EX A-1.xls close, and a duplicate file named MediaLoft Cafe Budget opens, as shown in Figure A-9.

Clues to Use

Creating a new workbook

You can create your own worksheets from scratch by opening a new workbook. To create a new workbook, click the New button 🗋 on the Standard toolbar. You can also use the Getting Started or New Workbook task panes to open a new workbook. Click the Go to New Workbook task pane button 🗋 in the Getting Started task pane to open the New Workbook task pane, then click the Blank Workbook button 🗋 to open a new workbook.

FIGURE A-7: Open dialog box

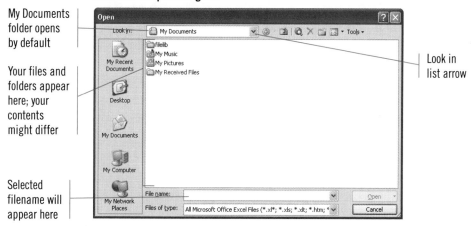

My Documents folder opens by default

Your files and folders appear here; your contents might differ

Selected filename will appear here

Look in list arrow

FIGURE A-8: Save As dialog box

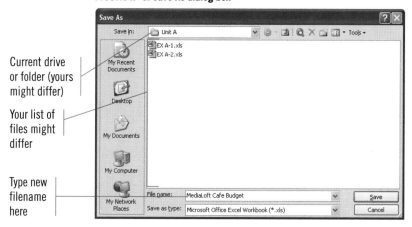

Current drive or folder (yours might differ)

Your list of files might differ

Type new filename here

FIGURE A-9: MediaLoft Café Budget workbook

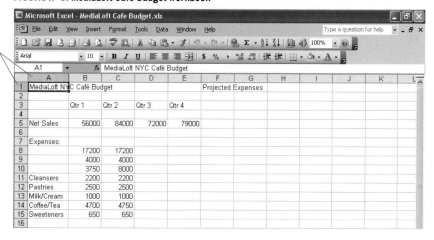

Orange column and row headers define the active cell

Clues to Use

Opening a workbook using a template

You can create a workbook by entering data and formats into a blank workbook, or you can use predesigned workbooks called templates that are included with Excel. Templates let you automatically create workbooks such as balance sheets, expense statements, loan amortizations, sales invoices, or timecards. Templates save you time because they contain labels, values, formulas, and formatting. To open a new workbook based on a template, click the Other Task Panes list arrow from the Getting Started task pane, then click New Workbook. Click the On my computer link under the Templates section, then click the Spreadsheet Solutions tab in the Templates dialog box. Click one of the samples, save it under a new name, then add your own information. You may need to have the Office CD available to install the templates. You can also find more templates by clicking the Templates home page link.

Entering Labels and Values

Labels help you identify the data in worksheet rows and columns, making your worksheet more readable and understandable. You should try to enter all labels in your worksheet before entering the data. Labels can contain text and numerical information not used in calculations, such as dates, times, or addresses. Labels are left-aligned by default. **Values**, which include numbers, formulas, and functions, are used in calculations. Excel recognizes an entry as a value when it is a number, or begins with one of these special symbols: +, -, =, @, #, or $. All values are right-aligned by default. When you ask Excel to total data in a column, it ignores those cells that have numbers within labels (such as 2006 Sales), and only totals those cells that contain values. When a cell contains both text and numbers, Excel recognizes the entry as a label. ▟▚▚▟▟ You notice that Jim's budget worksheet is missing some data. You want to enter labels identifying the rest of the expense categories, and the values for Qtr 3 and Qtr 4 into the MediaLoft Café Budget worksheet.

STEPS

1. **Click cell A8 to make it the active cell**

   Notice that the cell address A8 appears in the Name box. As you work, the mouse pointer takes on a variety of appearances, depending on where it is and what the program is doing. Table A-2 lists and identifies some mouse pointers. The labels in cells A8:A15 identify the expenses.

   > **TROUBLE**
   >
   > If you notice a mistake in a cell entry after entering it, double-click the cell, use [Backspace] or [Delete], make your corrections, then press [Enter]. You can also click Edit on the menu bar, point to Clear, then click Contents to remove a cell's contents.

2. **Type Salary, as shown in Figure A-10, then click the Enter button ✓ on the formula bar**

   As you type, the word "Enter" appears in the status bar. Clicking the Enter button indicates that you are finished typing or changing your entry, and the word "Ready" appears in the status bar. Because the cell is still selected, its contents still appear in the formula bar. You can also confirm a cell entry by pressing [Enter], [Tab], or one of the keyboard arrow keys. These three methods also select an adjacent cell. To confirm an entry and leave the same cell selected, you can press [Ctrl][Enter]. If a label does not fit in a cell, Excel displays the remaining characters in the next cell to the right, as long as it is empty. Otherwise, the label is **truncated**, or cut off.

3. **Click cell A9, type Rent, press [Enter] to confirm the entry and move the cell pointer to cell A10, type Advertising in cell A10, then press [Enter]**

   The remaining expense values have to be added to the worksheet for Quarters 3 and 4.

4. **Click cell D8, press and hold down the left mouse button, drag ✛ to cell E8 then down to cell E15, then release the mouse button**

   You have selected a **range**, which consists of two or more adjacent cells. The active cell is still cell D8, and the cells in the range are shaded in blue.

   > **QUICK TIP**
   >
   > To enter a number that will not be used as part of a calculation, such as a telephone number, type an apostrophe (') before the number.

5. **Type 17200, press [Enter], type 4000 in cell D9, press [Enter], type 3750 in cell D10, press [Enter], type 2200 in cell D11, press [Enter], type 2500 in cell D12, press [Enter], type 1000 in cell D13, press [Enter], type 4750 in cell D14, press [Enter], type 650 in cell D15, then press [Enter]**

   You often enter data in multiple columns and rows; selecting a range makes working with data entry easier because pressing [Enter] makes the next cell in the range active. You have entered all the values in the Qtr 3 column. The cell pointer is now in cell E8.

   > **QUICK TIP**
   >
   > The **AutoCalculate value** displays the sum of the selected values in the status bar.

6. **Type the remaining values for cells E8 through E15 as shown in Figure A-11**

   Before confirming a cell entry, you can click the Cancel button on the formula bar or press [Esc] to cancel or delete the entry.

7. **Click cell D8, type 17250, then press [Enter]**

8. **Press [Ctrl][Home] to return to cell A1**

9. **Click the Save button 🔲 on the Standard toolbar**

   You can also press [Ctrl][S] to save a worksheet.

FIGURE A-10: Worksheet with first label entered

Name box

Cancel button

Enter button

Formula bar

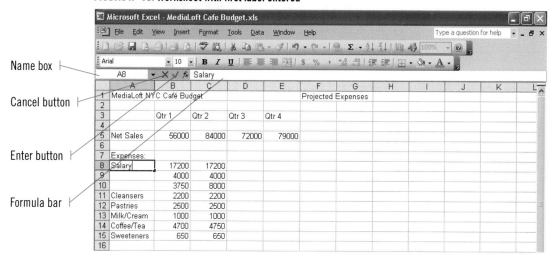

FIGURE A-11: Worksheet with new labels and values

Type these values

Labels entered

Values entered

AutoCalculate value

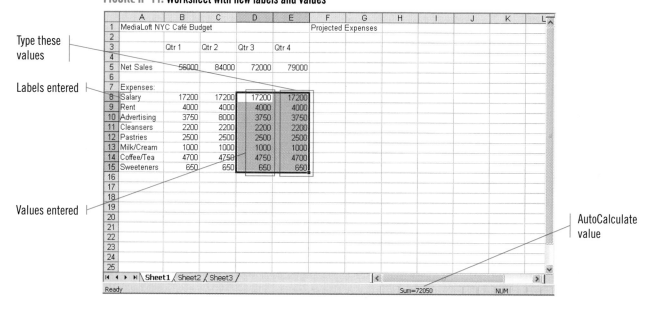

TABLE A-2: Commonly used pointers

name	pointer	use to
Normal		Select a cell or range; indicates Ready mode
Copy		Create a duplicate of the selected cell(s)
Fill handle		Create an alphanumeric series in a range
I-beam		Edit contents of formula bar
Move		Change the location of the selected cell(s)

Clues to Use

Navigating a worksheet

With over a million cells available to you, it is important to know how to move around, or navigate, a worksheet. You can use the arrow keys on the keyboard (↑, ↓, ←, or →) to move a cell at a time, or use [Page Up] or [Page Down] to move a screen at a time. To move a screen to the left press [Alt][Page Up]; to move a screen to the right press [Alt][Page Down]. You can also use the mouse pointer to click the desired cell. If the desired cell is not visible in the worksheet window, use the scroll bars or the Go To command on the Edit menu to move the location into view. To return to the first cell in a worksheet, click cell A1, or press [Ctrl][Home].

Excel 2003

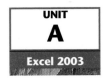

Naming and Moving a Sheet

Each workbook initially contains three worksheets, named Sheet1, Sheet2, and Sheet3. The sheet name appears on the sheet tab. When you open a workbook, the first worksheet is the active sheet. To move from sheet to sheet, you can click any sheet tab at the bottom of the worksheet window. The sheet tab scrolling buttons, located to the left of the sheet tabs, allow you to display hidden sheet tabs. To make it easier to identify the sheets in a workbook, you can rename each sheet and add color to the tabs. You can also organize them in a logical way. For instance, to better track performance goals, you could name each workbook sheet for an individual salesperson; then you could move the sheets so they appeared in alphabetical order. ▓▓▓▓ You have added data to Sheet1 of the budget workbook, which contains information on projected expenses. Jim tells you that Sheet2 contains data for the actual expenses. You want to be able to easily identify the actual expenses and the projected expenses, so you want to name the two sheets in the workbook, add color to distinguish them, then change their order.

STEPS

1. **Click the Sheet2 tab**

   Sheet2 becomes active; this is the worksheet that contains the actual quarterly expenses. Its tab moves to the front, and Sheet1 moves to the background.

2. **Click the Sheet1 tab**

   Sheet1, which contains the projected expenses, becomes active again. Once you have confirmed which sheet is which, you can assign them each a name that identifies their contents.

QUICK TIP

You can also rename a sheet by right-clicking the tab, clicking Rename on the shortcut menu, typing the new name, then pressing [Enter].

3. **Double-click the Sheet2 tab**

   Sheet 2 becomes the active sheet with the default sheet name of Sheet2 selected on the sheet tab.

4. **Type Actual, then press [Enter]**

   The new name automatically replaces the default name on the tab. Worksheet names can have up to 31 characters, including spaces and punctuation.

5. **Right-click the Actual tab, then click Tab Color on the shortcut menu**

   The Format Tab Color dialog box opens, as shown in Figure A-12.

QUICK TIP

To delete a worksheet, select the worksheet you want to delete, click Edit on the menu bar, then click Delete Sheet. To insert a worksheet, click Insert on the menu bar, then click Worksheet.

6. **Click the red color (first column, third row), click OK, double-click the Sheet1 tab, type Projected, then press [Enter]**

   Notice that when you renamed Sheet1, the color of the entire Actual tab changed to red. You decide to rearrange the order of the sheets, so that Actual comes before Projected.

7. **Click the Actual sheet tab and hold down the mouse button, then drag it to the left of the Projected sheet tab**

   As you drag, the pointer changes to ⬚▹, the sheet relocation pointer, and a small, black triangle shows its position. See Figure A-13. The first sheet in the workbook is now the Actual sheet. To see hidden sheets, click the far left tab scrolling button to display the first sheet tab; click the far right navigation button to display the last sheet tab. The left and right buttons move one sheet in their respective directions.

8. **Click the Projected sheet tab, enter your name in cell A20, then press [Ctrl][Home]**

   Your name identifies your worksheet as yours, which is helpful if you are sharing a printer.

9. **Click the Save button 🖫 on the Standard toolbar**

FIGURE A-12: Format Tab Color dialog box

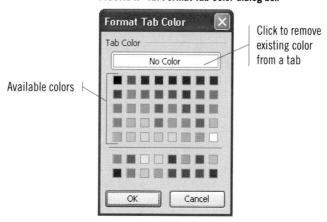

Click to remove existing color from a tab

Available colors

FIGURE A-13: Moving Actual sheet before Projected sheet

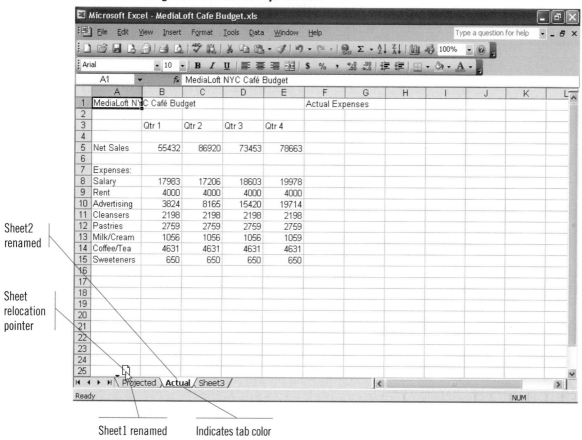

Sheet2 renamed

Sheet relocation pointer

Sheet1 renamed   Indicates tab color

Clues to Use

Copying worksheets

There are times when you may want to copy a worksheet. To copy it, press [Ctrl] as you drag the sheet tab, then release the mouse button before you release [Ctrl]. You can also move and copy worksheets between workbooks. You must have the workbook that you are copying to, as well as the workbook that you are copying from, open.

Select the sheet to copy or move, click Edit on the menu bar, then click Move or Copy sheet. Complete the information in the Move or Copy dialog box. Be sure to click the Create a copy check box if you are copying rather than moving the worksheet. Carefully check your calculation results whenever you move or copy a worksheet.

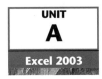

Previewing and Printing a Worksheet

After you complete a worksheet, you may want to print it to have a paper copy for reference or to give to others. You can also print a worksheet that is not complete to review your work when you are not at a computer. Before you print a worksheet, you should save any changes. That way, if anything happens to the file as it is being sent to the printer, you have your latest work saved. Then you should preview it to make sure it fits on the page the way you want. When you **preview** a worksheet, you see a copy of the worksheet exactly as it will appear on paper. See Table A-3 for a summary of printing tips. ▓▓▓ You are finished entering the labels and values into the MediaLoft budget. You have already saved your changes, so you preview the worksheet, then print a copy which you can review later.

STEPS

QUICK TIP

To print the worksheet using existing settings without previewing it, click the Print button 🖨 on the Standard toolbar.

1. **Make sure the printer is on and contains paper**

   If a file is sent to print and the printer is off, an error message appears on your screen.

2. **Click the Print Preview button 🔍 on the Standard toolbar**

   A miniature version of the worksheet appears in the Print Preview window, as shown in Figure A-14. If your worksheet requires more than one page, you can click the Next button or the Previous button to move between pages. Because your worksheet is only one page, the Next and Previous buttons are dimmed to signify they are inactive.

3. **Click Print**

   The Print dialog box opens, as shown in Figure A-15.

4. **Make sure that the Active sheet(s) option button is selected in the Print what section and that 1 appears in the Number of copies text box in the Copies section**

   Adjusting the value in the Number of copies text box enables you to print multiple copies. You can also print a selected range by clicking the Selection option button.

QUICK TIP

After previewing or printing a worksheet, dotted lines appear on the screen indicating individual page breaks in the printout. Page break positions vary with each printer.

5. **Click OK**

   A Printing dialog box appears briefly while the file is sent to the printer. Note that the dialog box contains a Cancel button. You can use it to cancel the print job while it is waiting in the print queue.

TABLE A-3: Worksheet printing tips

before you print	recommendation
Save the workbook	Make sure your work is saved before executing the command to print
Check the printer	Make sure that the printer is turned on and is online, that it has paper, and that there are no error messages or warning signals
Preview the worksheet	Check the formatted image for page breaks, page setup (vertical or horizontal), and overall appearance of the worksheet
Check the printer selection	Look in the Print dialog box to verify that the correct printer is selected
Check the Print what options	Look in the Print dialog box to verify that you are printing the active sheet, the entire workbook, or a range

FIGURE A-14: Print Preview window

Move to another page

Enlarge the screen image

Print the worksheet

Change print options

Zoom pointer

Return to worksheet

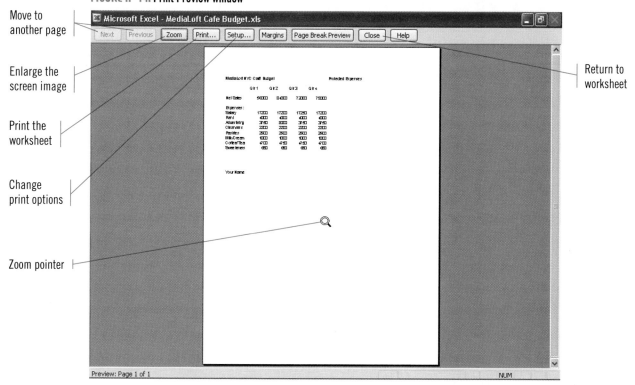

FIGURE A-15: Print dialog box

Your printer might differ

Prints the current worksheet

Indicates the number of copies to be printed

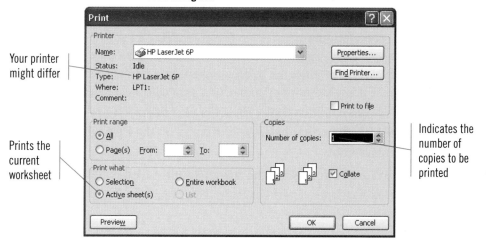

Using Zoom in Print Preview

When you are in the Print Preview window, you can enlarge the image by clicking the Zoom button. You can also position the Zoom pointer 🔍 over a specific part of the worksheet page, then click it to view that section of the page. Figure A-16 shows a magnified section of a document. While the image is zoomed in, use the scroll bars to view different sections of the page.

FIGURE A-16: Enlarging the preview using Zoom

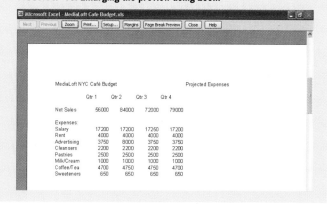

Excel 2003

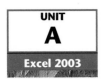
Getting Help

Excel features an extensive **Help system** that gives you immediate access to definitions, how to complete tasks, explanations, and useful tips. The Help task pane lets you search the Microsoft online Help database stored on the Web or the Excel Help database stored on your computer. You can type a **keyword**, a representative word on which Excel can search your area of interest, or you can access a question-and-answer format to research your Help topic. In addition, you can press [F1] at any time to display the Help task pane and get immediate assistance. Alternately, the **Type a question for help box** on the menu bar is always available for asking questions. You can click in the text box and type a question at any time to display related Help topics. Questions from your current Excel session are stored, and you can access them at any time by clicking the Type a question for help list arrow, then clicking the question of interest. ▓▓▓▓ Jim wants you to find out more about formulas so you can work more efficiently with them. He suggests you find out more information by using the Microsoft Excel Help task pane.

STEPS

> **QUICK TIP**
> You can also display the Microsoft Excel Help task pane from any open task pane. To do this, click the Other Task Panes list arrow, then click Help.

1. **Click the Microsoft Excel Help button ◉ on the Standard toolbar**

   The Excel Help task pane opens. You can get information by typing a keyword or question in the Search text box.

2. **Type Create a formula in the Search for text box**

   See Figure A-18.

3. **Click the Start searching button →**

   Excel searches for relevant topics from the Help files and displays a list of topics from which you can choose.

4. **Click Create a formula**

   A Help window containing information about creating formulas opens, as shown in Figure A-19. Microsoft Excel Help is an online feature that by default assumes you are connected to the Internet. If you are not connected to the Internet, then your search results might differ from Figure A-19. You may have fewer search results, reflecting those topics stored locally in the Excel Help database on your computer.

> **QUICK TIP**
> Clicking the Print button 🖨 in the Help window prints the information.

5. **Read the text, then click the Close button ⊠ on the Help window title bar**

   The Help window closes.

6. **Click the Close button ⊠ on the Search Results task pane to close it.**

   The task pane is no longer displayed in the worksheet window.

FIGURE A-18: Help task pane

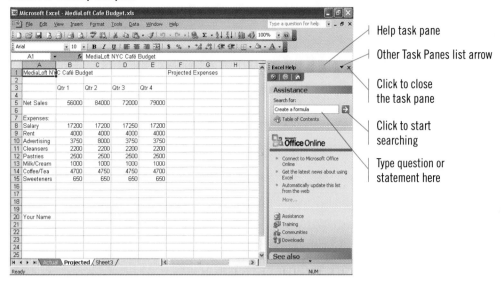

Help task pane

Other Task Panes list arrow

Click to close
the task pane

Click to start
searching

Type question or
statement here

FIGURE A-19: Help window

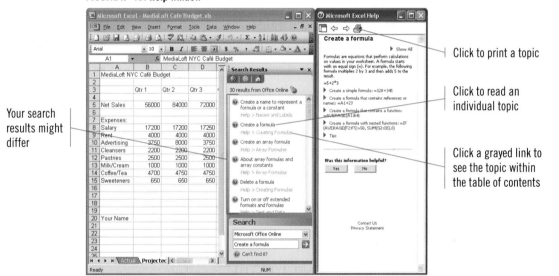

Your search
results might
differ

Click to print a topic

Click to read an
individual topic

Click a grayed link to
see the topic within
the table of contents

Clues to Use

Using the Office Assistant

If the Office Assistant is displayed, click it to access Help. If it is not displayed, click Help on the menu bar, then click Show the Office Assistant. (You may need to install additional components from your Microsoft Office CD in order to see the Office Assistant.) This feature provides help based on the text you type in the query box. To ask a question, click the Office Assistant. Type a question, statement, or word, as shown in Figure A-17, then click Search. The Search Results task pane searches the database and displays any matching topics. The animated Office Assistant provides Office Assistant Tips (indicated by a light bulb) on the current action you are performing. You can click the light bulb to display a dialog box containing relevant choices to which you can refer as you work. The default Office Assistant character is Clippit, but there are others from which you can choose. To change the appearance of the Office Assistant, right-click the Office Assistant, then click Options on the shortcut menu. Click the Gallery tab in the Options dialog box, click the Back and Next buttons until

you find an Assistant you want to use, then click OK. (You may need to insert your Microsoft Office CD to perform this task.)

FIGURE A-17: Office Assistant dialog box

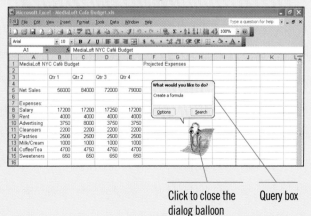

Click to close the
dialog balloon

Query box

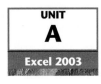

Closing a Workbook and Exiting Excel

When you have finished working, you need to save the workbook file and close it. When you have completed all your work in Excel you need to exit the program. You can exit Excel by clicking Exit on the File menu. ▰▰▰▰ You have completed your work on the MediaLoft budget. You want to close the workbook, then exit Excel.

STEPS

1. **Click File on the menu bar**

   The File menu opens. See Figure A-20.

2. **Click Close**

   Excel closes the workbook, asking if you want to save your changes; if you have made any changes be sure to save them. You can also click the workbook Close button instead of clicking Close on the File menu.

3. **Click File on the menu bar, then click Exit**

   You can also click the program Close button to exit the program. Excel closes, and you return to the desktop.

QUICK TIP
To exit Excel and close several files at once, click Exit on the File menu. Excel prompts you to save changes to each open workbook before exiting the program.

Program
control
menu box

Workbook
control
menu box

Close
command

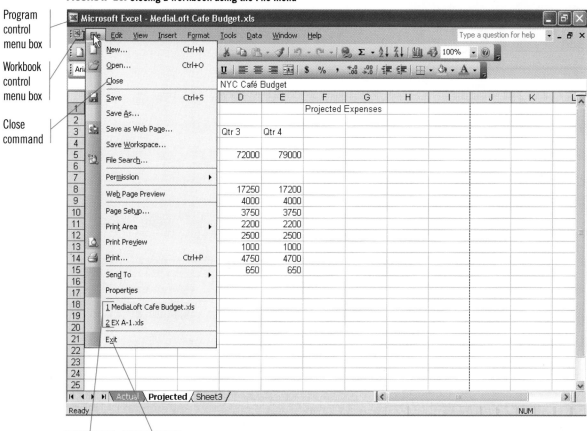

Your list
might differ

Exit command

Practice

▼ CONCEPTS REVIEW

Label the elements of the Excel worksheet window shown in Figure A-21.

FIGURE A-21

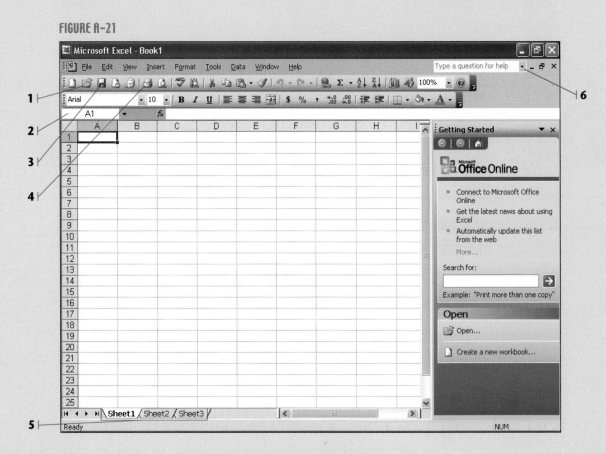

Match each term with the statement that best describes it.

7. Cell   a. Area that contains a grid of columns and rows

8. Worksheet window   b. The intersection of a column and row

9. Workbook   c. Allows you to enter or edit worksheet data

10. Name Box   d. Collection of worksheets

11. Cell pointer   e. Rectangle indicating the active cell

12. Formula bar   f. Displays the active cell address

Select the best answer from the list of choices.

13. **The following key(s) can be used to confirm cell entries, except:**
    a. [Enter].
    b. [Tab].
    c. [Esc].
    d. [Ctrl][Enter].

14. **Each of the following is true about labels, except:**
    a. They are left-aligned by default.
    b. They are not used in calculations.
    c. They are right-aligned by default.
    d. They can include numerical information.

15. **An electronic spreadsheet can perform all of the following tasks, except:**
    a. Display information visually.
    b. Calculate data accurately.
    c. Plan worksheet objectives.
    d. Recalculate updated information.

16. **What symbol is typed before a number to make the number a label?**
    a. '
    b. !
    c. "
    d. ;

17. **You can get Excel Help in any of the following ways, except:**
    a. Clicking Help on the menu bar, then clicking Microsoft Excel Help.
    b. Minimizing the program window.
    c. Clicking ⊚.
    d. Pressing [F1].

18. **Each of the following is true about values, except:**
    a. They can include labels.
    b. They are right-aligned by default.
    c. They are used in calculations.
    d. They can include formulas.

19. **Which button is used to preview a worksheet?**
    a. ▯
    b. ▯
    c. ▯
    d. ▯

20. **Each of the following is true about the Help feature, except:**
    a. You can use the Type a question for help text box.
    b. You can search your computer and Microsoft.com.
    c. You can change the appearance of the Office Assistant.
    d. It can complete certain tasks for you.

21. **Which feature is used to enlarge a Print Preview view?**
    a. Magnify
    b. Enlarge
    c. Amplify
    d. Zoom

▼ SKILLS REVIEW

1. **Define spreadsheet software.**
   a. Identify five disadvantages of using a nonelectronic spreadsheet.
   b. Identify five common business uses for electronic spreadsheets.

2. **Start Excel 2003.**
   a. Point to **All Programs** on the Start menu.
   b. Point to Microsoft Office, then click the **Microsoft Office Excel 2003** program icon.
   c. What appears when Excel opens?

▼ SKILLS REVIEW (CONTINUED)

3. View the Excel window.

   a. Identify as many elements in the Excel window without looking back in the unit.

   b. If the program and workbook are both maximized, which set of resizing buttons is used to minimize the workbook? (*Hint*: Would you use the upper or lower set?)

4. Open and save a workbook.

   a. Open the workbook EX A-2.xls from the drive and folder where your Data Files are located.

   b. Use the Create New Folder button in the Save As dialog box to create a folder called **Toronto** in the drive and folder where your Data Files are located.

   c. Save the workbook as **MediaLoft Toronto Café** in the **Toronto** folder where your Data Files are located.

   d. Close the file.

   e. Open it again from the new folder you created.

   f. Open a new workbook based on the Balance Sheet template: open the New Workbook task pane, click the On my computer link under the Templates section, display the Spreadsheet Solutions tab, then double-click Balance Sheet.

   g. Save the workbook as **MediaLoft Balance Sheet** in the drive and folder where your Data Files are stored, then close the workbook.

5. Enter labels and values.

   a. Enter the necessary labels shown in Table A-4. (The entry for "Water" should be in cell A4.)

   b. Enter the values shown in Table A-4.

   c. Clear the contents of cell A9 using the Edit menu, then type **Tea** in cell A9.

   d. Save the workbook using the Save button.

6. Name and move a sheet.

   a. Name the Sheet1 tab **Inventory**, then name the Sheet2 tab **Sales**.

   b. Move the Inventory sheet so it comes after the Sales sheet.

   c. Change the tab color of the Inventory sheet to yellow (third column, fourth row in the pallette).

   d. Change the tab color of the Sales sheet to aqua (fifth column, fourth row in the pallette).

TABLE A-4

	On-Hand	Cost Each	Sale Price
Water	32	10.03	
Coffee	52	13.71	
Bread	39	15.22	
Muffins	25	16.99	
Sweets	43	11.72	
Sodas	52	9.91	

7. Preview and print a worksheet.

   a. Make the Inventory sheet active.

   b. View it in Print Preview.

   c. Use the Zoom button to get a better look at your worksheet.

   d. Add your name to cell A11, then print one copy of the worksheet.

   e. Save the workbook.

8. Get Help.

   a. Display the Help task pane.

   b. Ask for information about defining a range.

   c. Print the information offered by the Help task pane using the Print button in the Help window.

   d. Close the Help window and task pane.

9. Close a workbook and exit Excel.

   a. Close the file using the Close command.

   b. Exit Excel.

▼ INDEPENDENT CHALLENGE 1

The Excel Help feature provides definitions, explanations, procedures, and other helpful information. It also provides examples and demonstrations to show you how Excel features work. Topics include elements such as the active cell, status bar, buttons, and dialog boxes, as well as detailed information about Excel commands and options.

a. Start Excel and open a blank workbook using the Getting Started task pane.

b. Display the Help task pane.

c. Find information about displaying toolbar buttons.

Advanced Challenge Exercise

■ Display the Office Assistant, if necessary, using the Show Office Assistant command on the Help menu.

■ Click the Office Assistant, then type a question about saving a workbook in another file format. (*Hint*: You may have to ask the Office Assistant more than one question.)

d. Print the information, close the Help window, then exit Excel.

▼ INDEPENDENT CHALLENGE 2

Spreadsheet software has many uses that can affect the way people work. The beginning of this unit discusses some examples of people using Excel. Use your own personal or business experiences to come up with five examples of how Excel can be used in a business setting.

a. Start Excel.

b. Write down five business tasks that you can complete more efficiently by using an Excel worksheet.

c. Sketch a sample of each worksheet. See Table A-5, a sample payroll worksheet, as a guide.

d. Open a new workbook and save it as **Sample Payroll** in the drive and folder where your Data Files are stored.

e. Give your worksheet a title in cell A1, then type your name in cell D1.

f. Enter the labels shown in Table A-5. Enter Hours Worked in column C and Hourly Wage in column E.

g. Create and enter your own sample data for Hours Worked and Hourly Wage in the worksheet. (The entry for "Dale Havorford" should be in cell A4.)

h. Save your work, then preview and print the worksheet.

i. Close the worksheet and exit Excel.

TABLE A-5

Employee Name	Hours Worked	Hourly Wage
Dale Havorford		
Chris Wong		
Sharon Martinez		
Belinda Swanson		
Total		

▼ INDEPENDENT CHALLENGE 3

You are the office manager for Christine's Car Parts, a small auto parts supplier. Although the company is just three years old, it is expanding rapidly, and you are continually looking for ways to make your job easier. Last year, you began using Excel to manage and maintain data on inventory and sales, which has greatly helped you to track information accurately and efficiently. The owner of the company has just approved your request to hire an assistant, who will be starting work in a week. You want to create a short training document that acquaints your new assistant with basic Excel skills.

    a. Start Excel.

    b. Create a new workbook and save it as **Training Workbook** in the drive and folder where your Data Files are located.

    c. Model your worksheet after the sample shown in Figure A-22. Enter a title for the worksheet in cell A1.

    d. Enter your name in cell D1.

    e. Create and enter values and labels for a sample spreadsheet. Make sure you have labels in column A.

    f. Change the name of Sheet1 to Sample Data, then change the tab color of the Sample Data worksheet to another color.

    g. Preview the worksheet, then print it.

Advanced Challenge Exercise

- Open a workbook based on a template from the Spreadsheet Solutions tab in the Templates dialog box. (You may need to insert your Office CD in order to do this.)
- Preview the worksheet, then print it.
- Save the workbook as **Template Sample**.

    h. Close the file(s) and exit Excel.

FIGURE A-22

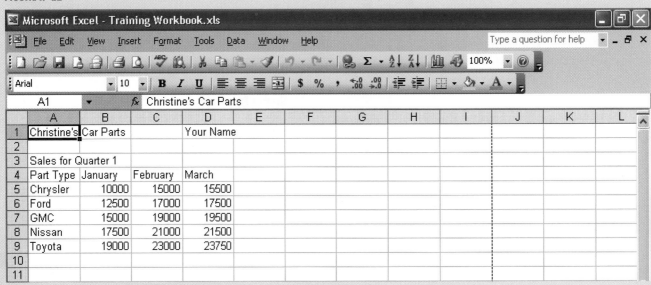

▼ INDEPENDENT CHALLENGE 4

You can use the World Wide Web to help make informed purchasing decisions. Your supervisor has just given you approval for buying a new computer. While cost is not a limiting factor, you do need to provide a list of hardware and software requirements. You can use data found on the World Wide Web, and use Excel to create a worksheet that details your purchase decision.

a. Connect to the Internet, then use your favorite search engine to find your own information sources on computer hardware and software you can purchase.

b. Locate data for the type of system you want by using at least two different vendor's Web sites. When you find systems that meet your needs, print out the information. Be sure to identify each system's key features, such as the processor chip, hard drive capacity, RAM, and monitor size.

c. When you are finished gathering data, disconnect from the Internet.

d. Start Excel, open a new workbook, then save it in the drive and folder where your Data Files are stored as **New Computer Data**.

e. Enter the manufacturers' names in columns and computer features (RAM, etc.) in rows. List the systems you found through your research, including the features you want (e.g., CD-ROM drive, etc.) and the cost for each system.

f. Indicate on the worksheet your final purchase decision by including descriptive text in a prominent cell. Enter your name in one of the cells.

g. Save, preview, then print your worksheet.

h. Close the file and exit Excel.

▼ VISUAL WORKSHOP

Create a worksheet similar to Figure A-23 using the skills you learned in this unit. Save the workbook as **Carrie's Camera and Darkroom** in the drive and folder where your Data Files are stored. Type your name in cell A11, then preview and print the worksheet.

FIGURE A-23

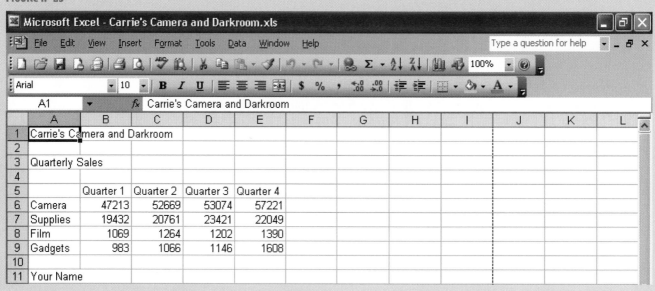

Building and Editing Worksheets

OBJECTIVES

Plan and design a worksheet
Edit cell entries
Enter formulas
Create complex formulas
Introduce Excel functions
Use Excel functions
Copy and move cell entries
Understand relative and absolute cell references
Copy formulas with relative cell references
Copy formulas with absolute cell references

If you have a SAM user profile, you may have access to hands-on instruction, practice, and assessment of the skills covered in this unit. Log in to your SAM account and go to your assignments page to see what your instructor has assigned.

Using your understanding of Excel basics, you can now plan and build your own worksheets. When you build a worksheet, you enter labels, values, and formulas into worksheet cells. Once you create a worksheet, you can save it in a workbook file and then print it. The MediaLoft Marketing Department has asked Jim Fernandez for an estimate of the average number of author appearances this summer. Marketing hopes that the number of appearances will increase 20% over last year's figures. Jim asks you to create a worksheet that summarizes appearances for last year and forecasts the summer appearances for this year.

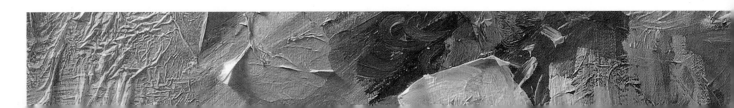

Planning and Designing a Worksheet

Before you start entering data into a worksheet, you need to know the purpose and approximate layout of the worksheet. ▓▓▒▒▒ To increase store traffic and sales, MediaLoft encourages authors to come to stores and sign their books. Jim wants to forecast MediaLoft's 2006 summer author appearances. The goal, already identified by the Marketing Department, is to increase the year 2005 signings by 20%. Using the planning guidelines below, Jim works with you to plan this worksheet and create it in Excel.

DETAILS

In planning and designing a worksheet it is important to:

- **Determine the purpose of the worksheet and give it a meaningful title**

  You need to forecast summer appearances for 2006. Jim suggests you title the worksheet "Summer 2006 MediaLoft Author Events Forecast."

- **Determine your worksheet's desired results, or output**

  Jim needs to begin scheduling author events and will use these forecasts to determine staffing and budget needs if the number of author events increases by 20%. He also wants to calculate the average number of author events because the Marketing Department uses this information for corporate promotions.

- **Collect all the information, or input, that will produce the results you want**

  Jim helps you by gathering together the number of author events that occurred at four stores during the 2005 summer season, which runs from June through August.

- **Determine the calculations, or formulas, necessary to achieve the desired results**

  Jim states you will first need to total the number of events at each of the selected stores during each month of the summer of 2005. Then you will need to add these totals together to determine the grand total of summer appearances. Because you need to determine the goal for the 2006 season, the 2005 monthly totals and grand total are multiplied by 1.2 to calculate the projected 20% increase for the 2006 summer season. Jim suggests you use the Average function to determine the average number of author appearances for the Marketing Department.

- **Sketch on paper how you want the worksheet to look; identify where to place the labels and values**

  Jim suggests you put the store locations in rows and the months in columns. Jim creates a sketch, in which he enters the data and notes the location of the monthly totals and the grand total. Below the totals, he writes out the formula for determining a 20% increase in 2005 appearances. He also includes a label for the calculations of the average number of events. Jim's sketch of this worksheet is shown in Figure B-1.

- **Create the worksheet**

  Jim begins creating the worksheet for you, by entering the labels first, to establish the structure of the worksheet. He then enters the values—the data summarizing the events—into the worksheet. Finally, he enters the formulas necessary to calculate totals, averages, and forecasts. These values and formulas will be used to calculate the necessary output. The worksheet Jim creates is shown in Figure B-2.

FIGURE B-1: Worksheet sketch showing labels, values, and calculations

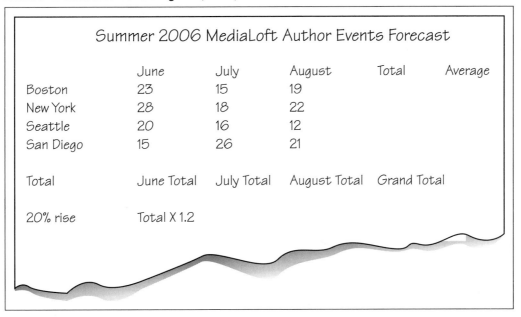

Summer 2006 MediaLoft Author Events Forecast

	June	July	August	Total	Average
Boston	23	15	19		
New York	28	18	22		
Seattle	20	16	12		
San Diego	15	26	21		
Total	June Total	July Total	August Total	Grand Total	
20% rise	Total X 1.2				

FIGURE B-2: Forecasting worksheet

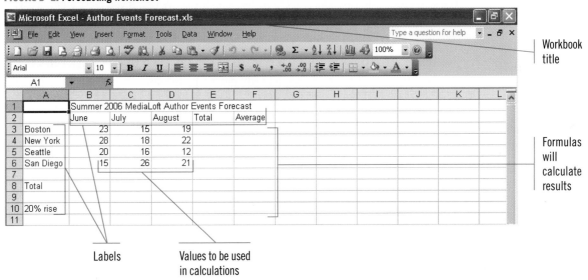

BUILDING AND EDITING WORKSHEETS EXCEL B-3

Editing Cell Entries

You can change the contents of a cell at any time. To edit the contents of a cell, you first select the cell you want to edit. Then you have two options: you can click the formula bar or press [F2]. This puts Excel into Edit mode. Alternately, you can double-click any cell and start editing. To make sure you are in Edit mode, look at the **mode indicator** on the far left of the status bar. ▓▓▓▓ After planning and creating the worksheet with Jim, you notice that he entered the wrong value for the August Seattle events, and that Houston should replace San Diego. You can edit these entries to correct them.

STEPS

QUICK TIP
In the Open dialog box, you can double-click the filename to open the workbook in one step.

1. **Start Excel, open the file EX B-1.xls from the drive and folder where your Data Files are stored, then save it as Author Events Forecast**

2. **Click cell D5, then click to the right of 12 in the formula bar**
   This cell contains August events for the Seattle store, which you want to change to reflect the correct numbers. Excel goes into Edit mode, and the mode indicator on the status bar displays "Edit." A blinking vertical line called the **insertion point** appears in the formula bar, and if you move the mouse pointer to the formula bar, the pointer changes to I, which is used for editing. See Figure B-3.

QUICK TIP
The Undo button 🔄 allows you to reverse up to 16 previous actions, one at a time.

3. **Press [Backspace], type 8, then click the Enter button ✓ on the formula bar**
   The value in cell D5 is changed from 12 to 18, and cell D5 remains selected.

4. **Click cell A6, then press [F2]**
   Excel returns to Edit mode, and the insertion point appears in the cell.

5. **Press and hold [Shift], press [Home], then release [Shift]**
   The contents of the cell is selected, and the next typed character will replace the selection.

6. **Type Houston, then press [Enter]**
   The label changes to Houston, and cell A7 becomes the active cell. If you make a mistake, you can click the Cancel button ✗ on the formula bar *before* confirming the cell entry. If you notice the mistake *after* you have confirmed the cell entry, click the Undo button 🔄 on the Standard toolbar.

QUICK TIP
Double-clicking when the pointer is to the left of the cell's contents positions the insertion point to the left of the data.

7. **Position the ✛ pointer to the left of 26 in cell C6, then double-click cell C6**
   Double-clicking a cell also puts Excel into Edit mode with the insertion. point in the cell.

8. **Press [Delete] twice, then type 19**
   The number of book signings for July in Houston has been corrected. See Figure B-4.

9. **Click ✓ to confirm the entry, then click the Save button 💾 on the Standard toolbar**

FIGURE B-3: Worksheet in Edit mode

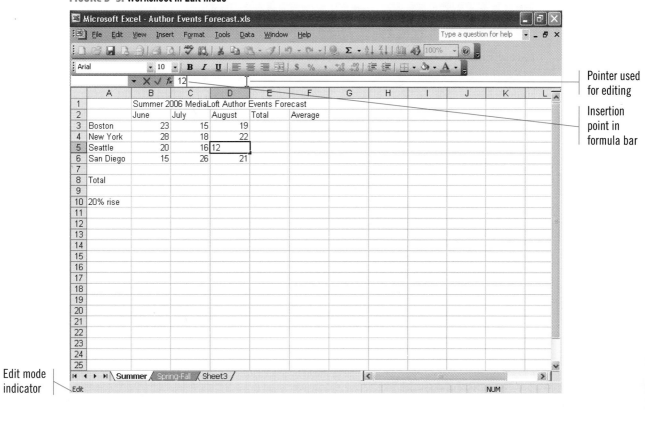

Pointer used for editing

Insertion point in formula bar

Edit mode indicator

FIGURE B-4: Edited worksheet

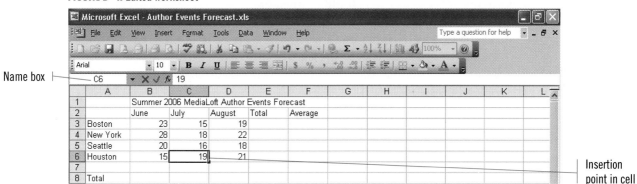

Name box

Insertion point in cell

Clues to Use

Recovering a lost workbook file

Sometimes while you are using Excel, you may experience a power failure or your computer may "freeze," making it impossible to continue working. If this type of interruption occurs, Excel has a built-in recovery feature that allows you to open and save files that were open at the time of the interruption. When you restart Excel after an interruption, the Document Recovery task pane opens on the left side of your screen displaying both original and recovered versions of the files that were open. If you're not sure which file to open (original or recovered), it's usually better to open the recovered file because it will have retained the latest information. You can, however, open and review all the versions of the file that were recovered and save the best one. Each file listed in the Document Recovery task pane has a list arrow with options that allow you to open the file, save the file, delete the file, or show repairs made to the file.

Entering Formulas

You use **formulas** to perform numeric calculations such as adding, multiplying, and averaging. Formulas in an Excel worksheet usually start with the equal sign (=), called the **formula prefix**, followed by cell addresses and range names. Arithmetic formulas use one or more **arithmetic operators** to perform calculations; see Table B-1 for a list of common arithmetic operators. Using a cell address or range name in a formula is called **cell referencing**. If you change a value in a cell, any formula containing that cell reference will be automatically recalculated using the new value. ✦✦✦✦✦ You need to total the values for the monthly author events for June, July, and August. You create formulas to perform these calculations.

STEPS

1. **Click cell B8**

   This is the cell where you want to enter the calculation that totals the number of June events.

2. **Type = (the equal sign)**

   Placing an equal sign at the beginning of an entry tells Excel that a formula is about to be entered, rather than a label or a value. "Enter" appears in the status bar. The total number of June events is equal to the sum of the values in cells B3, B4, B5, and B6.

   > **TROUBLE**
   > If you type an incorrect character, press [Backspace], then type the correct character.

3. **Type b3+b4+b5+b6**

   Compare your worksheet to Figure B-5. Each cell address in the equation is shown in a matching color in the worksheet. For example, the cell address B3 is written in blue in the equation and is outlined in blue in the worksheet. This makes it easy to identify each cell in a formula.

   > **TROUBLE**
   > If the formula instead of the result appears in the cell after you click ✓, make sure you began the formula with = (the equal sign).

4. **Click the Enter button ✓ on the formula bar**

   The result, 86, appears in cell B8. Cell B8 remains selected, and the formula appears in the formula bar. Excel is not case sensitive: it doesn't matter if you type uppercase or lowercase characters when you enter cell addresses. Typing cell addresses is only one way of creating a formula. A more accurate method involves **pointing** at cells using the mouse, then using the keyboard to supply arithmetic operators.

5. **Click cell C8, type =, click cell C3, type +, click cell C4, type +, click cell C5, type +, click cell C6, then click ✓**

   When you clicked cell C3, a moving border surrounded the cell. This **moving border** indicates the cell used in the calculation. Moving borders can appear around a single cell or a range of cells. The total number of author appearances for July is 68 and appears in cell C8. The pointing method of creating a formula is more accurate than typing, because it is easy to type a cell address incorrectly. You also need to enter a total for the August events in cell D8.

6. **Click cell D8, type =, click cell D3, type +, click cell D4, type +, click cell D5, type +, click cell D6, then click ✓**

   The total number of appearances for August is 80 and appears in cell D8. Compare your worksheet to Figure B-6.

7. **Click the Save button 🖫 on the Standard toolbar**

FIGURE B-5: Worksheet showing cells in a formula

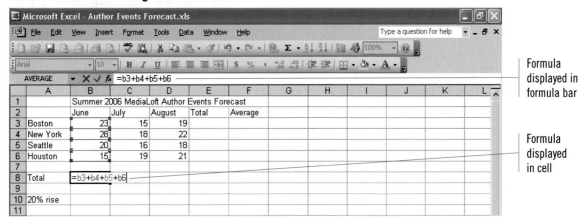

Formula displayed in formula bar

Formula displayed in cell

FIGURE B-6: Completed formulas

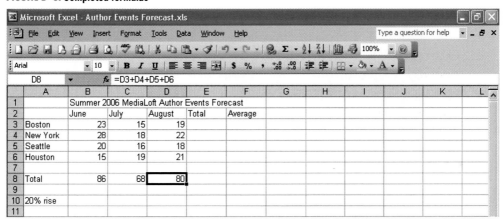

TABLE B-1: Excel arithmetic operators

operator	purpose	example
+	Addition	=A5+A7
–	Subtraction or negation	=A5–10
*	Multiplication	=A5*A7
/	Division	=A5/A7
%	Percent	=35%
^ (caret)	Exponent	=6^2 (same as 6^2)

Excel 2003

Creating Complex Formulas

The formula you entered is a simple formula containing one arithmetic operator, the plus sign. You can create a **complex formula**—an equation that uses more than one type of arithmetic operator. For example, you may need to create a formula that uses addition and multiplication. You can use arithmetic operators to separate tasks within a complex equation. In formulas containing more than one arithmetic operator, Excel uses the order of precedence rules to determine which operation to perform first. You want to total the values for the monthly author events for June, July, and August, and forecast what the 20% increase in appearances will be. You can create a complex formula to perform these calculations.

STEPS

1. **Click cell B10, type =, click cell B8, then type *.2**

   This part of the formula calculates 20% of the cell contents by multiplying the June total by .2 (or 20%). Because this part of the formula uses multiplication, it is calculated first according to the rules of precedence.

QUICK TIP

Press [Esc] to turn off a moving border and deselect the range.

2. **Type +, then click cell B8**

   The second part of the formula adds the 20% increase to the original value of the cell. The mode indicator says Point, indicating you can add more cell references. Compare your worksheet to Figure B-7.

3. **Click the Enter button ✔ on the formula bar**

   The result, 103.2, appears in cell B10.

4. **Click cell C10, type =, click cell C8, type *.2, type +, click cell C8, then click ✔**

   The result, 81.6, appears in cell C10.

5. **Click cell D10, type =, click cell D8, type *.2, type +, click D8, then click ✔**

   The result, 96, appears in cell D10. Compare your completed worksheet to Figure B-8.

6. **Click the Save button 🖫 on the Standard toolbar**

Clues to Use

Order of precedence in Excel formulas

A formula can include several mathematical operations. When you work with formulas that have more than one operator, the order of precedence is very important. If a formula contains two or more operators, such as 4+.55/4000*25, the computer performs the calculations in a particular sequence based on these rules: Operations inside parentheses are calculated before any other operations. Exponents are calculated next, then any multiplication and division—from left to right. Finally, addition and subtraction are calculated from left to right. In the example 4+.55/4000*25, Excel performs the arithmetic operations by first dividing 4000 into .55, then multiplying the result by 25, then adding 4. You can change the order of calculations by using parentheses. For example, in the formula (4+.55)/4000*25, Excel would first add 4 and .55, then divide that amount by 4000, then finally multiply by 25.

FIGURE B-7: Elements of a complex formula

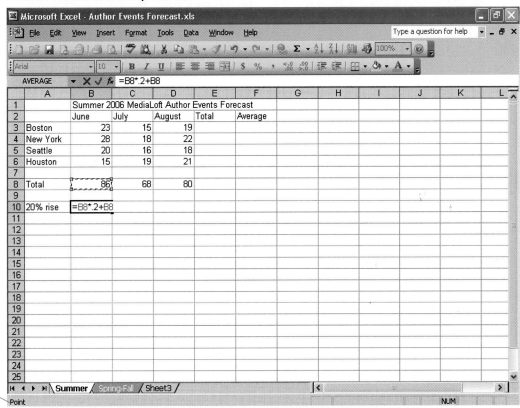

FIGURE B-8: Multiple complex formulas

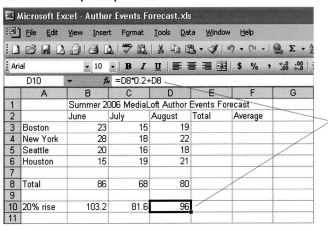

Formula calculates a 20% increase over the value in cell D8 and displays the result in cell D10

Clues to Use

Editing formulas

You edit formulas the same way you edit cell entries: you click the cell containing the formula then edit it in the formula bar; you can also double-click a cell or press [F2] to enter Edit mode, and then edit the formula in the cell. After you are in Edit mode, use the arrow keys to move the insertion point left or right in the formula. Use [Backspace] or [Delete] to delete characters to the left or right of the insertion point, then type or point to new cell references or operators.

Introducing Excel Functions

Functions are predefined worksheet formulas that enable you to perform complex calculations easily. Like formulas, functions always begin with the formula prefix = (the equal sign). You can type functions, or you can use the Insert Function button on the formula bar to select the function you need from a dialog box. The **AutoSum button** on the Standard toolbar enters the most frequently used function, SUM. A function can be used by itself within a cell, or as part of a formula. For example, to calculate monthly sales tax, you could create a formula that adds a range of cells (using the SUM function) and then multiplies the total by a decimal. ▒▓░░ You use the SUM function to calculate the grand totals in the worksheet.

STEPS

1. **Click cell E3**

   This is where you want the total of all Boston author events for June, July, and August to appear.

2. **Click the AutoSum button ∑ on the Standard toolbar**

   The formula =SUM(B3:D3) appears in the formula bar and a moving border surrounds cells in the worksheet, as shown in Figure B-9.

3. **Click the Enter button ✓ on the formula bar**

   The result, 57, appears in cell E3. By default, AutoSum adds the values in the cells above the cell pointer. If there are one or fewer values there, AutoSum adds the values to its left—in this case, the values in cells B3, C3, and D3. The information inside the parentheses is the **argument**, or the information Excel uses to calculate the function result. In this case, the argument is the range B3:D3.

4. **Click cell E4, click ∑, then click ✓**

   The total for the New York events, 68, appears in cell E4.

5. **Click cell E5, then click ∑**

   AutoSum sets up a function to add the two values in the cells above the active cell, but this time the default argument is not correct.

6. **Click cell B5 and hold down the mouse button, drag to cell D5 to select the range B5:D5, then click ✓**

   As you drag, the argument in the SUM function changes to reflect the selected range, and a yellow **Argument ScreenTip** shows the function syntax. You can click any part of the Argument ScreenTip to display Help on the function.

7. **Click cell E6, type =SUM(, click cell B6 and drag to cell D6, then click ✓**

8. **Click cell E8, type =SUM(, click cell B8 and drag to cell D8, then click ✓**

9. **Click cell E10, type =SUM(, click cell B10 and drag to cell D10, click ✓, then click the Save button 🖫 on the Standard toolbar**

   Compare your screen to Figure B-10.

FIGURE B-9: Formula and moving border

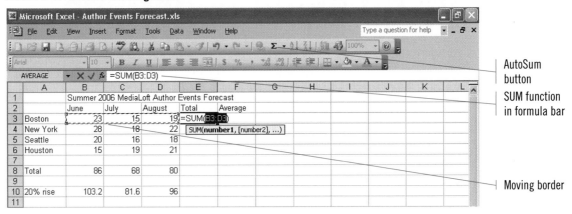

- AutoSum button
- SUM function in formula bar
- Moving border

FIGURE B-10: Worksheet with SUM functions entered

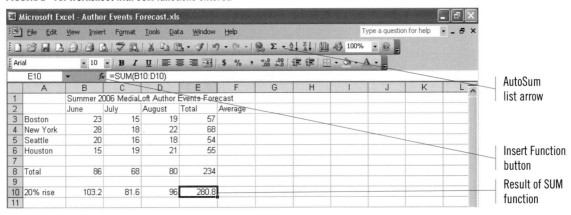

- AutoSum list arrow
- Insert Function button
- Result of SUM function

Excel 2003

Clues to Use

Using the MIN and MAX functions

Other commonly used functions include MIN and MAX. You use the MIN function to calculate the minimum, or smallest, value in a selected range; the MAX function calculates the maximum, or largest, value in a selected range. The MAX function is included in the Most Recently Used function category in the Insert Function dialog box, while both the MIN and MAX function can be found in the Statistical category. These functions are particularly useful in larger worksheets and can be selected using the Insert Function button on the formula bar or the AutoSum list arrow on the Standard toolbar.

Using Excel Functions

Functions can be typed directly from the keyboard, or by using the Insert Function button on the formula bar. Clicking this button opens the Insert Function dialog box, which provides a guided method of choosing a function, describes what each function does, and helps you choose which cells to select to complete each equation. ⬛ You need to use the AVERAGE function to calculate the average number of author events per store.

STEPS

1. **Click cell F3, then click the Insert Function button ƒₓ on the formula bar**

   The Insert Function dialog box opens, as shown in Figure B-11. Here you can select a function from a list. See Table B-2 for frequently used functions. The function you need to calculate averages—named AVERAGE—appears in the Most Recently Used function category.

2. **Click AVERAGE in the Select a function list box, then click OK**

   The Function Arguments dialog box opens.

3. **Type B3:D3 in the Number 1 text box, as shown in Figure B-12, then click OK**

   The value 19 appears in cell F3.

4. **Click cell F4, click ƒₓ to open the Insert Function dialog box, verify that AVERAGE is selected in the Select a function list, click OK, type B4:D4, then click OK**

5. **Click cell F5, click ƒₓ, click AVERAGE if necessary, click OK, type B5:D5, then click OK**

6. **Click cell F6, click ƒₓ, click AVERAGE if necessary, click OK, type B6:D6, then click OK**

   The result for Boston (cell F3) is 19; the result for New York (cell F4) is 22.66667; the result for Seattle (cell F5) is 18; and the result for Houston (cell F6) is 18.33333, giving you the averages for all four stores. See Figure B-13.

7. **Enter your name in cell A25, then click the Save button 💾 on the Standard toolbar**

8. **Click the Print button 🖨 on the Standard toolbar**

TABLE B-2: Frequently used functions

function	description
SUM (argument)	Calculates the sum of the arguments
AVERAGE (argument)	Calculates the average of the arguments
MAX (argument)	Displays the largest value among the arguments
MIN (argument)	Displays the smallest value among the arguments
COUNT (argument)	Calculates the number of values in the arguments
PMT (rate, number of payments, loan amount)	Calculates loan payment amounts
IF (condition, if true, if false)	Determines a value if a condition is true or false
TODAY ()	Returns the current date using a date format

FIGURE B-11: Insert Function dialog box

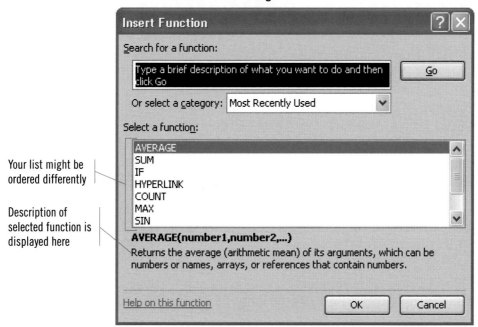

Your list might be ordered differently

Description of selected function is displayed here

FIGURE B-12: Function Arguments dialog box

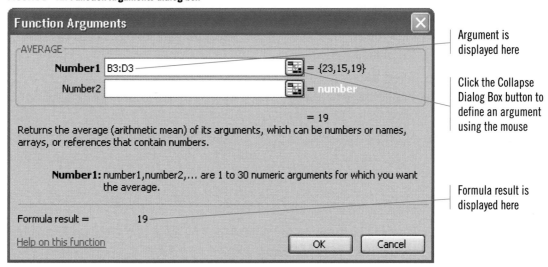

Argument is displayed here

Click the Collapse Dialog Box button to define an argument using the mouse

Formula result is displayed here

FIGURE B-13: Completed functions

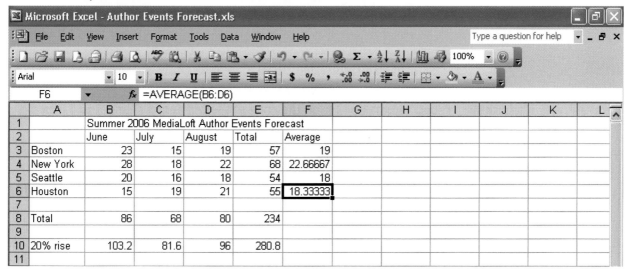

Copying and Moving Cell Entries

You can copy or move information from one cell or range in your worksheet to another using either the Cut, Copy, and Paste buttons, or the Excel drag-and-drop feature. When you cut or move information, the original data does not remain in the original location. You can also cut, copy, and paste labels and values from one worksheet to another. ▓▓▓▓ You need to include the 2006 forecast for spring and fall author events. Jim has already entered the spring data in the second worksheet in the workbook, and asks you to finish entering the labels and data for the fall. You copy information from the spring report to the fall report.

STEPS

1. **Click the Spring-Fall sheet tab of the Author Events Forecast workbook**

   The store names in cells A6:A7 are incorrect.

2. **Click the Summer sheet tab, select the range A5:A6, then click the Copy button 🗋 on the Standard toolbar**

   The selected range (A5:A6) is copied to the **Office Clipboard**, a temporary storage area that holds the selected information you copy or cut. A moving border surrounds the selected range until you press [Esc] or copy additional information to the Clipboard. The information you copied remains in the selected range.

3. **Click the Spring-Fall sheet tab, select the range A6:A7, then click the Paste button 🗋 on the Standard toolbar**

4. **Select the range A4:A9, then click 🗋**

   The Clipboard task pane opens when you copy a selection to the already occupied Clipboard. You can use the Clipboard task pane to copy, cut, store, and paste up to 24 items. Each item in the pane displays its contents.

5. **Click cell A13, click [Boston New York Seattle Houston Total] in the Clipboard task pane to paste the contents in cell A13, then click the Close button ☒ in the task pane title bar to close it**

   The item is copied into the range A13:A18. When pasting an item from the Clipboard into the worksheet, you only need to specify the upper-left cell of the range where you want to paste the selection. The Total label in column E is missing from the fall forecast.

6. **Click cell E3, position the pointer on any edge of the cell until the pointer changes to ⬚, then press and hold down [Ctrl]**

   The pointer changes to the Copy pointer ⬚.

7. **While still pressing [Ctrl], press and hold the left mouse button, drag the cell contents to cell E12, release the mouse button, then release [Ctrl]**

   As you dragged, an outline of the cell moved with the pointer, as shown in Figure B-14, and a ScreenTip appeared tracking the current position of the item as you moved it. When you released the mouse button, the Total label appeared in cell E12. This **drag-and-drop technique** is useful for copying cell contents. You can also use drag and drop to move data to a new cell.

8. **Click cell C1, position the pointer on the edge of the cell until it changes to ⬚, then drag the cell contents to A1**

   You don't use [Ctrl] when moving information with drag and drop. You can easily enter the fall events data into the range B13:D16.

9. **Select the range B13:D16, then using the information shown in Figure B-15, enter the author events data for the fall into this range, then click the Save button 🖫 on the Standard toolbar**

   The **AutoCalculate** area in the status bar displays "Sum=245," which is the sum of the values in the selected range.

FIGURE B-14: Using drag and drop to copy information

Copy button

Paste button

Copied cell

Outline of
copied cell

Drag-and-drop
pointer with
ScreenTip

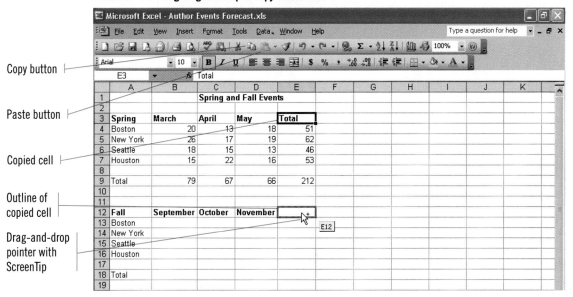

FIGURE B-15: Worksheet with fall author event data entered

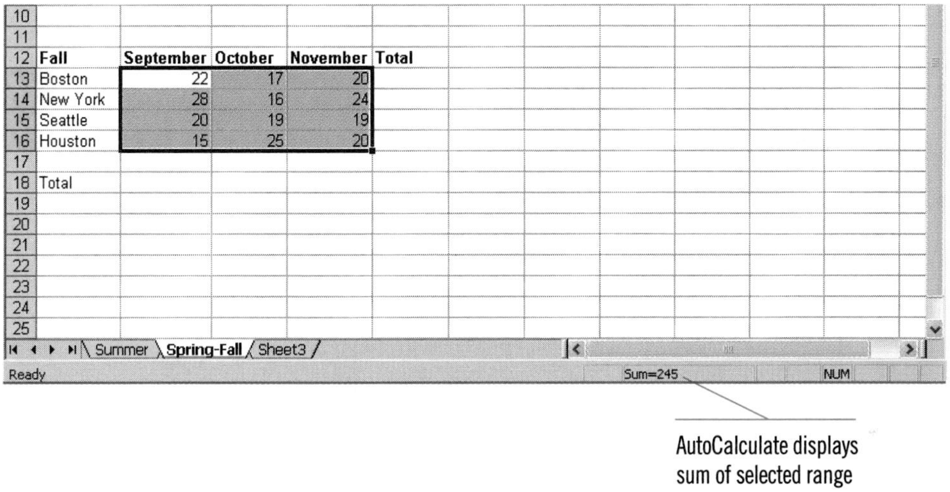

AutoCalculate displays
sum of selected range

Clues to Use

Using the Office Clipboard

The Office Clipboard, shown in the task pane in Figure B-16, lets you copy and paste multiple items such as text, images, tables, or Excel ranges within or between Microsoft Office applications. The Office Clipboard can hold up to 24 items copied or cut from any Office or Windows-compatible program. The Clipboard task pane displays the items stored on the Office Clipboard. You choose whether to delete the first item from the Clipboard when you copy the 25th item. The collected items remain on the Office Clipboard and are available to you until you close all open Office programs. You can specify when and where to show the Office Clipboard task pane by clicking the Options list arrow at the bottom of the Clipboard task pane.

FIGURE B-16: Office Clipboard task pane

Clipboard entry from
another program

Understanding Relative and Absolute Cell References

As you work in Excel, you will often want to reuse formulas in different parts of the worksheet. This will save you time because you won't have to retype them. For example, you may want to perform a what-if analysis showing one set of sales figures using a lower forecast in one part of the worksheet and another set using a higher forecast in another area. But when you copy formulas, it is important to make sure that they refer to the correct cells. To do this, you need to understand relative and absolute cell references. Jim often reuses formulas in different parts of his worksheets to examine different possible outcomes, so he wants you to understand relative and absolute cell references.

DETAILS

- ### Use relative references when cell relationships remain unchanged

    When you create a formula that references other cells, Excel normally does not "record" the exact cell references, but instead the relationship to the cell containing the formula. For example, in Figure B-17, cell E5 contains the formula: =SUM(B5:D5). When Excel retrieves values to calculate the formula in cell E5, it actually looks for "the cell three columns to the left of the formula, which in this case is cell B5," "the cell two columns to the left of the formula," and so on. This way, if you copy the cell to a new location such as cell E6, the results will reflect the new formula location, and will automatically retrieve the values in cells B6, C6, and D6. This is called **relative cell referencing**, because Excel is recording the input cells *in relation to* the formula cell.

    In most cases, you will use relative cell references, which is the Excel default. In Figure B-17, the formulas in E5:E9 and in B9:E9 contain relative cell references. They total the "three cells to the left of" or the "four cells above" the formulas.

- ### Use absolute cell references when one relationship changes

    There are times when you want Excel to retrieve formula information from a specific cell, and you don't want that cell to change when you copy the formula to a new location. For example, you might have a price in a specific cell that you want to use in all formulas, regardless of their location. If you used relative cell referencing, the formula results would be incorrect, because Excel would use a different cell every time you copied the formula. Therefore you need to use an **absolute cell reference**, a reference that does not change when you copy the formula.

    You create an absolute cell reference by placing a $ (dollar sign) before both the column letter and the row number for the cell's address, using the [F4] function key on the keyboard. Figure B-18 displays the formulas used in Figure B-17. The formulas in cells B15 to D18 use absolute cell references to refer to a potential sales increase of 50%, shown in cell B12.

Clues to Use

Using a mixed reference

Sometimes when you copy a formula, you'll want to change the row reference, but keep the column reference the same. This type of cell referencing combines elements of both absolute and relative referencing and is called a **mixed reference**. When copied, the mixed reference C$14 changes the column relative to its new location, but prevents the row from changing. In the mixed reference $C14, the column would not change, but the row would be updated relative to its location. Like the absolute reference, a mixed reference can be created using the [F4] function key. With each press of the [F4] key, you cycle through all the possible combinations of relative, absolute, and mixed references ($C$14, C$14, $C14, C14).

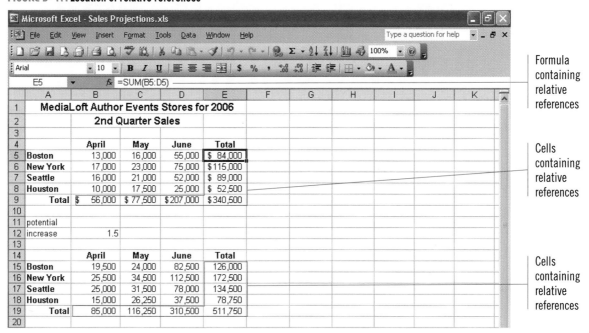

Formula
containing
relative
references

Cells
containing
relative
references

Cells
containing
relative
references

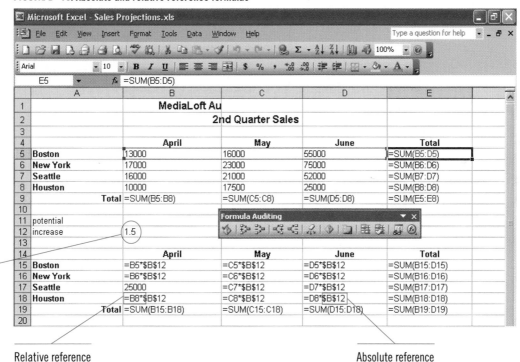

Cell
referenced
in absolute
formulas

Relative reference

Absolute reference

Clues to Use

Printing worksheet formulas

As you create a worksheet, you may find it valuable to print the sheet showing the formulas rather than the cell contents. You can do this by clicking Tools on the menu bar, clicking Options, then clicking the View tab in the Options dialog box. Make sure a check is displayed in the Formulas check box, then click OK. When the

Options dialog box closes, the cells are expanded to display the formulas, as shown in Figure B-18, and you can print the worksheet. To return the worksheet to its normal appearance, reopen the Options dialog box and deselect the Formulas check box.

Excel 2003

Copying Formulas with Relative Cell References

Copying and moving formulas allows you to reuse formulas you've already created. Copying formulas, rather than retyping them, is faster and helps to prevent typing errors. You can use the Copy and Paste commands or the Fill Right method to copy formulas. ▧▧▧ You want to copy the formulas that total the author appearances by region and by month from the spring to the fall.

STEPS

1. **Click cell E4, then click the Copy button ▣ on the Standard toolbar**

   The formula for calculating the total number of spring Boston author events is copied to the Clipboard. Notice that the formula =SUM(B4:D4) appears in the formula bar.

QUICK TIP

To specify components of the copied cell or range prior to pasting, click Edit on the menu bar, then click Paste Special. You can selectively copy formulas, values, and other more complex features.

2. **Click cell E13, then click the Paste button ▣ on the Standard toolbar**

   The formula from cell E4 is copied into cell E13, where the new result of 59 appears. Notice in the formula bar that the cell references have changed, so that the range B13:D13 appears in the formula. This formula contains relative cell references, which tell Excel to copy the formula to a new cell, but to substitute new cell references so that the relationship of the cells to the formula in its new location remains unchanged. In this case, Excel adjusted the formula so that cells D13, C13, and B13—the three cell references immediately to the left of E13—replaced cells D4, C4, and B4, the three cell references to the left of E4. Notice that the lower-right corner of the active cell contains a small square, called the **fill handle**. You can use the fill handle to copy labels, formulas, and values. This option is called **AutoFill**.

3. **Position the pointer over the fill handle until it changes to ✛, press and hold the left mouse button, then drag the fill handle to select the range E13:E16**

   See Figure B-19.

4. **Release the mouse button**

   A formula similar to the one in cell E13 now appears in the range E14:E16. Again, because the formula uses relative cell references, cells E14 through E16 correctly display the totals for the fall author events. After you release the mouse button, the **AutoFill Options button** appears. If you move the pointer over it and click its list arrow, you can specify what you want to fill and whether or not you want to include formatting.

5. **Click cell B9, click Edit on the menu bar, then click Copy**

TROUBLE

If the Clipboard task pane opens, click the Close button. If the Office Assistant appears, right-click it, then click Hide.

6. **Click cell B18, click Edit on the menu bar, then click Paste**

   See Figure B-20. The formula for calculating the September events appears in the formula bar. You also need totals to appear in cells C18, D18, and E18. You could use the fill handle again, but another option is the Fill command on the Edit menu.

7. **Select the range B18:E18**

8. **Click Edit on the menu bar, point to Fill, then click Right**

   The rest of the totals are filled in correctly. Compare your worksheet to Figure B-21.

9. **Click the Save button ▣ on the Standard toolbar**

FIGURE B-19: Selected range using the fill handle

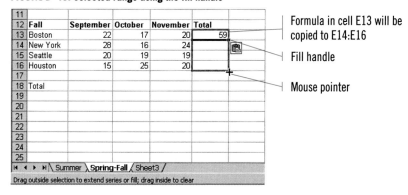

Formula in cell E13 will be copied to E14:E16

Fill handle

Mouse pointer

FIGURE B-20: Copied formula

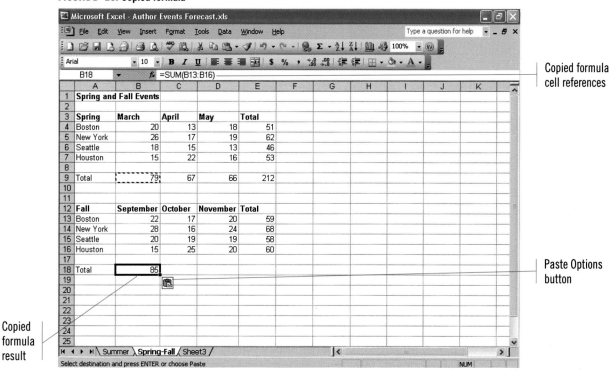

Copied formula cell references

Paste Options button

Copied formula result

FIGURE B-21: Completed worksheet with all formulas copied

	Fall	September	October	November	Total
12	Fall	September	October	November	Total
13	Boston	22	17	20	59
14	New York	28	16	24	68
15	Seattle	20	19	19	58
16	Houston	15	25	20	60
17					
18	Total	85	77	83	245
19					
20					
21					
22					
23					
24					
25					

Clues to Use

Filling cells with sequential text or values

Often, you'll need to fill cells with sequential text: months of the year, days of the week, years, or text plus a number (Quarter 1, Quarter 2,...). You can easily fill cells using sequences by dragging the fill handle. As you drag the fill handle, Excel automatically extends the existing sequence. (The contents of the last filled cell appear in the ScreenTip.) Use the Fill Series command on the Edit menu to examine all of the available fill series options.

Copying Formulas with Absolute Cell References

When copying formulas, you might want a cell reference to always refer to a particular cell address. In such an instance, you would use an absolute cell reference. An absolute cell reference always refers to a specific cell address when the formula is copied. You create an absolute reference by placing a dollar sign ($) before the row letter and column number of the address (for example $A$1). ▰▰▰▰ The staff in the Marketing Department hopes the number of author events will increase by 20% over last year's figures. Jim asks you to add a column that calculates a possible increase in the number of spring events in 2006. You can then do a what-if analysis and recalculate the spreadsheet several times, changing the percentage by which the number of appearances might increase each time.

STEPS

1. **Click cell G1, type Change, then press [→]**

   You can store the increase factor that will be used in the what-if analysis in cell H1.

2. **Type 1.1, then press [Enter]**

   The value in cell H1 represents a 10% increase in author events.

3. **Click cell G3, type What if?, then press [Enter]**

4. **In cell G4, type =, click E4, type *, click H1, then click the Enter button ☑ on the formula bar**

   The result, 56.1, appears in cell G4. This value represents the total spring events for Boston if there is a 10% increase. Jim wants you to perform a what-if analysis for all the stores.

QUICK TIP

Before you copy or move a formula, check to see if you need to use an absolute cell reference.

5. **Drag the fill handle to extend the selection from G4 to G7**

   The resulting values in the range G5:G7 are all zeros. When you copy the formula it adjusts so that the formula in cell G5 is =E5*H2. Because there is no value in cell H2, the result is 0, an error. You need to use an absolute reference in the formula to keep the formula from adjusting itself. That way, it will always reference cell H1. You can change the relative cell reference to an absolute cell reference by using [F4].

6. **Click cell G4, press [F2] to change to Edit mode, then press [F4]**

   When you press [F2], the range finder outlines the arguments of the equation in blue and green. When you press [F4], dollar signs appear, changing the H1 cell reference to an absolute reference. See Figure B-22.

7. **Click ☑, then drag the fill handle to extend the selection to range G4:G7**

   The formula correctly contains an absolute cell reference, and the value of G4 remains unchanged at 56.1. The correct values for a 10% increase appear in cells G4:G7. You complete the what-if analysis by changing the value in cell H1 to indicate a 20% increase in events.

8. **Click cell H1, type 1.2, then click ☑**

   The values in the range G4:G7 change to reflect the 20% increase. Compare your completed worksheets to Figure B-23. Because events only occur in whole numbers, the appearance of the numbers can be changed later.

9. **Enter your name in cell A25, click the Save button ◲ on the Standard toolbar, click the Print button ◳ on the Standard toolbar, close the workbook, then exit Excel**

FIGURE B-22: **Absolute cell reference in cell G4**

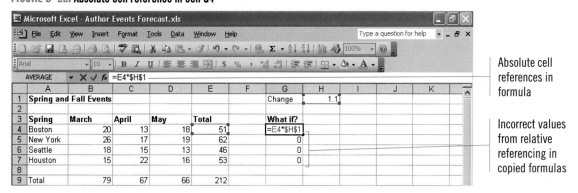

FIGURE B-22: **Absolute cell reference in cell G4**

Absolute cell references in formula

Incorrect values from relative referencing in copied formulas

FIGURE B-23: **Completed worksheets**

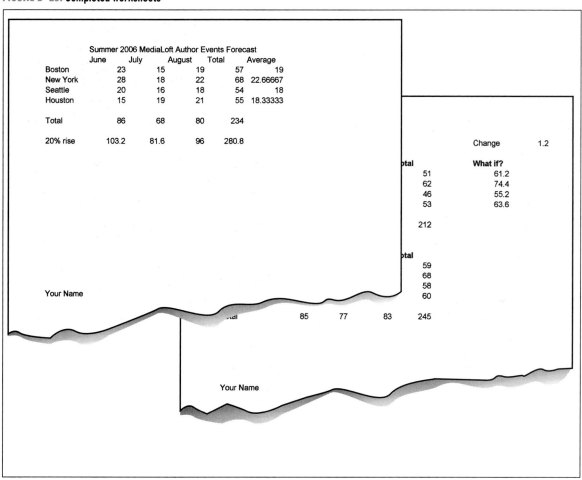

Excel 2003

Clues to Use

Inserting and deleting selected cells

As you add formulas to your workbook, you may need to insert or delete cells, not entire rows or columns. When you do this, Excel automatically adjusts cell references to reflect their new locations. To insert cells, click Insert on the menu bar, then click Cells. The Insert dialog box opens, asking if you want to insert a cell and move the selected cell down or to the right of the new one. To delete one or more selected cells, click Edit on the menu bar, click Delete, and in the Delete dialog box, indicate which way you want to move the adjacent cells. When using this option, be careful not to disturb row or column alignment that may be necessary to make sense of the worksheet.

Practice

▼ CONCEPTS REVIEW

Label each element of the Excel worksheet window shown in Figure B-24.

FIGURE B-24

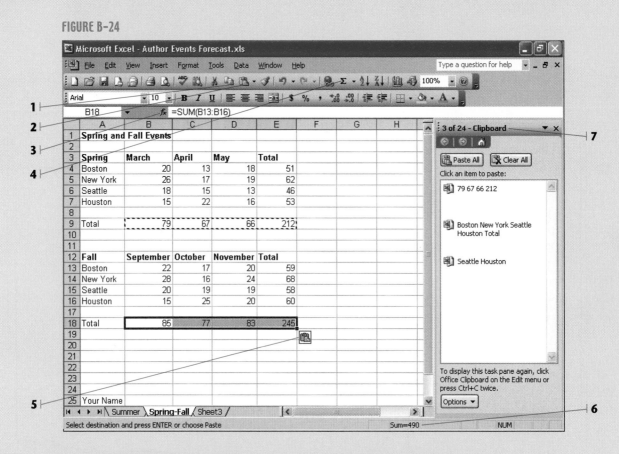

Match each term or button with the statement that best describes it.

8. 🔲

9. **Function**

10. **Formula**

11. **Fill handle**

12. 🔲

a. A predefined formula that provides a shortcut for commonly used calculations

b. A cell entry that performs a calculation in an Excel worksheet

c. Used to copy labels, formulas, and values

d. Adds the selected range to the Office Clipboard

e. Used to paste cells

Select the best answer from the list of choices.

13. Which button is used to enter data in a cell?

a.

c.

b.

d

14. What type of cell reference changes when it is copied?

a. Circular

c. Looping

b. Absolute

d. Relative

15. What character is used to make a reference absolute?

a. $

c. @

b. ^

d. &

▼ SKILLS REVIEW

1. Plan and design a worksheet.

a. Using the scenario of tracking quarterly sales at a formal-wear rental shop, determine what sort of output would be required.

b. Determine what kind of input would be required.

c. What sort of formulas might be needed?

d. Make a paper sketch of how the worksheet might look.

2. Edit cell entries.

a. Start Excel, open the workbook EX B-2.xls from the drive and folder where your Data Files are stored, then save it as **Office Furnishings**.

b. Change the quantity of Tables to **27**.

c. Change the price of Desks to **285**.

d. Change the quantity of Easels to **18**.

e. Enter your name in cell A40, then save the workbook.

3. Enter formulas.

a. In cell B6, use the pointing method to enter the formula **B2+B3+B4+B5**.

b. In cell D2, enter the formula **B2*C2**.

c. Save your work.

4. Create complex formulas.

a. In cell B8, enter the formula **(B2+B3+B4+B5)/4**.

b. In cell C8, enter the formula **(C2+C3+C4+C5)/4**.

c. Save your work.

5. Introduce Excel functions.

a. Delete the contents of cell B6.

b. In cell B6, use the AutoSum feature to calculate the sum of B2:B5.

c. Save your work.

6. Use Excel functions.

a. Enter the label **Min Price** in cell A9.

b. In cell C9, enter the function **MIN(C2:C5)**.

c. Enter the label **Max Price** in cell A10.

d. Create a formula in cell C10 that determines the maximum price of for the range C2:C5.

e. Save your work.

7. Copy and move cell entries.

a. Select the range **A1:C6**, then copy the range to cell A12.

b. Select the range **D1:E1**, then use drag and drop to copy the range to cell D12.

c. Move the contents of cell G1 to cell E9, then save your work.

▼ SKILLS REVIEW (CONTINUED)

8. Understand relative and absolute cell references.

   a. Write a brief description of the difference between a relative and absolute reference.

   b. Provide a sketched example of a relative and absolute reference.

9. Copy formulas with relative cell references.

   a. Copy the formula in D2 into cells D3:D5.

   b. Copy the formula in D2 into cells D13:D16.

   c. Save the worksheet.

10. Copy formulas with absolute cell references.

   a. In cell E10, enter the value **1.375**.

   b. In cell E2, create a formula containing an absolute reference that multiplies D2 and E10.

   c. Use the fill handle to copy the formula in E2 into cells **E3:E5**.

   d. Use the Copy and Paste buttons to copy the formula in E2 into cells **E13:E16**.

   e. Use the Delete command on the Edit menu to delete cells A13:E13, shifting the cells up.

   f. Change the amount in cell E10 to **3.45**.

   g. Select cells A1:E1 and insert cells, shifting cells down.

   h. Enter **Inventory Estimate** in cell A1.

   i. Save, preview, print, and close the workbook, then exit Excel.

▼ INDEPENDENT CHALLENGE 1

You are the box office manager for the Young Brazilians Jazz Band, a popular new group. Your responsibilities include tracking seasonal ticket sales for the band's concerts and anticipating ticket sales for the next season. The group sells four types of tickets: reserved, general, senior, and student tickets.

The 2006–2007 season includes five scheduled concerts: Spring, Summer, Fall, Winter, and Thaw. You will plan and build a worksheet that tracks the sales of each of the four ticket types for all five concerts.

   a. Think about the results you want to see, the information you need to build into these worksheets, and what types of calculations must be performed.

   b. Sketch sample worksheets on a piece of paper to indicate how the information should be laid out. What information should go in the columns? What information should go in the rows?

   c. Start Excel, open a new workbook, then save it as **Young Brazilians** in the drive and folder where your Data Files are stored.

   d. Plan and build a worksheet that tracks the sales of each of the four ticket types for all five concerts. Build the worksheets by entering a title, row labels, column headings, and formulas.

   e. Enter your own sales data that shows that no concert sold more than 400 tickets, and the Reserved category was the most popular.

   f. Calculate the total ticket sales for each concert, the total sales for each of the four ticket types, and the total sales for all tickets.

   g. Name the worksheet **Sales Data** and color the worksheet tab red.

   h. Copy the Sales Data worksheet to a blank worksheet, name the copied worksheet **5% Increase**, then color the sheet tab aqua.

   i. Modify the 5% Increase sheet so that a 5% increase in sales of all ticket types is shown in a separate column with an appropriate column label. See Figure B-25 for a sample worksheet.

   j. Enter your name in a cell in each worksheet.

   k. Save your work, preview and print the worksheets, then close the workbook and exit Excel.

FIGURE B-25

	A	B	C	D	E	F	G	H	I	J	K	L
1			2006-2007 Season									
2			Young Brazilians Jazz Band					Increase				
3								1.05				
4		Reserved	General	Senior	Student							
5	Concerts	Seating	Admission	Citizens	Tickets	Totals		What if?				
6	Spring	285	50	40	20	395		414.75				
7	Summer	135	25	35	20	215		225.75				
8	Fall	130	50	25	20	225		236.25				
9	Winter	160	100	30	20	310		325.5				
10	Thaw	250	75	35	20	380		399				
11	Total	960	300	165	100	1525		1601.25				
12												

▼ INDEPENDENT CHALLENGE 2

The Beautiful You Salon is a small but growing beauty salon that has hired you to organize its accounting records using Excel. The owners want you to track the salon's expenses using Excel. Before you were hired, one of the bookkeepers entered last year's expenses in a workbook, but the analysis was never completed.

a. Start Excel, open the workbook EX B-3.xls, then save it as **Beautiful You Finances** in the drive and folder where your Data Files are stored. The worksheet includes labels for functions such as the Average, Maximum, and Minimum amounts of each of the expenses in the worksheet.

b. Think about what information would be important for the bookkeeping staff to know.

c. Create your sketch using the existing worksheet as a foundation.

d. Create formulas in the Total column and row using the AutoSum function.

e. Rename Sheet1 **Expenses** and add a color to the sheet tab.

Advanced Challenge Exercise

- Create formulas in the Average, Maximum, and Minimum columns and rows using the appropriate functions, dragging to select the range.
- Create a formula using the COUNT function that determines the total number of expense categories listed per quarter.

f. Enter your name in a worksheet cell, then compare your screen to the sample worksheet shown in Figure B-26.

g. Preview the worksheet, then print it.

h. Save the workbook, then close the workbook and exit Excel.

FIGURE B-26

	A	B	C	D	E	F	G	H	I	J	K	L
1	Beautiful You Salon											
2												
3	Operating Expenses for 2006											
4												
5	Expense	Quarter 1	Quarter 2	Quarter 3	Quarter 4	Total	Average	Maximum	Minimum			
6	Rent	4750	4750	4750	4750	19000	4750	4750	4750			
7	Utilities	8624	7982	7229	8096	31931	7982.75	8624	7229			
8	Payroll	23456	26922	25876	29415	105669	26417.25	29415	23456			
9	Insurance	8355	8194	8225	8327	33101	8275.25	8355	8194			
10	Education	4749	3081	6552	4006	18388	4597	6552	3081			
11	Inventory	29986	27115	25641	32465	115207	28801.75	32465	25641			
12	Total	79920	78044	78273	87059	323296						
13												
14	Average	13320	13007.33	13045.5	14509.83							
15	Maximum	29986	27115	25876	32465							
16	Minimum	4749	3081	4750	4006							
17	Count	6										

▼ INDEPENDENT CHALLENGE 3

You have been promoted to computer lab manager at Learn-It-All, a local computer training center. It is your responsibility to make sure there are enough computers for students during scheduled classes. Currently, you have five classrooms: four with IBM PCs and one with Macintoshes. Classes are scheduled Monday, Wednesday, and Friday in two-hour increments from 9 a.m. to 5 p.m. (the lab closes at 7 p.m.), and each room can currently accommodate 32 computers.

You plan and build a worksheet that tracks the number of students who can currently use the available computers per room. You create your enrollment data. Using an additional worksheet, you show the impact of an enrollment increase of 25%.

a. Think about how to construct these worksheets to create the desired output.

b. Sketch sample paper worksheets to indicate how the information should be laid out.

c. Start Excel, open a new workbook, then save it as **Learn-it-All** in the drive and folder where your Data Files are stored.

d. Create a worksheet by entering a title, row labels, column headings, data, and formulas. Name the sheet to easily identify its contents.

e. Create a second sheet by copying the information from the initial sheet.

f. Name the second sheet to easily identify its contents.

g. Add color to each sheet tab, then compare your screen to the sample shown in Figure B-27.

h. Enter your name in a cell in each sheet.

i. Save your work, preview and print each worksheet, then close the workbook and exit Excel.

FIGURE B-27

	A	B	C	D	E	F	G	H	I	J
1	Computer Lab Schedule - Increased enrollment									
2										
3	Monday	PC room #1	PC room #2	PC room #3	PC room #4	Mac room #1				
4	9:00	40	40	40	40	40				
5	11:00	40	40	40	40	40				
6	1:00	40	40	40	40	40				
7	3:00	40	40	40	40	40				
8	5:00	40	40	40	40	40				
9		200	200	200	200	200				
10										
11	Wednesday	PC room #1	PC room #2	PC room #3	PC room #4	Mac room #1				
12	9:00	40	40	40	40	40				
13	11:00	40	40	40	40	40				
14	1:00	40	40	40	40	40				
15	3:00	40	40	40	40	40				
16	5:00	40	40	40	40	40				
17		200	200	200	200	200				
18										
19	Friday	PC room #1	PC room #2	PC room #3	PC room #4	Mac room #1				
20	9:00	40	40	40	40	40				
21	11:00	40	40	40	40	40				
22	1:00	40	40	40	40	40				
23	3:00	40	40	40	40	40				
24	5:00	40	40	40	40	40				
25		200	200	200	200	200				

Actual \ **Increased** / Sheet3 /

Ready   NUM

▼ INDEPENDENT CHALLENGE 4

Your company is opening a branch office in Great Britain and your boss is a fanatic about keeping the thermostats at a constant temperature during each season of the year. Because she grew up in the United States, she is only familiar with Fahrenheit temperatures and doesn't know how to convert them to Celsius. She has asked you to find out the Celsius equivalents for the thermostatic settings she wants to use. She prefers the temperature to be 65 degrees F in the winter, 62 degrees F in the spring, 75 degrees F in the summer, and 70 degrees F in the fall. You can use the Web and Excel to determine the new settings.

a. Start Excel, open a new workbook, then save it as **Temperature Conversions** in the drive and folder where your Data Files are stored.

b. Use your favorite search engine to find your own information sources on calculating temperature conversions.

c. Think about how to create an Excel equation that can perform the conversion.

d. Create column and row titles using Table B-3 to get started.

e. In the appropriate cell, create an equation that calculates the conversion of a Fahrenheit temperature to a Celsius temperature.

f. Copy the equation, then paste it in the remaining Celsius cells.

TABLE B-3

Temperature Conversions		
Season	Fahrenheit	Celsius
Spring	62	
Winter	65	
Summer	75	
Fall	70	

Advanced Challenge Exercise

- Copy the contents of Sheet1 to Sheet2.
- In Sheet2, change the display so the formulas are visible, then print it.

g. Enter your name in one of the cells in each sheet, preview Sheet1, then print it.

h. Save the workbook, then close the files and exit Excel.

▼ VISUAL WORKSHOP

Create a worksheet similar to Figure B-28 using the skills you learned in this unit. Save the workbook as **Annual Budget** in the drive and folder where your Data Files are stored. Enter your name in cell A13, then preview and print the worksheet.

FIGURE B-28

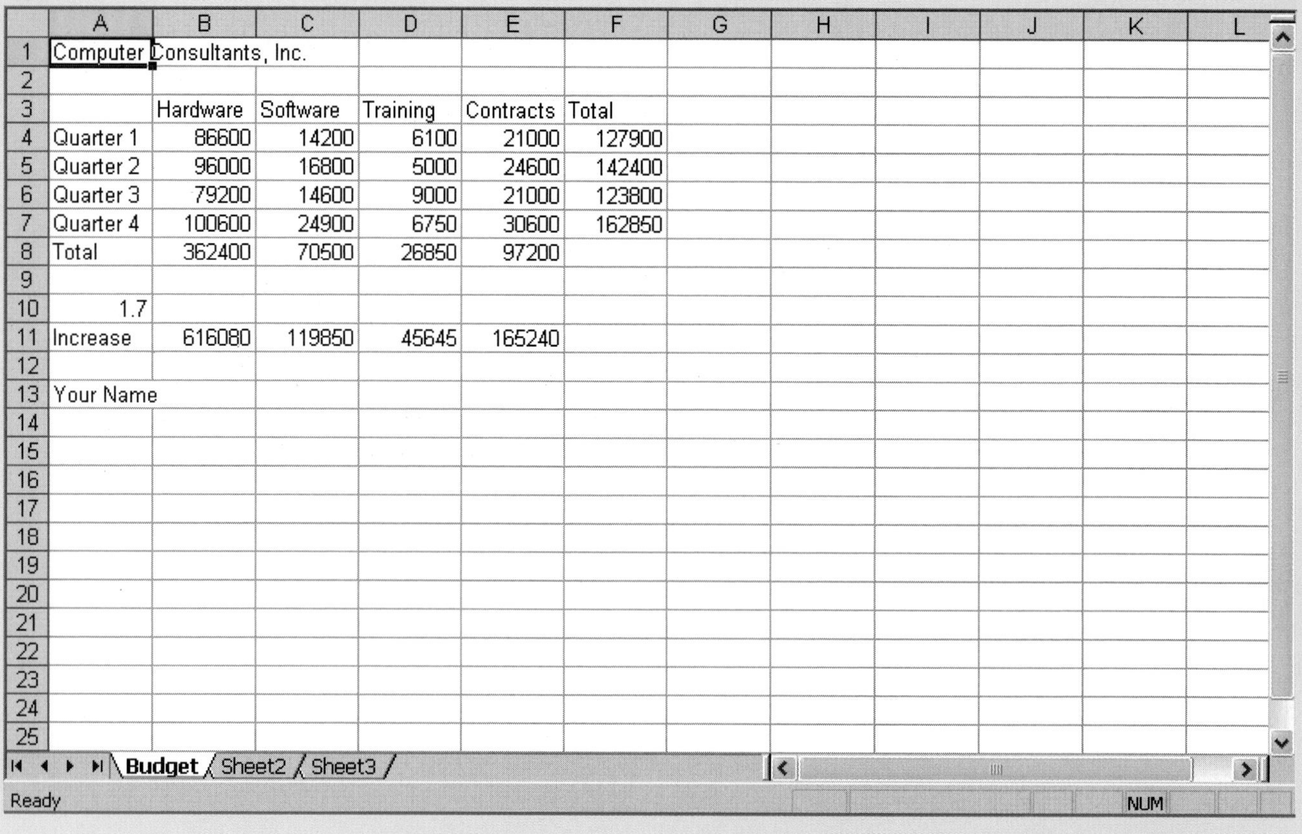

	A	B	C	D	E	F	G	H	I	J	K	L
1	Computer Consultants, Inc.											
2												
3		Hardware	Software	Training	Contracts	Total						
4	Quarter 1	86600	14200	6100	21000	127900						
5	Quarter 2	96000	16800	5000	24600	142400						
6	Quarter 3	79200	14600	9000	21000	123800						
7	Quarter 4	100600	24900	6750	30600	162850						
8	Total	362400	70500	26850	97200							
9												
10	1.7											
11	Increase	616080	119850	45645	165240							
12												
13	Your Name											
14												
15												
16												
17												
18												
19												
20												
21												
22												
23												
24												
25												

| ◄ ► ►| \ **Budget** / Sheet2 / Sheet3 /

Ready   NUM

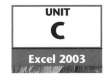

Formatting a Worksheet

OBJECTIVES

Format values
Use fonts and font sizes
Change attributes and alignment
Adjust column widths
Insert and delete rows and columns
Apply colors, patterns, and borders
Use conditional formatting
Check spelling

If you have a SAM user profile, you may have access to hands-on instruction, practice, and assessment of the skills covered in this unit. Log in to your SAM account and go to your assignments page to see what your instructor has assigned.

You can use Excel formatting features to make a worksheet more attractive, to make it easier to read, or to emphasize key data. You do this by using different colors and fonts for the cell contents, adjusting column and row widths, and inserting and deleting columns and rows. ▨▨▨ The marketing managers at MediaLoft have asked Jim Fernandez to create a workbook that lists advertising expenses for all MediaLoft stores. Jim has prepared a worksheet for the New York City store containing this information, which he can adapt later for use in other stores. He asks you to use formatting to make the worksheet easier to read and to call attention to important data.

Formatting Values

If you enter a value in a cell and you don't like the way the data appears, you can adjust the cell's format. A cell's **format** determines how labels and values appear in it, such as boldface, italic, with or without dollar signs or commas, and the like. Formatting changes only the way a value or label appears; it does not alter cell data in any way. To format a cell, first select it, then apply the formatting. You can format cells and ranges before or after you enter data. 🔳🔳🔳 The Marketing Department has requested that Jim begin by listing the New York City store's advertising expenses. Jim developed a worksheet that lists advertising invoices, entered all the information, and now he wants you to format some of the labels and values. Because some of the changes might also affect column widths, you make all formatting changes before widening the columns.

STEPS

1. **Start Excel, open the file EX C-1.xls from the drive and folder where your Data Files are stored, then save it as Ad Expenses.**
   The NYC advertising worksheet appears in Figure C-1. You can display numeric data in a variety of ways, such as with decimals or leading dollar signs. Excel provides a special format for currency, which adds two decimal places and a dollar sign.

2. **Select the range E4:E32, then click the Currency Style button $ on the Formatting toolbar**
   Excel adds dollar signs and two decimal places to the Cost data. Excel automatically resizes the column to display the new formatting. Another way to format dollar values is to use the comma format, which does not include the dollar sign ($).

3. **Select the range G4:I32, then click the Comma Style button , on the Formatting toolbar**
   The values in columns G, H, and I display the comma format. You can also format percentages by using the Formatting toolbar.

4. **Select the range J4:J32, click the Percent Style button % on the Formatting toolbar, then click the Increase Decimal button ⬆️ on the Formatting toolbar to show one decimal place**
   The data in the % of Total column is now formatted with a percent sign (%) and one decimal place. You decide that you prefer the percentages rounded to the nearest whole number.

5. **Click the Decrease Decimal button ⬇️ on the Formatting toolbar**
   You can also apply a variety of formats to dates in a worksheet.

6. **Select the range B4:B31, click Format on the menu bar, click Cells, then if necessary click the Number tab in the Format Cells dialog box**
   The Format Cells dialog box opens with the Date category already selected on the Number tab. See Figure C-2.

7. **Select the format 14-Mar-01 in the Type list box, then click OK**
   The dates in column B appear in the format you selected. You decide you don't need the year to appear in the Inv. Due column. You can quickly open the Format Cells dialog box by right-clicking a selected range.

8. **Select the range C4:C31, right-click the range, click Format Cells on the shortcut menu, click 14-Mar in the Type list box in the Format Cells dialog box, then click OK**
   Compare your worksheet to Figure C-3.

9. **Click the Save button 💾 on the Standard toolbar**

FIGURE C-1: Advertising expense worksheet

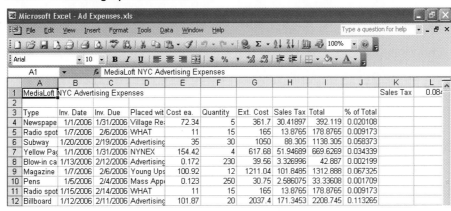

FIGURE C-2: Format Cells dialog box

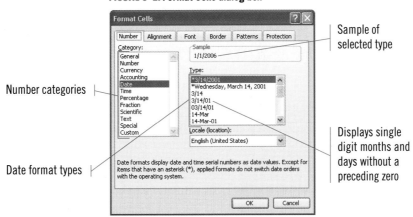

Number categories

Date format types

Sample of selected type

Displays single digit months and days without a preceding zero

FIGURE C-3: Worksheet with formatted values

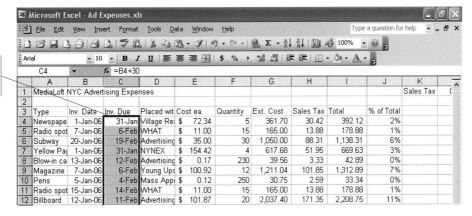

Dates formatted to appear without year

Excel 2003

Using Fonts and Font Sizes

A **font** is the name for a collection of characters (letters, numerals, symbols, and punctuation marks) with a similar, specific design. The **font size** is the physical size of the text, measured in units called points. A **point** is equal to 1/72 of an inch. The default font in Excel is 10-point Arial. You can change the font, the size, or both of any worksheet entry or section by using the Format command on the menu bar or by using the Formatting toolbar. Table C-1 shows several fonts in different sizes. ▓▓▓▓▓ Now that the data is formatted, Jim wants you to change the font and size of the labels and the worksheet title so that they stand out more from the data.

STEPS

1. **Press [Ctrl][Home] to select cell A1**

2. **Right-click cell A1, click Format Cells on the shortcut menu, then click the Font tab in the Format Cells dialog box**
   See Figure C-4.

3. **Scroll down the Font list to see an alphabetical listing of the fonts available on your computer, click Times New Roman in the Font list box, click 24 in the Size list box, then click OK**
   The title font appears in 24-point Times New Roman, and the Formatting toolbar displays the new font and size information. The column headings should stand out more from the data.

4. **Select the range A3:J3, then click the Font list arrow** `Arial ▾` **on the Formatting toolbar**
   Notice that the font names on this font list are displayed in the font they represent.

QUICK TIP
Once you've clicked the Font list arrow, you can quickly locate a font in the list by typing the first few characters in its name.

5. **Click Times New Roman in the Font list, click the Font Size list arrow** `10 ▾` **on the Formatting toolbar, then click 14 in the Font Size list**
   Compare your worksheet to Figure C-5. Notice that some of the column headings are now too wide to appear fully in the column. Excel does not automatically adjust column widths to accommodate cell formatting; you have to adjust column widths manually. You'll learn to do this in a later lesson.

6. **Click the Save button 🖫 on the Standard toolbar**

TABLE C-1: Types of fonts

font	12 point	24 point
Arial	Excel	Excel
Playbill	Excel	Excel
Comic Sans MS	Excel	Excel
Times New Roman	Excel	Excel

FIGURE C-4: Font tab in the Format Cells dialog box

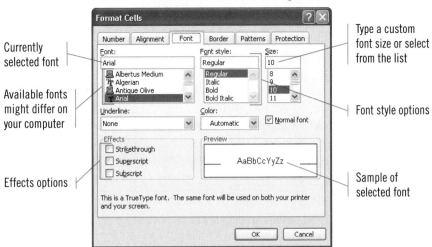

Currently selected font

Available fonts might differ on your computer

Effects options

Type a custom font size or select from the list

Font style options

Sample of selected font

FIGURE C-5: Worksheet with formatted title and labels

Font and size of active cell or range

Title appears in 24-point Times New Roman

Column headings now 14-point Times New Roman

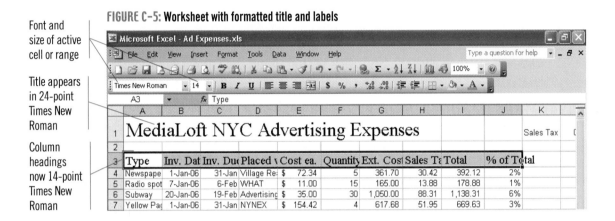

Clues to Use

Inserting and adjusting clip art

You can add clips to your worksheets to make them look more professional. A **clip** is an individual media file, such as art, sound, animation, or a movie. **Clip art** refers to images such as a corporate logo, a picture, or a photo; Excel comes with many clips that you can use. To add clip art to your worksheet, click Insert on the menu bar, point to Picture, then click Clip Art. The Insert Clip Art task pane appears. Here you can search for clips by typing one or more keywords (words related to your subject) in the Search text box, then clicking Search. Clips that relate to your keywords appear in the Clip Art task pane, as shown in Figure C-6. Click the image you want. (If you have a standard Office installation and have an active Internet connection, you will have more images available.) You can also add your own images to a worksheet by clicking Insert on the menu bar, pointing to Picture, then clicking From File. Navigate to the file you want, then click Insert. To resize an image, drag its lower-right corner. To move an image, drag it to a new location.

FIGURE C-6: Results of Clip Art search

UNIT C
Excel 2003

Changing Attributes and Alignment

Attributes are styling formats such as bold, italics, and underlining that you can apply to affect the way text and numbers look in a worksheet. You can also change the **alignment** of labels and values in cells to be left, right, or center. You can apply attributes and alignment options using the Formatting toolbar or using the Alignment tab of the Format Cells dialog box. See Table C-2 for a list and description of the available attribute and alignment toolbar buttons. Now that you have applied new fonts and font sizes to the worksheet labels, Jim wants you to further enhance the worksheet's appearance by adding bold and underline formatting and centering some of the labels.

STEPS

1. **Press [Ctrl][Home] to select cell A1, then click the Bold button B on the Formatting toolbar**
   The title appears in bold.

> **QUICK TIP**
> Use formatting shortcuts on any selected range: [Ctrl][B] to bold, [Ctrl][I] to italicize, and [Ctrl][U] to underline.

2. **Click cell A3, then click the Underline button U on the Formatting toolbar**
   Excel underlines the text in the column heading in the selected cell.

3. **Click the Italics button I on the Formatting toolbar, then click B**
   The word "Type" appears in boldface, underlined, italic type. Notice that the Bold, Italics, and Underline buttons are all selected.

> **QUICK TIP**
> Overuse of any attribute can be distracting and make a workbook less readable. Be consistent, adding emphasis the same way throughout.

4. **Click I**
   Excel removes italics from cell A3, but the bold and underline formatting attributes remain.

5. **Click the Format Painter button on the Formatting toolbar, then select the range B3:J3**
   Bold formatting is added to the rest of the labels in the column headings. The title would look better if it were centered over the data columns.

6. **Select the range A1:J1, then click the Merge and Center button on the Formatting toolbar**
   The Merge and Center button creates one cell out of the 10 cells across the row, then centers the text in that newly created large cell. The title "MediaLoft NYC Advertising Expenses" is centered across the 10 columns you selected. You can change the alignment within individual cells using toolbar buttons; you can split merged cells into their original components by selecting the merged cells, then clicking.

> **QUICK TIP**
> To clear all formatting for a selected range, click Edit on the menu bar, point to Clear, then click Formats.

7. **Select the range A3:J3, then click the Center button on the Formatting toolbar**
   Compare your screen to Figure C-7. Although they may be difficult to read, notice that all the headings are centered within their cells.

8. **Click the Save button on the Standard toolbar**

Clues to Use

Rotating and indenting cell entries
In addition to applying fonts and formatting attributes, you can rotate or indent cell data within a cell to further change its appearance. You can rotate text within a cell by altering its alignment. To change alignment, select the cells you want to modify, click Format on the menu bar, click Cells, then click the Alignment tab in the Format Cells dialog box. Click a position in the Orientation box, or type a number in the Degrees text box to change from the default horizontal alignment, then click OK. You can indent cell contents using the Increase Indent button on the Formatting toolbar, which moves cell contents to the right one space, or the Decrease Indent button, which moves cell contents to the left one space.

FIGURE C-7: Worksheet with formatting attributes applied

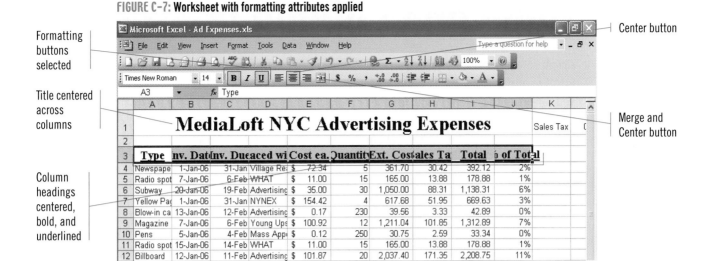

Formatting buttons selected

Center button

Title centered across columns

Merge and Center button

Column headings centered, bold, and underlined

TABLE C-2: Attribute and alignment buttons on the Formatting toolbar

button	description	button	description
B	Bolds text		Aligns text on the left side of the cell
I	Italicizes text		Centers text horizontally within the cell
U	Underlines text		Aligns text on the right side of the cell
	Adds lines or borders		Centers text across columns, and combines two or more selected, adjacent cells into one cell

Clues to Use

Using AutoFormat

Excel has 16 predefined worksheet formats to make formatting your worksheets easier and to give you the option of consistently styling your worksheets. AutoFormats are designed for worksheets with labels in the left column and top rows, and totals in the bottom row or right column. To use AutoFormat, select the data to be format-ted—or place your mouse pointer anywhere within the range to be selected (Excel can automatically detect a range of cells)—click Format on the menu bar, click AutoFormat, select a format from the sample boxes in the AutoFormat dialog box, as shown in Figure C-8, then click OK.

FIGURE C-8: AutoFormat dialog box

Samples of available formats

Adjusting Column Widths

As you continue formatting a worksheet, you might need to adjust column widths to accommodate a larger font size or style. The default column width is 8.43 characters wide, a little less than one inch. With Excel, you can adjust the column width for one or more columns by using the mouse or the Column command on the Format menu. Table C-3 describes the commands available on the Format Column menu. █████ Jim notices that some of the labels in column A have been truncated and don't fit in the cells. He asks you to adjust the widths of the columns so that the labels appear in their entirety.

STEPS

1. **Position the pointer on the line between the column A and column B headings**

   The **column heading** is the orange box at the top of each column containing a letter. The pointer changes to ✛, as shown in Figure C-9. You position the pointer on the right edge of the column that you are adjusting. The Yellow Pages entries are the widest in the column.

QUICK TIP
To reset columns to the default width, click the column headings to select the columns, click Format on the menu bar, point to Column, click Standard Width in the Column Width dialog box, then click OK.

2. **Click and drag the ✛ pointer to the right until the column displays the Yellow Pages entries fully**

   You can use the **AutoFit** feature and your mouse to resize a column so it automatically accommodates the widest entry in a cell.

3. **Position the pointer on the column line between columns B and C headings until it changes to ✛, then double-click**

   Column B automatically widens to fit the widest entry, in this case, the column label.

4. **Use AutoFit to resize columns C, D, and J**

   You can also use the Column Width command on the Format menu to adjust several columns to the same width.

5. **Select the range F5:I5**

   Columns can be adjusted by selecting any cell in the column.

6. **Click Format on the menu bar, point to Column, click Width to open the Column Width dialog box, then move the dialog box, if necessary, by dragging it by its title bar so you can see the selected columns**

   The column width measurement is based on the number of characters in the Normal font (in this case, Arial).

TROUBLE
If "######" appears after you adjust a column of values, the column is too narrow to display the contents. Increase the column width until the values appear.

7. **Type 11 in the Column Width text box, then click OK**

   The column widths change to reflect the new setting. See Figure C-10.

8. **Click the Save button 🖬 on the Standard toolbar**

TABLE C-3: Format Column commands

command	description
Width	Sets the width to a specific number of characters
AutoFit Selection	Fits to the widest entry
Hide	Hide(s) column(s)
Unhide	Unhide(s) column(s)
Standard Width	Resets width to default widths

FIGURE C-9: Preparing to change the column width

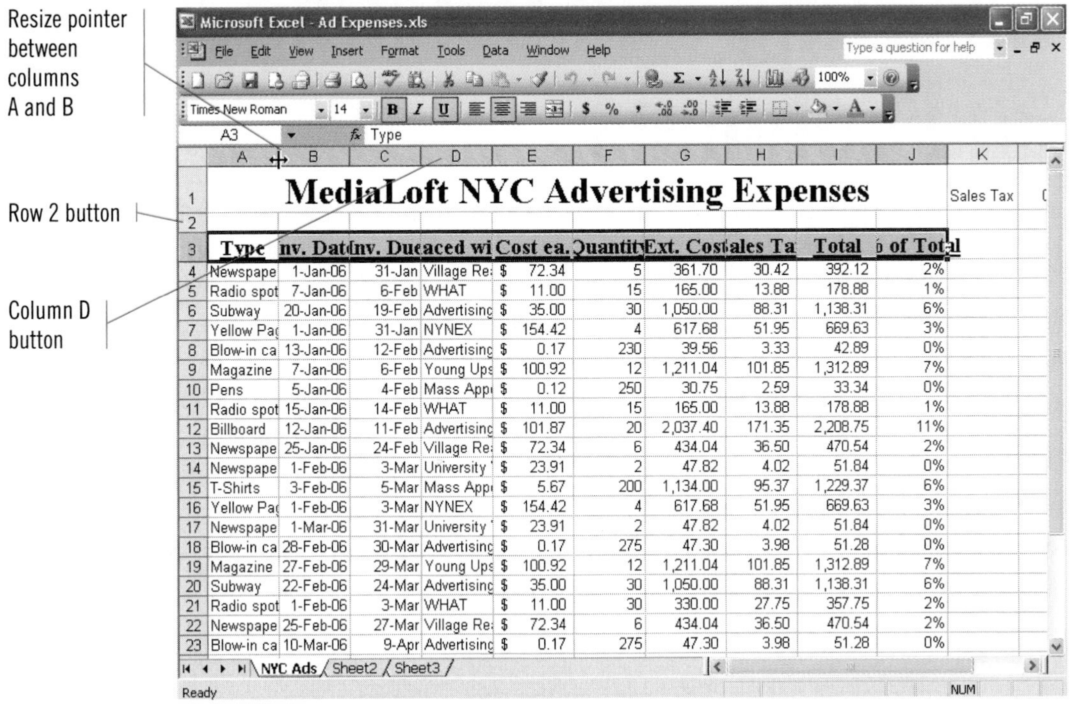

Resize pointer between columns A and B

Row 2 button

Column D button

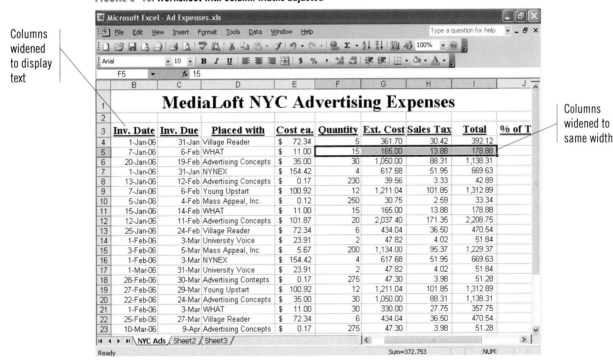

FIGURE C-10: Worksheet with column widths adjusted

Columns widened to display text

Columns widened to same width

Clues to Use

Specifying row height

The Row Height command on the Format menu allows you to customize row height to improve readability. Row height is calculated in points, the same units of measure used for fonts. The row height must exceed the size of the font you are using. Normally, you don't need to adjust row heights manually. If you format something in a row to be a larger point size, Excel adjusts the row to fit the largest point size in the row. You can also adjust row height by placing the ⊕ pointer under the row heading and dragging to the desired height.

FORMATTING A WORKSHEET EXCEL C-9

Inserting and Deleting Rows and Columns

As you modify a worksheet, you might find it necessary to insert or delete rows and columns to keep your worksheet current. For example, you might need to insert rows to accommodate new inventory products or remove a column of yearly totals that are no longer necessary. Excel inserts rows above the cell pointer and inserts columns to the left of the cell pointer. When you insert a new row, the contents of the worksheet shift down from the newly inserted row. When you insert a new column, the contents of the worksheet shift to the right from the point of the new column. To insert a single row, you can also right-click the row heading immediately below where you want the new row, then click Insert. To insert multiple rows, drag across row headings to select the same number of rows as you want to insert. You have already improved the appearance of the worksheet by formatting the labels and values. Now Jim asks you to improve the overall appearance of the worksheet by inserting a row between the last row of data and the totals. Also, you have located a row of inaccurate data and an unnecessary column that you need to delete.

STEPS

1. Right-click cell A32, then click Insert on the shortcut menu

The Insert dialog box opens. See Figure C-11. You can choose to insert a column or a row, or you can shift the data in the cells in the active column right or in the active row down. An additional row between the last row of data and the totals will visually separate the totals.

> **QUICK TIP**
>
> Inserting or deleting rows or columns can cause problems in formulas that contain absolute cell references. After adding rows or columns to a worksheet, be sure to proof your formulas.

2. Click the Entire row option button, then click OK

A blank row appears between the totals and the Billboard data, and the formula result in cell E33 has not changed. The Insert Options button 🖑 now appears beside cell A33. When you place ⌀ over 🖑, you can click the Insert Options list arrow and select from the following options: Format Same As Above, Format Same As Below, or Clear Formatting.

3. Click the row 27 heading

Hats from Mass Appeal Inc. are no longer part of the advertising campaign. All of row 27 is selected, as shown in Figure C-12.

> **QUICK TIP**
>
> Use the Edit menu, or right-click the selected row and click Delete to remove a selected row. Pressing [Delete] on the keyboard removes the contents of a selected row; the row itself remains.

4. Click Edit on the menu bar, then click Delete

Excel deletes row 27, and all rows below this shift up one row.

5. Click the column J heading

The percentage information is calculated elsewhere and is no longer necessary in this worksheet.

6. Click Edit on the menu bar, then click Delete

Excel deletes column J. The remaining columns to the right shift left one column.

7. Click the Save button 🖫 on the Standard toolbar

Clues to Use

Hiding and unhiding columns and rows

As you work with a worksheet, you may find that you need to make one or more columns or rows invisible. You can hide a selected column by clicking Format on the menu bar, pointing to Column, then clicking Hide. A hidden column is indicated by a black vertical line in its original position. You can display a hidden column by selecting the columns on either side of the black line, clicking Format on the menu bar, pointing to Column, and then clicking Unhide. (To hide/unhide one or more rows, substitute Row for the Column command.)

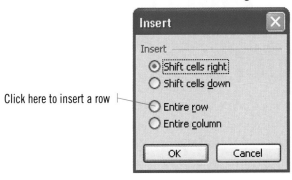

FIGURE C-11: **Insert dialog box**

Click here to insert a row

FIGURE C-12: **Worksheet with row 27 selected**

Row 27
heading

Inserted row

Insert Options
button might
appear in a
different
location, or
not at all

20	Subway	22-Feb-06	24-Mar	Advertising Concepts	$	35.00	30	1,050.00	88.31	1,138
21	Radio spot	1-Feb-06	3-Mar	WHAT	$	11.00	30	330.00	27.75	357
22	Newspaper	25-Feb-06	27-Mar	Village Reader	$	72.34	6	434.04	36.50	470
23	Blow-in cards	10-Mar-06	9-Apr	Advertising Concepts	$	0.17	275	47.30	3.98	51
24	Radio spot	15-Feb-06	17-Mar	WHAT	$	11.00	25	275.00	23.13	298
25	Pens	15-Mar-06	14-Apr	Mass Appeal, Inc.	$	0.12	250	30.75	2.59	33
26	Yellow Pages	1-Mar-06	31-Mar	NYNEX	$	154.44	4	617.76	51.95	669
27	Hats	20-Mar-06	19-Apr	Mass Appeal, Inc.	$	7.20	250	1,800.00	151.38	1,951
28	Subway	20-Mar-06	19-Apr	Advertising Concepts	$	35.00	30	1,050.00	88.31	1,138
29	Newspaper	1-Apr-06	1-May	University Voice	$	23.91	2	47.82	4.02	51
30	Subway	10-Apr-06	10-May	Advertising Concepts	$	35.00	30	1,050.00	88.31	1,138
31	Billboard	28-Mar-06	27-Apr	Advertising Concepts	$	101.87	20	2,037.40	171.35	2,208
32										
33					$1,355.24		2034	17,987.90	1,512.78	19,500
34										
35										
36										

|◄ ◄ ► ►| \ **NYC Ads** / Sheet2 / Sheet3 /

Ready   Sum=81782.06007   NUM

Excel 2003

Clues to Use

Adding and editing comments

Much of your Excel work may be in collaboration with teammates with whom you share worksheets. You can share ideas with other worksheet users by adding comments within selected cells. To include a comment in a worksheet, click the cell where you want to place the comment, click Insert on the menu bar, then click Comment. A resizable text box containing the computer user's name opens in which you can type your comments. A small, red triangle appears in the upper-right corner of a cell containing a comment. If the comments are not already displayed, workbook users can point to the triangle to display the comment. To see all worksheet comments, as shown in Figure C-13, click View on the menu bar, then click Comments. To edit a comment, click the cell containing the comment, click Insert on the menu bar, then click Edit Comment. To delete a comment, right-click the cell containing the comment, then click Delete Comment on the shortcut menu.

FIGURE C-13: **Comments in worksheet**

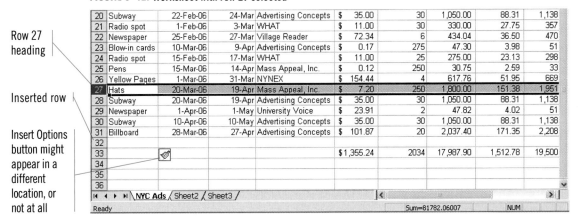

Applying Colors, Patterns, and Borders

You can use colors, patterns, and borders to enhance the overall appearance of a worksheet and to make it easier to read. You can add these enhancements by using the Patterns or Borders tabs in the Format Cells dialog box or by using the Borders and Color buttons on the Formatting toolbar. You can apply color or patterns to the background of a cell, to a range, or to cell contents. You can also apply borders to all the cells in a worksheet or only to selected cells to call attention to individual cells or groups of cells. See Table C-4 for a list of border buttons and their functions. Jim asks you to add a pattern, a border, and color to the title of the worksheet to give the worksheet a more professional appearance.

STEPS

1. **Press [Ctrl][Home] to select cell A1, then click the Fill Color list arrow on the Formatting toolbar**
   The color palette appears.

> **QUICK TIP**
> Use color sparingly. Too much color can divert the reader's attention from the worksheet data.

2. **Click the Turquoise color (fourth row, fifth column)**
   Cell A1 has a turquoise background, as shown in Figure C-14. Cell A1 spans columns A through I because of the Merge and Center command used for the title.

3. **Right-click cell A1, then click Format Cells on the shortcut menu**
   The Format Cells dialog box opens.

4. **Click the Patterns tab if it is not already displayed**
   See Figure C-15. Adding a pattern to cells can add to the visual interest of your worksheet.

5. **Click the Pattern list arrow, click the Thin Diagonal Crosshatch pattern (third row, last column), then click OK**
   A border also enhances a cell's appearance. Unlike underlining, which is a text-formatting tool, borders extend to the width of the cell.

> **QUICK TIP**
> You can also draw cell borders using the mouse pointer. Click the Borders list arrow on the Formatting toolbar, click Draw Borders, then drag to create borders or boxes.

6. **Click the Borders list arrow on the Formatting toolbar, then click the Thick Bottom Border (second row, second column) on the Borders palette**
   It can be difficult to view a border in a selected cell.

7. **Click cell A3**
   The border is a nice enhancement. Font color can also help distinguish information in a worksheet.

> **QUICK TIP**
> The default color on the Fill Color and Font Color buttons changes to the last color you selected.

8. **Select the range A3:I3, click the Font Color list arrow on the Formatting toolbar, then click the Blue color (second row, third column from the right) on the palette**
   The text changes color, as shown in Figure C-16.

9. **Click the Save button on the Standard toolbar**

Clues to Use

Formatting columns or rows

You can save yourself time by formatting an entire column or row using any of the categories that appear in the Format Cells dialog box. You might, for example, want to format all the cells within a column to accept telephone numbers, social security numbers, zip codes, or custom number formats. Click the column or row heading—located at the top of a column or beginning of a row—to select the entire column or row. You can format a selected column or row by clicking Format on the menu bar, clicking Cells, then clicking the appropriate tab in the Format Cells dialog box.

FIGURE C-14: Background color added to cell

Cell A1 with turquoise background

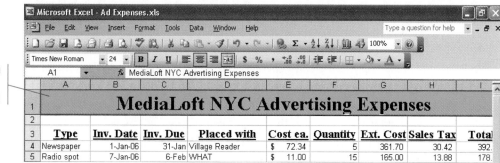

FIGURE C-15: Patterns tab in the Format Cells dialog box

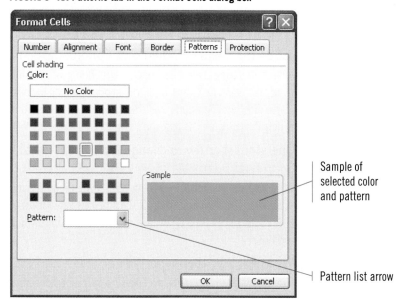

Sample of selected color and pattern

Pattern list arrow

FIGURE C-16: Worksheet with colors, patterns, and border

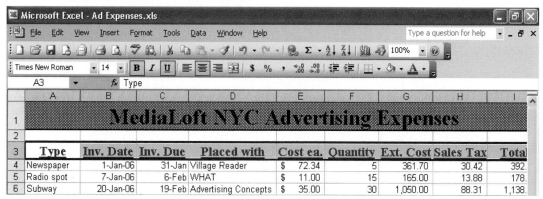

TABLE C-4: Border buttons

button	function	button	function	button	function
	No Border		Bottom Double Border		Top and Thick Bottom Border
	Bottom Border		Thick Bottom Border		All Borders
	Left Border		Top and Bottom Border		Outside Borders
	Right Border		Top and Double Bottom Border		Thick Box Border

Using Conditional Formatting

Formatting makes worksheets look professional and helps distinguish different types of data. You can have Excel automatically apply formatting depending on specific values in cells. You might, for example, want advertising costs above a certain number to appear in red boldface and lower values to appear in blue. Automatically applying formatting attributes based on cell values is called **conditional formatting**. If the data meets your criteria, Excel applies the formats you specify. ▰▰▰▰ Jim wants the worksheet to include conditional formatting so that total advertising costs greater than $175 appear in boldface red type. He asks you to create the conditional format in the first cell in the Total cost column.

STEPS

1. **Click cell** G4

   Use the scroll bars if necessary, to make column G visible.

TROUBLE

If the Office Assistant appears, close it by clicking the No, don't provide help now button.

2. **Click** Format **on the menu bar, then click** Conditional Formatting

   The Conditional Formatting dialog box opens. Depending on the logical operator you've selected (such as "greater than" or "not equal to"), the Conditional Formatting dialog box displays different input boxes. You can define up to three different conditions, and then assign formatting attributes to each one. You define the condition first. The default setting for the first condition is "Cell Value Is" "between."

3. **Click the** Operator list arrow **to change the current condition, then click** greater than or equal to

   Because you changed the operator from "between," which required text boxes for two values, only one value text box now appears. The first condition is that the cell value must be greater than or equal to some value. See Table C-5 for a list of options. The value can be a constant, formula, cell reference, or date. That value is set in the third box.

4. **Click the** Value text box, **then type** 175

   Now that you have assigned the value, you need to specify what formatting you want for cells that meet this condition.

5. **Click** Format, **click the** Color list arrow **in the Format Cells dialog box, click the** Red color **(third row, first column), click** Bold **in the Font style list box, then click** OK

6. **Compare your settings to Figure C-17, then click** OK **to close the Conditional Formatting dialog box**

   The value in cell G4, 361.70, is formatted in bold red numbers because it is greater than 175, meeting the condition to apply the format. You can copy conditional formats the same way you would copy other formats.

7. **Verify that** cell G4 is selected, click the Format Painter button ✅ on the Standard toolbar, **then drag** ⬩🖌 **to select the range** G5:G30

8. **Click cell** G4

   Compare your results to Figure C-18. All cells with values greater than or equal to 175 in column G appear in bold red text.

9. **Press** [Ctrl][Home] **to select cell A1, then click the** Save button 🖫 on the Standard toolbar

TABLE C-5: Conditional formatting options

option	mathematical equivalent	option	mathematical equivalent
Between	$X>Y<Z$	Greater than	$Z>Y$
Not between	$B>C<A$	Less than	$Y<Z$
Equal to	$A=B$	Greater than or equal to	$A>=B$
Not equal to	$A≠B$	Less than or equal to	$Z<=Y$

FIGURE C-17: Completed Conditional Formatting dialog box

Operator list arrow

Enter value in the
Value text box

Click to define format
of cells that meet the
condition

Click to add additional condition(s)

Click to delete existing condition(s)

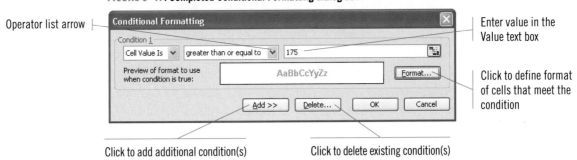

FIGURE C-18: Worksheet with conditional formatting

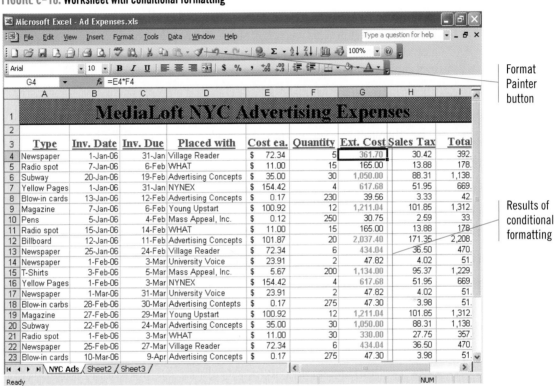

Format
Painter
button

Results of
conditional
formatting

Clues to Use

Deleting conditional formatting

Because it's likely that the conditions you define will change, you can delete any conditional format you define. Select the cell(s) containing conditional formatting, click Format on the menu bar, click Conditional Formatting, then click Delete in the Conditional Formatting dialog box. The Delete Conditional Format dialog box opens, as shown in Figure C-19. Select the check boxes for any of the conditions you want to delete, click OK, then click OK again. The previously assigned formatting is deleted—leaving the cell's contents intact.

FIGURE C-19: Delete Conditional Format dialog box

Checking Spelling

A single misspelled word can cast doubt on the validity and professional value of your entire workbook. Excel includes a spelling checker to help you ensure that the words in your worksheet are spelled correctly. The spelling checker scans your worksheet, displays words it doesn't find in its built-in dictionary, and when possible, suggests replacements. To check other sheets in a multiple-sheet workbook, you need to display each sheet and run the spelling checker again. Because the built-in dictionary cannot possibly include all the words that anyone needs, you can add words to the dictionary, such as your company name, an acronym, or an unusual technical term. The spelling checker will no longer consider that word misspelled. Any words you've added to the dictionary using Word, Access, or PowerPoint are also available in Excel. Because he will distribute this workbook to the marketing managers, Jim asks you to check its spelling.

STEPS

TROUBLE
If a language other than English is being used, the Spelling dialog box lists the name of that language in its title bar.

1. **Click the Spelling button 🔤 on the Standard toolbar**

   The Spelling: English (U.S.) dialog box opens, as shown in Figure C-21, with MediaLoft selected as the first misspelled word in the worksheet. For any word, you have the option to Ignore or to Ignore All cases that the spell checker flags, or to Add the word to the dictionary.

2. **Click Ignore All for MediaLoft**

   The spelling checker found the word "cards" misspelled and offers "crabs" as an alternative.

3. **Scroll through the Suggestions list, click cards, then click Change**

   The word "Concepts" is also misspelled, and the spelling checker suggests the correct spelling.

4. **Click Change**

   When no more incorrect words are found, Excel displays a message indicating that all the words on the worksheet have been checked.

5. **Click OK**

6. **Enter your name in cell A34, then press [Ctrl][Home]**

QUICK TIP
You can set **AutoCorrect** to correct spelling as you type. Click Tools on the menu bar, then click AutoCorrect Options.

7. **Click the Save button 💾 on the Standard toolbar, then preview the worksheet**

8. **In the Preview window, click Setup to open the Page Setup dialog box, under Scaling click Fit to option button to print the worksheet on one page, click OK, click Print, then click OK**

   Compare your printout to Figure C-22.

9. **Click File on the menu bar, then click Exit to close the workbook without saving changes and exit Excel**

Clues to Use

Using e-mail to send a workbook

Once you have checked for spelling errors, you can use e-mail to send an entire workbook from within Excel. To send a workbook as an e-mail message attachment, open the workbook, click File on the menu bar, point to Send To, then click Mail Recipient (as Attachment). You supply the To and optional Cc information, as shown in Figure C-20, then click Send.

FIGURE C-20: E-mailing an Excel workbook

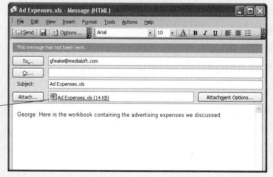

Workbook is automatically attached to message

FIGURE C-21: Spelling English dialog box

Misspelled word

Type replacement word here or click a suggestion

Click to ignore all occurrences of misspelled word

Click to add word to dictionary

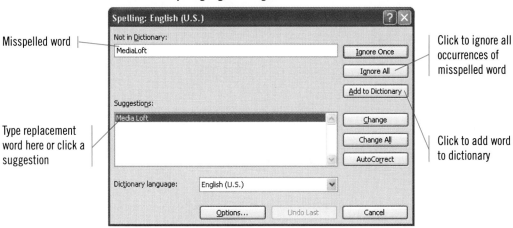

FIGURE C-22: Completed worksheet

MediaLoft NYC Advertising Expenses

Sales Tax 0.0841

Type	Inv. Date	Inv. Due	Placed with	Cost ea.	Quantity	Ext. Cost	Sales Tax	Total
Newspaper	1-Jan-06	31-Jan	Village Reader	$ 72.34	5	361.70	30.42	392.12
Radio spot	7-Jan-06	6-Feb	WHAT	$ 11.00	15	165.00	13.88	178.88
Subway	20-Jan-06	19-Feb	Advertising Concepts	$ 35.00	30	1,050.00	88.31	1,138.31
Yellow Pages	1-Jan-06	31-Jan	NYNEX	$ 154.42	4	617.68	51.95	669.63
Blow-in cards	13-Jan-06	12-Feb	Advertising Concepts	$ 0.17	230	39.56	3.33	42.89
Magazine	7-Jan-06	6-Feb	Young Upstart	$ 100.92	12	1,211.04	101.85	1,312.89
Pens	5-Jan-06	4-Feb	Mass Appeal, Inc.	$ 0.12	250	30.75	2.59	33.34
Radio spot	15-Jan-06	14-Feb	WHAT	$ 11.00	15	165.00	13.88	178.88
Billboard	12-Jan-06	11-Feb	Advertising Concepts	$ 101.87	20	2,037.40	171.35	2,208.75
Newspaper	25-Jan-06	24-Feb	Village Reader	$ 72.34	6	434.04	36.50	470.54
Newspaper	1-Feb-06	3-Mar	University Voice	$ 23.91	2	47.82	4.02	51.84
T-Shirts	3-Feb-06	5-Mar	Mass Appeal, Inc.	$ 5.67	200	1,134.00	95.37	1,229.37
Yellow Pages	1-Feb-06	3-Mar	NYNEX	$ 154.42	4	617.68	51.95	669.63
Newspaper	1-Mar-06	31-Mar	University Voice	$ 23.91	2	47.82	4.02	51.84
Blow-in cards	28-Feb-06	30-Mar	Advertising Concepts	$ 0.17	275	47.30	3.98	51.28
Magazine	27-Feb-06	29-Mar	Young Upstart	$ 100.92	12	1,211.04	101.85	1,312.89
Subway	22-Feb-06	24-Mar	Advertising Concepts	$ 35.00	30	1,050.00	88.31	1,138.31
Radio spot	1-Feb-06	3-Mar	WHAT	$ 11.00	30	330.00	27.75	357.75
Newspaper	25-Feb-06	27-Mar	Village Reader	$ 72.34	6	434.04	36.50	470.54
Blow-in cards	10-Mar-06	9-Apr	Advertising Concepts	$ 0.17	275	47.30	3.98	51.28
Radio spot	15-Feb-06	17-Mar	WHAT	$ 11.00	25	275.00	23.13	298.13
Pens	15-Mar-06	14-Apr	Mass Appeal, Inc.	$ 0.12	250	30.75	2.59	33.34
Yellow Pages	1-Mar-06	31-Mar	NYNEX	$ 154.44	4	617.76	51.95	669.71
Subway	20-Mar-06	19-Apr	Advertising Concepts	$ 35.00	30	1,050.00	88.31	1,138.31
Newspaper	1-Apr-06	1-May	University Voice	$ 23.91	2	47.82	4.02	51.84
Subway	10-Apr-06	10-May	Advertising Concepts	$ 35.00	30	1,050.00	88.31	1,138.31
Billboard	28-Mar-06	27-Apr	Advertising Concepts	$ 101.87	20	2,037.40	171.35	2,208.75
				$ 1,348.04	1784	16,187.90	1,361.40	17,549.30

Your Name

Practice

▼ CONCEPTS REVIEW

Label each element of the Excel worksheet window shown in Figure C-23.

FIGURE C-23

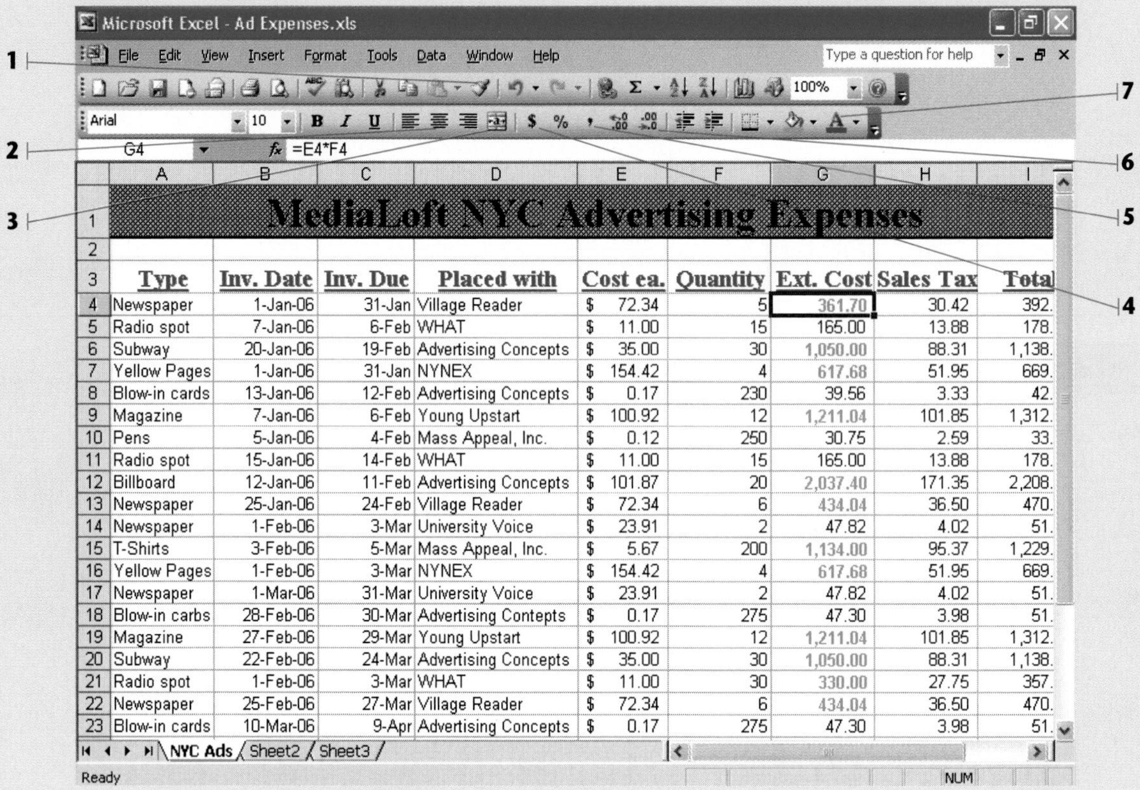

Match each command or button with the statement that best describes it.

8. $
9. (button)
10. ABC✓
11. **Cells command on the Format menu**
12. **Conditional Formatting**
13. **Delete command on the Edit menu**

a. Changes appearance of a cell depending on result
b. Erases the contents of a cell
c. Used to check the spelling in a worksheet
d. Used to change the appearance of selected cells
e. Pastes the contents of the Clipboard into the current cell
f. Changes the format to Currency

Select the best answer from the list of choices.

14. What is the name of the feature used to resize a column to its widest entry?

    a. AutoResize

    b. AutoFormat

    c. AutoFit

    d. AutoAdjust

15. Which button center-aligns the contents of a single cell?

    a.

    b.

    c.

    d.

16. Which button increases the number of decimal places in selected cells?

    a.

    b.

    c.

    d.

17. Which of the following is an example of the comma format?

    a. 5555.55

    b. 55.55%

    c. 5,555.55

    d. $5,555.55

18. How many conditional formats can be created in any cell?

    a. 1

    b. 2

    c. 3

    d. 4

19. Which feature applies formatting attributes according to cell contents?

    a. AutoFormat

    b. Comments

    c. Conditional Formatting

    d. Merge and Center

20. Each of the following operators can be used in conditional formatting, *except*:

    a. Equal to.

    b. Greater than.

    c. Similar to.

    d. Not between.

▼ SKILLS REVIEW

1. Format values.

a. Start Excel and open a new workbook.

b. Enter the information from Table C-6 in your worksheet. Begin in cell A1, and do not leave any blank rows or columns.

c. Save this workbook as **MediaLoft GB Sales** in the drive and folder where your Data Files are stored.

d. Select the range of values in the Average Price column.

e. Format the range using the Currency Style button.

f. Apply the Comma format to the Average Price and Quantity data, and reduce the number of decimals in the Quantity column to 0.

g. Insert formulas in the Totals column (multiply the Average Price by the Quantity).

h. Apply the Currency format to the Totals data.

i. Save your work.

TABLE C-6

MediaLoft Great Britain Quarterly Sales Projections			
Department	Average Price	Quantity	Totals
Sports	30	2250	
Computers	42	3185	
History	37	1325	
Personal Growth	29	2070	

2. Use fonts and font sizes.

a. Select the range of cells containing the column labels.

b. Change the font of the column labels to Times New Roman.

c. Increase the font size of the column labels and the label in cell A1 to 14 point.

d. Resize the columns as necessary.

e. Save your changes.

3. Change attributes and alignment.

a. Select the worksheet title **MediaLoft Great Britain**, then use the Bold button to apply the bold attribute.

b. Use the Merge and Center button to center the title and the Quarterly Sales Projections labels over columns A through D.

c. Select the label **Quarterly Sales Projections**, then apply underlining to the label.

d. Add the bold attribute to the labels in the Department column.

e. Use the Format Painter to paste the format from the data in the Department column to the Department and Totals labels.

f. Add the italics attribute to the Average Price and Quantity labels.

g. Select the range of cells containing the column titles, then center them.

h. Return the underlined, merged and centered Quarterly Sales Projections label to its original alignment.

i. Move the Quarterly Sales Projections label to cell D2 and change the alignment to Align Right.

j. Save your changes.

4. Adjust column widths.

    a. Use the Format menu to change the width of the Average Price column to **25**.

    b. Use the AutoFit feature to resize the Average Price column.

    c. Use the Format menu to resize the Department column to **18** and the Quantity column to **15**.

    d. Change the text in cell C3 to **Sold**, then use AutoFit to resize the column.

    e. Save your changes.

5. Insert and delete rows and columns.

    a. Insert a new row between rows 4 and 5.

    b. Add MediaLoft Great Britain's newest department—**Children's Corner**—in the newly inserted row. Enter **35** for the average price and **1225** for the number sold.

    c. Add the following comment to cell A5: **New department**. Display the comment, if necessary.

    d. Add a formula in cell D5 that multiplies the Average Price column by the Sold column.

    e. Add a new column between the Department and Average Price columns with the title **Location**.

    f. Delete the History row.

    g. Edit the comment in cell A5 so it reads "New department. Needs promotion."

    h. Save your changes.

6. Apply colors, patterns, and borders.

    a. Add an outside border around the Average Price and Sold data.

    b. Apply a light green background color to the labels in the Department column.

    c. Apply a gold background to the column labels in cells **A3:E3**.

    d. Change the color of the font in the column labels in cells A3:E3 to blue.

    e. Add a 12.5% Gray pattern fill to the title in cell A1. (*Hint*: Use the Patterns tab in the Format Cells dialog box to locate the 12.5% Gray pattern.)

    f. Enter your name in cell A20, then save your work.

    g. Preview and print the worksheet, then close the workbook.

7. Use conditional formatting.

    a. Open the file EX C-2.xls from the drive and folder where your Data Files are stored, then save it as **Monthly Operating Expenses**.

    b. Create conditional formatting that changes a monthly data entry to blue if the value is **greater than 2500**, and changes the monthly data entry to red if the value is **less than 700**.

    c. Create a third conditional format that changes the monthly data to green if a value is **between 1000 and 2000**.

    d. Use the Bold button and Center button to format the column headings and row titles.

    e. Make Column A wide enough to accommodate the contents of cells **A4:A9**.

    f. Create formulas in cells F4:F9 and cells B11:F11. Use the Comma Style with no decimals in these cells.

    g. AutoFit the remaining columns.

    h. Use Merge and Center in row 1 to center the title over columns A–F.

    i. Format the title in cell A1 using 14-point text. Fill the cell with a color and pattern of your choice.

    j. Delete the third conditional format.

    k. Enter your name in cell A20, then apply a green background to it and make the text color yellow.

    l. Use the Edit menu to clear the cell formats from the cell with your name, then save your changes.

8. Check spelling.

    a. Check the spelling in the worksheet using the spelling checker, correcting any spelling errors.

    b. Save your changes, then preview and print the workbook.

    c. Close the workbook, then exit Excel.

▼ INDEPENDENT CHALLENGE 1

Beautiful You, a small beauty salon, has been using Excel for several months. Now that the salon's accounting records are in Excel, the manager would like you to work on the inventory. Although more items will be added later, the worksheet has enough items for you to begin your modifications.

a. Start Excel, open the file EX C-3.xls from the drive and folder where your Data Files are stored, then save it as **BY Inventory**.

b. Create a formula that calculates the value of the inventory on hand for each item.

c. Use an absolute reference to calculate the sale price of each item, using the markup percentage shown.

d. Add the bold attribute to the column headings.

e. Make sure all columns are wide enough to display the data and headings.

f. Change the On Hand Value and Sale Price columns so they display the Currency style with two decimal places.

g. Change the Price Paid column so it displays the Comma style with two decimal places.

h. Add a row under #2 Curlers for **Nail Files**, price paid **$0.25**, sold **individually (each)**, with **59** on hand.

i. Verify that all the formulas in the worksheet are correct. Adjust any items as needed, and check the spelling.

j. Use conditional formatting to call attention to items with a quantity of 25 or fewer on hand. Use boldfaced red text.

k. Add an outside border around the data in the Item column.

l. Delete the row with #3 Curlers.

m. Enter your name in an empty cell, then save the file.

n. Preview and print the worksheet, compare your work to the sample shown in Figure C-24, close the workbook, then exit Excel.

FIGURE C-24

	A	B	C	D	E	F	G	H	I	J
1	Beautiful You Salon						markup ->	1.35		
2										
3	**Item**	**Price Paid**	**Sold by**	**On Hand**	**On Hand Value**	**Sale Price**				
4	#2 Curlers	13.80	box	53	$ 731.40	$ 18.63				
5	Nail Files	0.25	each	59	$ 14.75	$ 0.34				
6	Hair dryers	4.25	each	75	$ 318.75	$ 5.74				
7	Nail polish	3.92	each	62	$ 243.04	$ 5.29				
8	Conditioner	2.99	each	35	$ 104.65	$ 4.04				
9	Scrumptious shampoo	8.30	each	25	$ 207.50	$ 11.21				
10	Clips	2.25	box	33	$ 74.25	$ 3.04				
11	Pins	4.75	box	36	$ 171.00	$ 6.41				
12	#1 Curlers	2.10	box	37	$ 77.70	$ 2.84				
13	Jumbo conditioner	10.65	each	22	$ 234.30	$ 14.38				
14	#472 color	16.32	each	13	$ 212.16	$ 22.03				
15										
16										
17										
18										
19										
20	Your Name									
21										
22										
23										
24										
25										

|◄ ◄ ► ►|\Sheet1 / Sheet2 / Sheet3 /

Ready   NUM

▼ INDEPENDENT CHALLENGE 2

You volunteer several hours each week with the Community Action Center. You would like to examine the membership list, and decide to use formatting to make the existing data look more professional and easier to read.

a. Start Excel, open the file EX C-4.xls from the drive and folder where your Data Files are stored, then save it as **Community Action**.

b. Remove any blank columns.

c. Format the Annual Revenue figures using the Currency format.

d. Make all columns wide enough to fit their data and headings.

e. Use formatting enhancements, such as fonts, font sizes, and text attributes to make the worksheet more attractive.

f. Center-align the column labels.

g. Use conditional formatting so that entries for Number of Employees that are greater than 50 appear in a contrasting color.

h. Adjust any items as necessary, then check the spelling.

i. Enter your name in an empty cell, then save your work.

j. Before printing, preview the file so you know what the worksheet looks like, then print a copy. Compare your work to the sample shown in Figure C-25.

k. Close the workbook, then exit Excel.

FIGURE C-25

	A	B	C	D	E	F	G
1	Community Action Center Members						
2							
3		Annual	Number of		Type of		
4	Member	Revenue	Employees	Status	Business		
5	Lisa's Photo Studio	$ 56,000.00	5	member	Restaurant		
6	Chip Technology	$ 492,600.00	175	member	Manufacturing, Microchips		
7	Computer Attic	$ 128,000.00	4	member	Computer Consultant		
8	Deluxe Auto Shop	$ 98,420.00	7	member	Automotive		
9	Front Office	$ 162,320.00	25	member	Employment Agency		
10	General Hospital	$ 1,154,000.00	480	member	Health		
11	Grande Table	$ 101,500.00	25	member	Restaurant		
12	Holiday Inn	$ 175,000.00	75	member	Hotel/Motel		
13	Midas Muffler	$ 106,000.00	22	member	Automotive		
14	Mill Shoppe	$ 346,000.00	165	member	Manufacturing, Furniture		
15	Reservation Inn	$ 272,000.00	42	member	Hotel/Motel		
16	State University	$ 975,630.00	422	member	Education		
17	Candy's Candy Shop	$ 100,500.00	3	non-member	Restaurant		
18	Dental Associates	$ 175,000.00	15	non-member	Health		
19	Dr. Rachel	$ 173,000.00	5	non-member	Health		
20	Dunkin' Donuts	$ 66,420.00	7	non-member	Restaurant		
21	Earl's Restaurant	$ 290,000.00	45	non-member	Restaurant		
22	First Federal Bank	$ 1,216,500.00	36	non-member	Bank		
23	Friendly Chevy	$ 289,000.00	17	non-member	Automotive		
24	Ken's Florist Shop	$ 89,900.00	10	non-member	Florist		
25	Moineka Muffler	$ 107,900.00	24	non-member	Automotive		

Sheet1 / Sheet2 / Sheet3 /

Ready   NUM

▼ INDEPENDENT CHALLENGE 3

Classic Instruments is a Miami-based company that manufactures high-quality pens and markers. As the finance manager, one of your responsibilities is to analyze the monthly reports from your five district sales offices. Your boss, Joanne Bennington, has just asked you to prepare a quarterly sales report for an upcoming meeting. Because several top executives will be attending this meeting, Joanne reminds you that the report must look professional. In particular, she asks you to emphasize the company's surge in profits during the last month and to highlight the fact that the Northeastern district continues to outpace the other districts.

a. Plan a worksheet that shows the company's sales during the first quarter. Assume that all pens are the same price. Make sure you include:

- The number of pens sold (units sold) and the associated revenues (total sales) for each of the five district sales offices. The five sales districts are: Northeastern, Midwestern, Southeastern, Southern, and Western.
- Calculations that show month-by-month totals and a three-month cumulative total
- Calculations that show each district's share of sales (percent of Total Sales)
- Formatting enhancements to emphasize the recent month's sales surge and the Northeastern district's sales leadership

b. Ask yourself the following questions about the organization and formatting of the worksheet: How can you calculate the totals? What formulas can you copy to save time and keystrokes? Do any of these formulas need to use an absolute reference? How do you show dollar amounts? What information should be shown in bold? Do you need to use more than one font? Should you use more than one point size?

c. Start Excel, then build the worksheet with your own price and sales data. Enter the titles and labels first, then enter the numbers and formulas. You can use the information in Table C-7 to get started.

TABLE C-7:

Classic Instruments
1st Quarter Sales Report

Office	Price	January Units Sold	Sales	February Units Sold	Sales	March Units Sold	Sales	Total Units Sold	Sales
Northeastern									
Midwestern									
Southeastern									
Southern									
Western									

d. Save the workbook as **Classic Instruments** in the drive and folder where your Data Files are stored.
e. Adjust the column widths as necessary.
f. Change the height of row 1 to 30 points.
g. Format labels and values, and change the attributes and alignment if necessary.
h. Resize columns and adjust the formatting as necessary.
i. Add a column that calculates a 24% increase in sales dollars. Use an absolute cell reference in this calculation.
j. Create a new column named Increase in Sales that adds the projected increase to the Total Sales. (*Hint*: Make sure the current formatting is applied to the new information.)

Advanced Challenge Exercise

- Use AutoFormat to add color and formatting to the data.
- Insert a clip art image in an appropriate location, adjusting its size and position as necessary.

k. Enter your name in an empty cell.
l. Check the spelling, then save your work.
m. Preview, then print the file in landscape orientation.
n. Close the file, then exit Excel.

▼ INDEPENDENT CHALLENGE 4

After saving for many years, you now have enough funds to take that international trip you have always dreamed about. Your well-traveled friends have told you that you should always have the local equivalent of $100 U.S. dollars in cash with you when you enter a country. You decide to use the Web to determine how much money you will need in each country.

a. Start Excel, open a new workbook, then save it as **Currency Conversions** in the drive and folder where your Data Files are stored.

b. Enter column and row labels using the information in Table C-8 to get started.

c. Use your favorite search engine to find your own information sources on currency conversions.

d. Find out how much cash is equivalent to **$1** in U.S. dollars for the following countries: **Australia**, **Canada**, **France**, **Germany**, **Sweden**, and the **United Kingdom**. Also enter the name of the currency used in each country.

e. Create an equation that calculates the equivalent of **$100** in U.S. dollars for each country in the list, using an absolute value in the formula.

f. Format the entries in columns B and C using the correct currency unit for each country, with two decimal places. (*Hint*: Use the Numbers tab in the Format cells dialog box; choose the appropriate currency format from the Symbol list, using two decimal places.)

g. Create a conditional format that changes the font attributes of the calculated amount in the "$100 US" column to bold and red if the amount is equals or exceeds **500 units** of the local currency.

h. Merge and center the title over the column headings.

i. Add any formatting attributes to the column headings, and resize the columns as necessary.

j. Add a background color to the title.

TABLE C-8

Currency Equivalents $100 in US dollars			
Country	$1 Equivalent	$100 US	Name of Units
Australia			
Canada			
France			
Germany			
Sweden			
United Kingdom			

Advanced Challenge Exercise

- Apply the AutoFormat of your choice to the conversion table.
- Delete the conditional format in the $100 US column.
- If you have access to an e-mail account, e-mail this workbook to your instructor as an attachment.

k. Enter your name in an empty worksheet cell.

l. Spell check, save, preview, then print the worksheet.

m. Close the workbook and exit Excel.

▼ VISUAL WORKSHOP

Create the worksheet shown in Figure C-26, using skills you learned in this unit. Open the file EX C-5.xls from the drive and folder where your Data Files are stored, then save it as **Projected March Advertising Invoices**. Create a conditional format in the Cost ea. column so that entries greater than 60 appear in red. (*Hint*: The only additional font used in this exercise is Times New Roman. It is 22 point in row 1, and 16 point in row 3.) Enter your name in cell A20, spell check the worksheet, then save and print your work.

FIGURE C-26

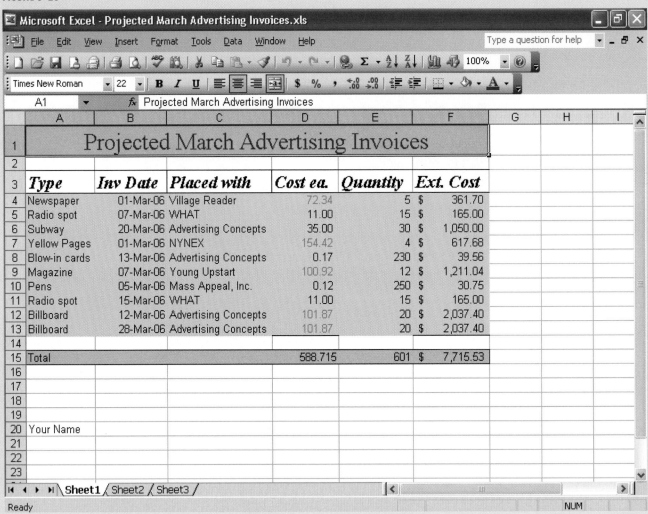

Working with Charts

OBJECTIVES

Plan and design a chart
Create a chart
Move and resize a chart
Edit a chart
Format a chart
Enhance a chart
Annotate and draw on a chart
Preview and print a chart

SAM If you have a SAM user profile, you may have access to hands-on instruction, practice, and assessment of the skills covered in this unit. Log in to your SAM account and go to your assignments page to see what your instructor has assigned.

Worksheets provide an effective way to organize information, but they are not always the best format for presenting data to others. Information in a selected range or worksheet can easily be displayed as a chart. **Charts**, often called graphs, allow you to communicate the relationships in your worksheet data in readily understandable pictures. In this unit, you will learn how to create a chart, how to edit a chart and change the chart type, how to add text annotations and arrows to a chart, and how to preview and print a chart. For the annual meeting, Jim Fernandez needs you to create a chart showing the six-month sales history for the MediaLoft stores in the Eastern Division. He wants to illustrate the growth trend in this division.

Planning and Designing a Chart

Before creating a chart, you need to plan the information you want your chart to show and how you want it to look. █████ In early June, the Marketing Department launched a regional advertising campaign for the Eastern Division. The results of the campaign were increased sales during the fall months. Jim wants you to create a chart for the annual meeting that illustrates the growth trend for sales in MediaLoft's Eastern Division stores and to highlight this sales increase.

DETAILS

Jim wants you to use the worksheet shown in Figure D-1 and the following guidelines to plan the chart:

- **Determine the purpose of the chart and identify the data relationships you want to communicate graphically**

  You want to create a chart that shows sales throughout MediaLoft's Eastern Division from July through December. In particular, you want to highlight the increase in sales that occurred as a result of the advertising campaign.

- **Determine the results you want to see, and decide which chart type is most appropriate to use**

  Different charts display data in distinctive ways. Some chart types are more appropriate for particular types of data and analyses. How you want your data displayed—and how you want that data interpreted—can help you determine the best chart type to use. Table D-1 describes several different types of charts, the corresponding button on the Chart Type palette located on the Chart toolbar, and indicates when each one is best used. Because you want to compare data (sales in multiple locations) over a time period (the months July through December), you decide to use a column chart.

- **Identify the worksheet data you want the chart to illustrate**

  You are using data from the worksheet titled MediaLoft Eastern Division Stores shown in Figure D-1. This worksheet contains the sales data for the four stores in the Eastern Division from July through December.

- **Sketch the chart, then use your sketch to decide where the chart elements should be placed**

  You sketch your chart as shown in Figure D-2. You put the months on the horizontal axis (the **x-axis**) and the monthly sales figures on the vertical axis (the **y-axis**). The x-axis is often called the **category axis** because it often contains the names of data groups, such as months or years. The y-axis is called the **value axis** because it often contains numerical values that help you interpret the size of chart elements. (In a 3-D chart, the y-axis is referred to as the z-axis.) The area inside the horizontal and vertical axes is called the **plot area**. The **tick marks** on the y-axis create a scale of measure for each value. Each value in a cell you select for your chart is a **data point**. In any chart, a **data marker** visually represents each data point, which in this case is a column. A collection of related data points is a **data series**. In this chart, there are four data series (Boston, Chicago, Kansas City, and New York), so you include a **legend** to make it easy to identify them.

FIGURE D-1: Worksheet containing sales data

Microsoft Excel - MediaLoft Sales-Eastern Division.xls

File Edit View Insert Format Tools Data Window Help

Type a question for help

Arial 12 B I U

A1 MediaLoft Eastern Division Stores

	A	B	C	D	E	F	G	H	I	J	K
1	MediaLoft Eastern Division Stores										
2	FY 2006 Sales Following Advertising Campaign										
3											
4											
5		July	August	September	October	November	December	Total			
6	Boston	18,750	13,050	18,600	22,500	22,500	20,750	$116,150			
7	Chicago	17,200	18,200	17,250	19,500	18,600	19,500	$110,250			
8	Kansas City	12,150	11,500	15,350	18,100	17,050	17,500	$ 91,650			
9	NYC	19,500	16,250	18,900	20,500	22,000	23,800	$120,950			
10	Total	$ 67,600	$ 59,000	$ 70,100	$ 80,600	$ 80,150	$ 81,550	$439,000			
11											

FIGURE D-2: Column chart sketch

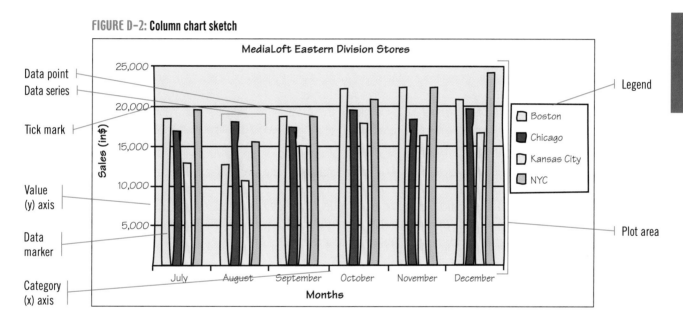

TABLE D-1: Commonly used chart types

type	button	description
Area		Shows how individual volume changes over time in relation to total volume
Bar		Compares distinct object levels over time using a horizontal format; sometimes referred to as a horizontal bar chart in other spreadsheet programs
Column		Compares distinct object levels over time using a vertical format; the Excel default; sometimes referred to as a bar chart in other spreadsheet programs
Line		Compares trends over even time intervals; appears similar to an area chart, but does not emphasize total
Pie		Compares sizes of pieces as part of a whole; used for a single series of numbers
XY (scatter)		Compares trends over uneven time or measurement intervals; used in scientific and engineering disciplines for trend spotting and extrapolation
Combination	none	Combines a column and line chart to compare data requiring different scales of measure

Creating a Chart

To create a chart in Excel, you first select the range containing the data you want to chart. Once you've selected a range, you can use the Excel **Chart Wizard** to lead you through the process of creating the chart. ▓▓▓▓ Using the worksheet containing the sales data for the Eastern Division, Jim asks you to create a chart that shows the growth trend that occurred.

STEPS

QUICK TIP
When charting any data, make sure all series are for the same time period.

1. **Start Excel, open the File EX D-1.xls from the drive and location where your Data Files are stored, then save it as MediaLoft Sales-Eastern Division**

   You want the chart to include the monthly sales figures for each of the Eastern Division stores, as well as month and store labels. You don't include the Total column and row because the monthly figures make up the totals, and these figures would skew the chart.

QUICK TIP
You can create a chart from noncontiguous cells by pressing and holding [Ctrl] while selecting each range.

2. **Select the range A5:G9, then click the Chart Wizard button 📊 on the Standard toolbar**

   The selected range contains the data you want to chart. The Chart Wizard opens. The Chart Wizard - Step 1 of 4 - Chart Type dialog box lets you choose the type of chart you want to create. The default chart type is a Clustered Column, as shown in Figure D-3. You can see a preview of the chart using your selected data by pressing and holding the Press and Hold to View Sample button.

3. **Click Next to accept Clustered Column, the default chart type**

   The Chart Wizard - Step 2 of 4 - Chart Source Data dialog box lets you choose the data to chart and whether the series appear in rows or columns. You want to chart the effect of sales for each store over the time period. Currently, the rows are appropriately selected as the data series, as specified by the Series in option button (located under the Data range). Because you selected the data before clicking the Chart Wizard button, Excel converted the range to absolute values and the correct range, =Sheet1!$A$5:$G$9, appears in the Data range text box.

4. **Click Next**

   The Chart Wizard - Step 3 of 4 - Chart Options dialog box shows a sample chart using the data you selected. The store locations (the rows in the selected range) are plotted against the months (the columns in the selected range), and Excel added the months as labels for each data series. A legend shows each location and its corresponding color on the chart. The Titles tab lets you add titles to the chart and its axes. Other tabs let you modify the axes, legend, and other chart elements.

5. **Click the Chart title text box, then type MediaLoft Sales - Eastern Division**

   After a moment, the title appears in the Sample Chart box. See Figure D-4.

6. **Click Next**

   In the Chart Wizard - Step 4 of 4 - Chart Location dialog box, you determine the placement of the chart in the workbook. You can display a chart as an object on the current sheet (called an **embedded chart**), on any other existing sheet, or on a newly created chart sheet. A **chart sheet** in a workbook contains only a chart, which is linked to the workbook data. The default selection—displaying the chart as an object in the sheet containing the data—will help Jim emphasize his point at the annual meeting.

QUICK TIP
If the Chart toolbar does not display, click View on the menu bar, point to Toolbars, and then click Chart.

7. **Click Finish**

   The column chart appears and the Chart toolbar opens, either docked or floating, as shown in Figure D-5. Your chart and the chart toolbar might be in different locations, and the chart may look slightly different. You adjust the chart's location and size in the next lesson. The **sizing handles**, the small squares at the corners and sides of the chart's border, indicate that the chart is selected. Any time a chart is selected, as it is now, a blue border surrounds the worksheet data range, a green border surrounds the row labels, and a purple border surrounds the column labels.

8. **Click the Save button 💾 on the Standard toolbar**

FIGURE D-3: First Chart Wizard dialog box

Selected chart

Chart types

Clustered column chart is the default

Chart sub-types for selected chart

Description of selected chart sub-type

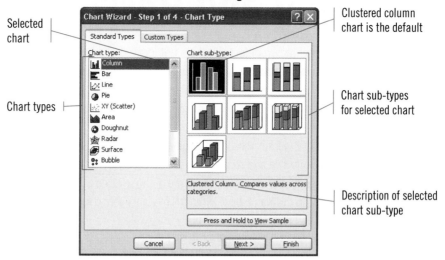

FIGURE D-4: Third Chart Wizard dialog box

Type the chart title here

Sample chart

Title added

Legend

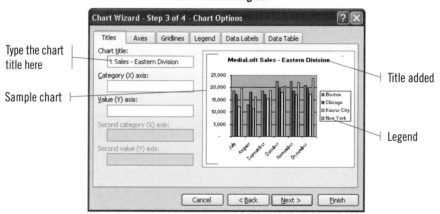

FIGURE D-5: Worksheet with column chart

Column labels

Row labels

Data range

Selected chart object

Chart toolbar

Title

Legend

Sizing handles

Month labels on the x-axis

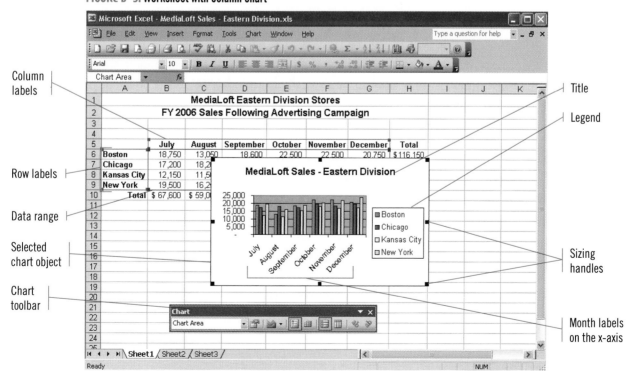

Moving and Resizing a Chart

Charts are graphics, or drawn objects, and are not located in a specific cell or at a specific range address. An **object** is an independent element on a worksheet. You can select an object by clicking within its borders to surround it with sizing handles. You can move a selected chart object anywhere on a worksheet without affecting formulas or data in the worksheet. However, any data changed in the worksheet is automatically updated in the chart. You can resize a chart to improve its appearance by dragging its sizing handles. You can even put a chart on another sheet, and it will still reflect the original data. Chart objects contain other objects, such as a title and legend, which you can move and resize. To move an object, select it, then drag it or cut and copy it to a new location. When you select a chart object, the name of the selected object appears in the Chart Objects list box on the Chart toolbar and in the Name box. 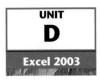 Jim wants you to increase the size of the chart, position it below the worksheet data, and reposition the legend.

STEPS

QUICK TIP

If you want to delete a chart, select it, then press [Delete].

1. **Make sure the chart is still selected, then position the pointer over the chart**

   The pointer shape ⬓ indicates that you can move the chart or use a sizing handle to resize it. For a table of commonly used chart pointers, refer to Table D-2. On occasion, the Chart toolbar obscures your view. You can dock the toolbar to make it easier to see your work.

2. **If the chart toolbar is floating, click the Chart toolbar's title bar, drag it to the right edge of the status bar until it docks, then release the mouse button**

   The toolbar is docked on the bottom of the screen.

3. **Place ⬓ on a blank area near the edge of the chart, press and hold the left mouse button, using ✛, drag the chart until its upper-left edge is at the top of row 13 and the left edge of the chart is at the left border of column A, then release the mouse button**

   As you drag the chart, you can see a dotted outline representing the chart's perimeter. The chart appears in the new location.

QUICK TIP

Resizing a chart doesn't affect the data in the chart, only the way the chart looks on the sheet.

4. **Position the pointer on the right-middle sizing handle until it changes to ↔, then drag the right edge of the chart to the right edge of column H**

   The chart is widened. See Figure D-6.

5. **Position the pointer over the upper-middle sizing handle until it changes to ↕, then drag it to the top edge of row 12**

6. **Scroll down the screen, position the pointer over the lower-middle sizing handle until it changes to ↕, then drag to position the bottom border of the chart at the bottom border of row 25**

   You can move the legend to improve the chart's appearance. You want to align the top of the legend with the top of the plot area.

QUICK TIP

Placing the mouse pointer over a chart object displays a ScreenTip identifying it, whether the chart is selected or not. If a chart—or any object in it—is selected, the ScreenTips still appear and the name of the selected chart object appears in the Chart Objects list box on the Chart toolbar and in the Name box.

7. **Click the legend to select it, then drag the legend upward using ⬓ so the top of the legend aligns with the top of the plot area**

   Sizing handles appear around the legend when you click it; "Legend" appears in the Chart Objects list box on the Chart toolbar as well as in the Name box, and a dotted outline of the legend border appears as you drag. Changing any label modifies the legend text.

8. **Click cell A9, type NYC, then click the Enter button ✓ on the formula bar**

   See Figure D-7. The legend changes to the text you entered. Because the chart is no longer selected, the chart toolbar no longer appears at the bottom of the screen.

9. **Click the Save button 🖫 on the Standard toolbar**

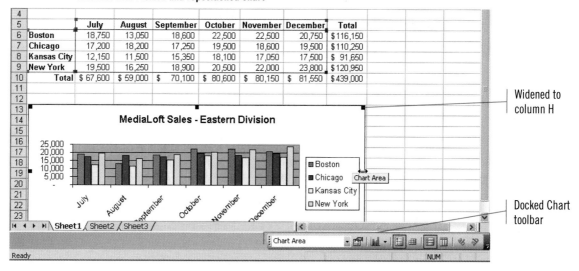

FIGURE D-6: Worksheet with resized and repositioned chart

Widened to column H

Docked Chart toolbar

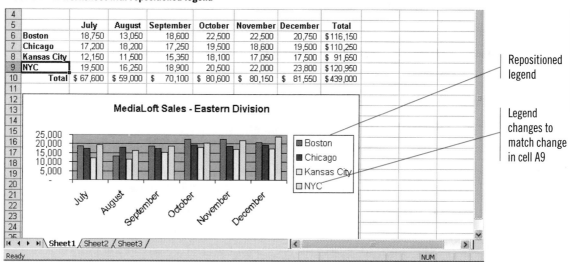

FIGURE D-7: Worksheet with repositioned legend

Repositioned legend

Legend changes to match change in cell A9

TABLE D-2: Commonly used pointers

name	pointer	use	name	pointer	use
Diagonal resizing	↗ or ↘	Change chart shape	I-beam	I	Edit chart text from corners
Draw	+	Create shapes	Move chart	✛	Change chart location
Horizontal resizing	↔	Change chart shape from left to right	Vertical resizing	↕	Changes chart shape from top to bottom

Clues to Use

Changing the location of a chart

Suppose you have created an embedded chart that you decide would look better on a chart sheet. You can make this change without recreating the entire chart. To change the location of a selected chart, click Chart on the menu bar, then click Location. If the chart is embedded, click the As new sheet option button, then click OK. If the chart is on its own sheet, click the As object in option button, then click OK.

Editing a Chart

Once you've created a chart, it's easy to modify it. You can change data values in the worksheet, and the chart is automatically updated to reflect the new data. You can also change a data point in a chart, and the corresponding data values in the worksheet are automatically updated. You can also easily change the type of chart displayed by using the buttons on the Chart toolbar. ▓▓▓▓ You look over your worksheet and realize the data for the Kansas City store in November and December is incorrect. After you correct this data, Jim asks you to see how the same data looks using different chart types.

STEPS

TROUBLE
If you cannot see the chart and data together on your screen, click View on the menu bar, click Zoom, then click 75%.

1. **If necessary, scroll the worksheet so that you can see both the chart and row 8 containing the Kansas City sales figures, click the** November Kansas City data point, **then click the data point again**

    Handles surround the data point. You can click and drag these handles to modify the plotted data value.

2. **Drag the upper handle until the ScreenTip displays 21000**

    The value in cell F8 displays 21000.

3. **Click cell** G8, **type** 23000, **then click the** Enter button ✓ **on the formula bar**

    The Kansas City columns for November and December reflect the increased sales figures. See Figure D-8. The totals in column H and row 10 are also updated.

4. **Select the chart by clicking a blank area within the chart border, then click the** Chart Type list arrow ◢▾ **on the Chart toolbar**

    The Chart Type buttons appear on the Chart Type palette. Table D-3 describes the principal chart types available.

QUICK TIP
As you work with charts, experiment with different formats for your charts until you get just the right look.

5. **Click the** Bar Chart button ▤ **on the palette**

    The column chart changes to a bar chart. See Figure D-9. You look at the bar chart, take some notes, then decide to see if the large increase in sales would be better presented with a three-dimensional column chart.

6. **Click** ◢▾, **then click the** 3-D Column Chart button ▦ **on the palette**

    A three-dimensional column chart appears. You notice that the three-dimensional column format is more crowded than the two-dimensional format, but it gives you a sense of volume.

QUICK TIP
The Chart Type button displays the last chart type selected.

7. **Click** ◢▾, **then click the** Column Chart button ▥ **on the palette**

8. **Click the** Save button ▤ **on the Standard toolbar**

TABLE D-3: Commonly used chart type buttons

click to display a	click to display a	click to display a	click to display a
◢ area chart	● pie chart	◣ 3-D area chart	▬ 3-D pie chart
▤ bar chart	⠿ (XY) scatter chart	▤ 3-D bar chart	◈ 3-D surface chart
▥ column chart	◉ doughnut chart	▦ 3-D column chart	▮ 3-D cylinder chart
▨ line chart	✦ radar chart	◣ 3-D line chart	▲ 3-D cone chart

FIGURE D-8: Worksheet with new data entered for Kansas City

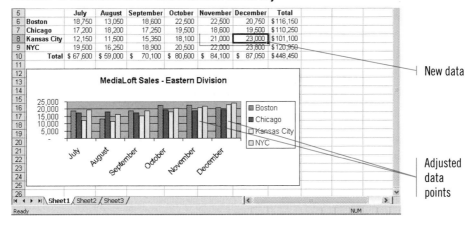

New data

Adjusted data points

FIGURE D-9: Bar chart

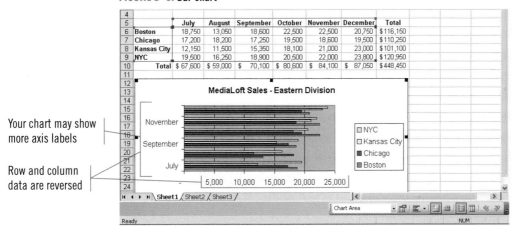

Your chart may show more axis labels

Row and column data are reversed

Clues to Use

Rotating a 3-D chart

In a three-dimensional chart, other data series in the same chart can sometimes obscure columns or bars. You can rotate the chart to obtain a better view. Click the chart, click the Corners object located at the tip of one of its axes, then drag the handle until a more pleasing view of the data series appears. See Figure D-10.

FIGURE D-10: 3-D chart rotated with improved view of data series

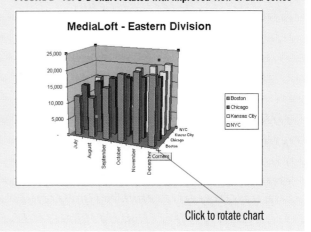

Click to rotate chart

Formatting a Chart

After you've created a chart using the Chart Wizard, you can easily modify its appearance. You can use the Chart toolbar and Chart menu to change the colors of data series and to add or eliminate a legend and gridlines. **Gridlines** are the horizontal and vertical lines in the chart that enable the eye to follow the value on an axis. ▰▰▰ Jim wants you to make some changes in the appearance of the chart. He wants to see if the chart looks better without gridlines, and he wants you to change the color of a data series.

STEPS

1. **Make sure the chart is still selected**

   Horizontal gridlines currently extend from the value axis tick marks across the chart's plot area.

   > **QUICK TIP**
   > The Chart menu only appears on the menu bar when a chart or one of its objects is selected.

2. **Click Chart on the menu bar, click Chart Options, click the Gridlines tab in the Chart Options dialog box, then click the Major Gridlines check box for the Value (Y) axis to remove the check mark**

   The gridlines disappear from the sample chart in the dialog box, as shown in Figure D-11.

3. **Click the Major gridlines check box for the Value (Y) axis to reselect it, then click the Minor gridlines check box for the Value (Y) axis**

   Both major and minor gridlines appear in the sample. **Minor gridlines** show the values between the tick marks.

4. **Click the Minor gridlines check box for the Value (Y) axis, then click OK**

   The minor gridlines disappear, leaving only the major gridlines on the value axis. You can change the color of the columns to better distinguish the data series.

5. **With the chart selected, double-click any light blue column in the NYC data series**

   Handles appear on all the columns in the NYC data series, and the Format Data Series dialog box opens, as shown in Figure D-12.

6. **Click the fuchsia color (fourth row, first column) on the Patterns tab, then click OK**

   All the columns for the series become fuchsia, and the legend changes to match the new color. Compare your formatted chart to Figure D-13.

7. **Click the Save button 🖫 on the Standard toolbar**

Clues to Use

Adding data labels to a chart

There are times when your audience might benefit by seeing data labels on a chart. These labels can indicate the series name, category name, and/or the value of one or more data points. Once your chart is selected, you can add this information to your chart by clicking

Chart on the menu bar, clicking Chart Options, then clicking the Data Labels tab in the Chart Options dialog box. You can also apply formatting to data labels, or delete individual data labels.

FIGURE D-11: Chart Options dialog box

Sample chart
appears without
gridlines

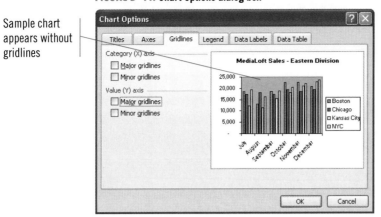

FIGURE D-12: Format Data Series dialog box

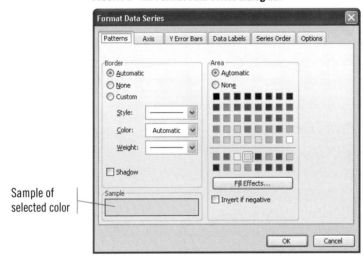

Sample of
selected color

FIGURE D-13: Chart with formatted data series

Gridlines
make it
easy to
follow axis
values

New data
series color

New color
appears in
legend

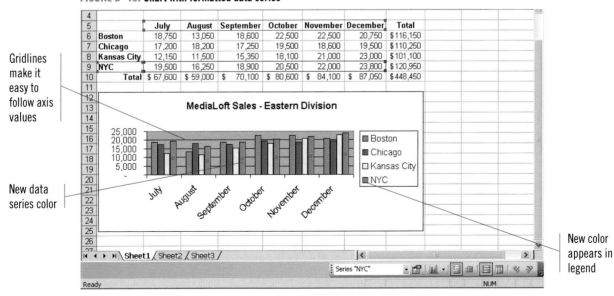

Enhancing a Chart

There are many ways to enhance a chart to make it easier to read and understand. You can create titles for the x-axis and y-axis, add graphics, or add background color. You can even format the text you use in a chart. Many enhancements can be made using the Chart toolbar buttons. These buttons are listed in Table D-4. ░░░░░ Jim wants you to improve the appearance of the chart by creating titles for the category axis and value axis and adding a drop shadow to the chart title.

STEPS

1. **Click a blank area of the chart to select the chart, click Chart on the menu bar, click Chart Options, click the Titles tab in the Chart Options dialog box, then type Months in the Category (X) axis text box**

   Descriptive text on the category axis helps readers understand the chart. The word "Months" appears below the month labels in the sample chart, as shown in Figure D-14.

> **QUICK TIP**
>
> To edit the text, position the pointer over the selected text box until it changes to I, click the text box, then edit the text.

2. **Type Sales (in $) in the Value (Y) axis text box, then click OK**

   A selected text box containing "Sales (in $)" appears rotated 90 degrees to the left of the value axis. Once the Chart Options dialog box is closed, you can move the value or title to a new position by clicking an edge of the object then dragging it.

3. **Press [Esc] on the keyboard to deselect the value axis title**

   Next you decide that a border with a drop shadow will enhance the chart title.

4. **Click the MediaLoft Sales – Eastern Division chart title to select it**

> **QUICK TIP**
>
> The Format button ▣ on the Chart toolbar opens a dialog box with the appropriate formatting options for the selected chart element. The ScreenTip for the button changes, depending on the selected object.

5. **Click the Format Chart Title button ▣ on the Chart toolbar to open the Format Chart Title dialog box, make sure the Patterns tab is selected, then click the Shadow check box to select it**

   A border with a drop shadow appears in the sample area.

6. **Click the Font tab in the Format Chart Title dialog box, click Times New Roman in the Font list, click Bold Italic in the Font style list, click OK, then press [Esc] on the keyboard to deselect the chart title**

   A border with a drop shadow appears around the chart title, and the chart title text is reformatted.

7. **Click any one of the months (on the category axis), click ▣, click the Font tab in the Format Axis dialog box if necessary, click 8 in the Size list if necessary, then click OK**

   The size of the category axis text decreases, making more of the plot area visible.

> **QUICK TIP**
>
> You can also double-click the text on the value axis to open the Format Axis Titles dialog box.

8. **Click any one of the sales values (on the value axis), click ▣, click the Font tab if necessary, click 8 in the Size list, click OK, then press [Esc] on the keyboard to deselect the value axis**

   The text on the value axis becomes smaller. Compare your chart to Figure D-15.

9. **Click the Save button ▣ on the Standard toolbar**

Clues to Use

Changing text alignment in charts

You can modify the alignment of axis text to make it fit better within the plot area. With a chart selected, double-click the axis text to be modified. The Format Axis dialog box opens. Click the Alignment tab, then change the alignment by typing the number of degrees in the Degrees text box, or by clicking a marker in the Degrees sample box. When you have made the desired changes, click OK.

FIGURE D-14: Sample chart with Category (X) axis text

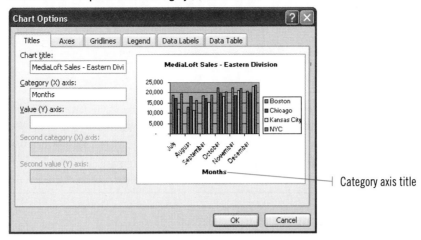

Category axis title

FIGURE D-15: Enhanced chart

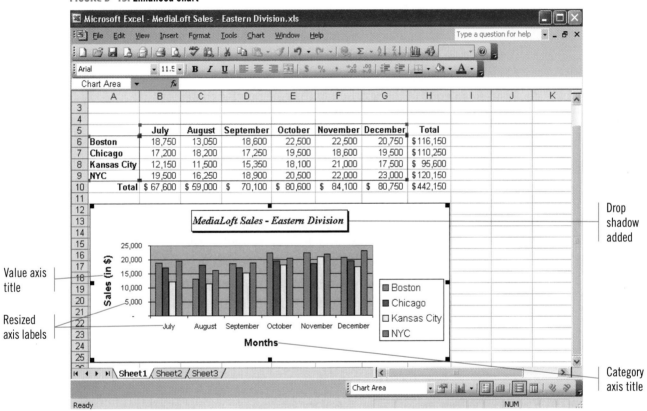

Value axis title

Resized axis labels

Drop shadow added

Category axis title

TABLE D-4: Chart enhancement buttons

button	use
	Displays the Format dialog box for the selected chart object
	Selects chart type (chart type on button changes to last chart type selected)
	Adds/deletes legend
	Creates a data table within the chart
	Charts data by row
	Charts data by column
	Angles selected text downward (clockwise)
	Angles selected text upward (counterclockwise)

Annotating and Drawing on a Chart

You can add arrows and text annotations to point out critical information in your charts. **Text annotations** are labels that you add to a chart to further describe your data. You can draw lines and arrows that point to the exact locations you want to emphasize. ▓▓▓▓▓ Jim wants you to add a text annotation and an arrow to highlight the October sales increase.

STEPS

1. **Make sure the chart is selected**

   To call attention to the Boston October sales increase, you can draw an arrow that points to the top of the Boston October data series with the annotation, "Due to ad campaign." With the chart selected, simply typing text in the formula bar creates annotation text.

TROUBLE

If the pointer changes to ⌶ or ↔, release the mouse button, click outside the text box area to deselect it, select the text box, then repeat Step 3.

2. **Type** Due to ad campaign, **then click the** Enter button ✔ **on the formula bar**

   As you type, the text appears in the formula bar. After you confirm the entry, the text appears in a selected text box on the chart.

3. **Point to an edge of the text box so that the pointer changes to** ✥

4. **Drag the** text box **above the chart, as shown in Figure D-16, then release the mouse button**

   You can add an arrow to point to a specific area or item in a chart by using the Drawing toolbar.

QUICK TIP

To annotate charts, you can also use the Callout shapes in the AutoShapes menu on the Drawing toolbar.

5. **Click the** Drawing button ⊿ **on the Standard toolbar if necessary to display the Drawing toolbar**

   The Drawing toolbar appears below the worksheet.

6. **Click the** Arrow button ↘ **on the Drawing toolbar, then move the pointer over the chart**

   The pointer changes to ╋, and the status bar displays "Click and drag to insert an AutoShape." When you draw an arrow, the point farthest from where you start has the arrowhead.

QUICK TIP

You can also insert text and an arrow in the data section of a worksheet by clicking the Text Box button ▣ on the Drawing toolbar, drawing a text box, typing the text, then adding the arrow.

7. **Position** ╋ **under the** t **in the word "to" in the text box, press and hold the left mouse button, drag the line to the Boston column in the October sales series, then release the mouse button**

   An arrow appears, pointing to Boston October sales. The arrow is a selected object in the chart; you can resize, format, or delete it just like any other object. Compare your finished chart to Figure D-17.

8. **Click** ⊿ **to close the Drawing toolbar**

9. **Click the** Save button 🖫 **on the Standard toolbar**

Clues to Use

Adding an organizational chart or other diagram type

In addition to charts, annotations, and drawn objects, you can create a variety of diagrams. Diagram types include an Organization Chart, Cycle, Radial, Pyramid, Venn, or Target diagram. To insert a diagram, click Insert on the menu bar, then click Diagram. In the Diagram Gallery dialog box, click a diagram type, then click OK. The diagram appears on the worksheet as an embedded object with sizing handles, and the Diagram toolbar opens. You can edit placeholder text and use the Diagram toolbar buttons to insert or modify shapes, change the layout or diagram type, or select an AutoFormat. A selected diagram shape can be formatted using the Drawing toolbar buttons.

FIGURE D-16: Repositioning text annotation

Outline of repositioned annotation

Selected text annotation

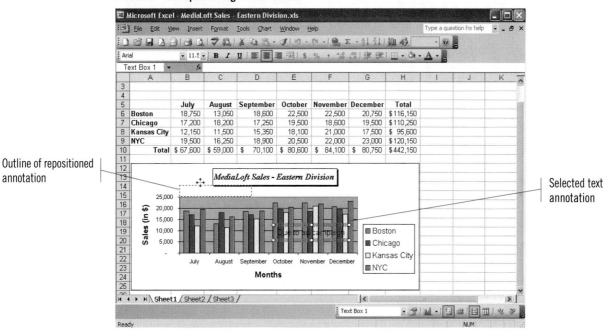

FIGURE D-17: Completed chart with text annotation and arrow

Repositioned text annotation

Arrow

Drawing toolbar

Boston October sales

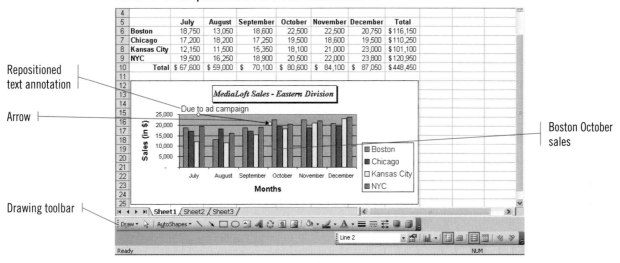

Clues to Use

Exploding a pie slice

Just as an arrow can call attention to a data series, you can emphasize a pie slice by exploding, or pulling it away from, the pie chart. Once the pie chart is selected, click the pie to select it, click the desired slice to select only that slice, then drag the slice away from the pie, as shown in Figure D-18. After you change the chart type, you may need to adjust arrows within the chart.

FIGURE D-18: Exploded pie slice

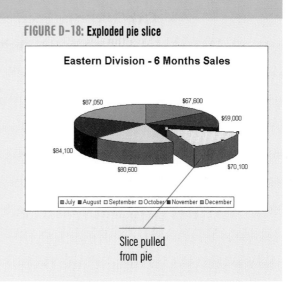

Slice pulled from pie

Previewing and Printing a Chart

After you complete a chart, you often need to print it. As with previewing a worksheet, previewing a chart lets you see what your chart looks like before you print it. You can print a chart by itself or as part of the worksheet. ████ Jim wants a printed version of the chart for the annual meeting. He wants you to print the worksheet and the chart together, so that the shareholders can see the actual sales numbers for the Eastern Division stores.

STEPS

1. **Press [Esc] on the keyboard to deselect the arrow and the chart, enter your name in cell A35, then press [Ctrl][Home] on the keyboard to select cell A1**

2. **Click the Print Preview button ▣ on the Standard toolbar**

   The Print Preview window opens. You decide the chart and data would fit better on the page if they were printed in **landscape** orientation—that is, with the text running the long way on the page. You use Page Setup to change the page orientation.

3. **Click Setup on the Print Preview toolbar to open the Page Setup dialog box, then click the Page tab, if necessary**

4. **Click the Landscape option button in the Orientation section, as shown in Figure D-19, then click OK**

   Because each page has a default left margin of 0.75", the chart and data will print too far over to the left of the page. You can change this setting using the Margins tab of the Page Setup dialog box.

5. **Click Setup on the Print Preview toolbar, click the Margins tab, click the Horizontally check box under Center on page, then click OK**

   The data and chart are positioned horizontally on the page. See Figure D-20.

6. **Click Print to display the Print dialog box, then click OK**

   The data and chart print, and you are returned to the worksheet. If you want, you can choose to preview (and print) only the chart.

7. **Select the chart, then click ▣**

   The chart appears in the Print Preview window. If you wanted to, you could print the chart by clicking the Print button on the Print Preview toolbar.

8. **Click Close on the Print Preview toolbar**

9. **Click the Save button ▣ on the Standard toolbar, close the workbook, then exit Excel**

FIGURE D-19: Page tab of the Page Setup dialog box

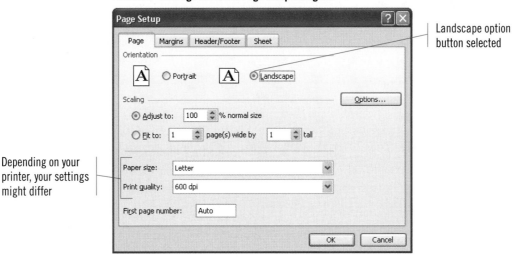

Landscape option button selected

Depending on your printer, your settings might differ

FIGURE D-20: Chart and data ready to print

Centered on page

Orientation changed to landscape

Chart and data will print on one page

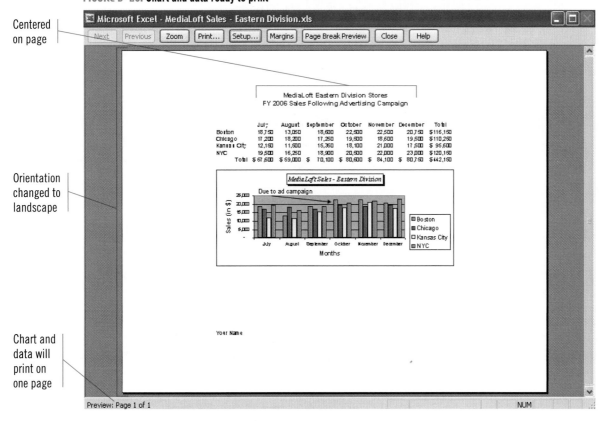

Clues to Use

Using the Page Setup dialog box for a chart

When a chart is selected, a different Page Setup dialog box opens than when neither the chart nor data is selected. The Center on Page options are not always available. To accurately position a chart on the page, you can click the Margins button on the Print Preview toolbar. Margin lines appear on the screen and show you exactly how the margins appear on the page. The exact placement appears in the status bar when you press and hold the mouse button on the margin line. You can drag the lines to the exact settings you want.

Practice

▼ CONCEPTS REVIEW

Label each element of the Excel chart shown in Figure D-21.

FIGURE D-21

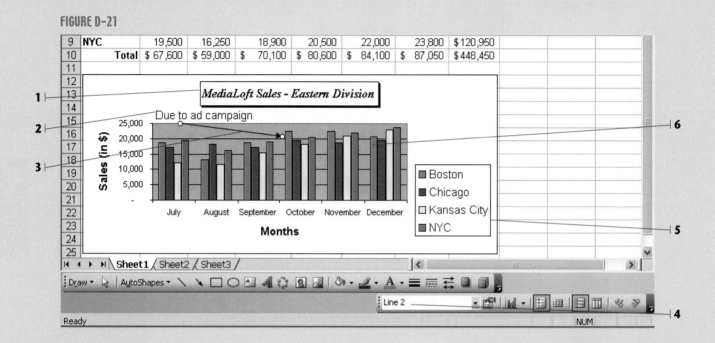

Match each chart type with the statement that best describes it.

7. **Combination**
8. **Column**
9. **Line**
10. **Area**
11. **Pie**

a. Shows how volume changes over time
b. Compares data as parts of a whole
c. Displays a column and line chart using different scales of measurement
d. Compares trends over even time intervals
e. Compares data over time—the Excel default

Select the best answer from the list of choices.

12. **Which pointer is used to resize a chart object?**
    a. I
    b. ↘
    c. ✥
    d. +

13. **The object in a chart that identifies patterns used for each data series is a:**
    a. Data point.
    b. Plot.
    c. Legend.
    d. Range.

14. **The orientation of a page whose dimensions are 11" wide by 8½" tall is:**
    a. Portrait.
    b. Longways.
    c. Landscape.
    d. Sideways.

15. **What is the term for a row or column on a chart?**
    a. Range address
    b. Axis title
    c. Chart orientation
    d. Data series

16. **In a 2-D chart, the category axis is the:**
    a. X-axis.
    b. Z-axis.
    c. D-axis.
    d. Y-axis.

17. **In a 2-D chart, the value axis is the:**
    a. X-axis.
    b. Y-axis.
    c. D-axis.
    d. Z-axis.

▼ SKILLS REVIEW

1. **Plan and design a chart.**
   a. Start Excel, open the Data File EX D-2.xls from the drive and folder where your Data Files are stored, then save it as **MediaLoft Vancouver Software Usage**.
   b. Sketch the type of chart you would use to plot this data.
   c. In what chart type is the y-axis referred to as the z-axis?
   d. What term is used to describe the visual representation of each data point?

2. **Create a chart.**
   a. Select the range containing the data and headings.
   b. Start the Chart Wizard.
   c. In the Chart Wizard, select a clustered column chart, then verify that the series are in rows, add the chart title **Software Usage by Department**, and make the chart an object on the worksheet.
   d. After the chart appears, save your work.

3. Move and resize a chart.

a. Make sure the chart is still selected.

b. Move the chart beneath the data.

c. Resize the chart so it extends to column J.

d. Use the Legend tab in the Chart Options dialog box to move the legend below the charted data.

e. Resize the chart so the bottom is at the top of row 25.

f. Save your work.

4. Edit a chart.

a. Change the value in cell B3 to **6**. Notice the change in the chart.

b. Select the chart.

c. Use the Chart Type list arrow to change the chart to a 3-D Column Chart.

d. Rotate the chart to move the data.

e. Change the chart back to a column chart.

f. Save your work.

5. Format a chart.

a. Make sure the chart is still selected.

b. Use the Chart Options dialog box to turn off the displayed gridlines.

c. Change the font used in the Category and Value labels to Times New Roman.

d. Turn on the major gridlines for the value axis.

e. Change the chart title's font to Times New Roman, with a font size of 18.

f. Save your work.

6. Enhance a chart.

a. Make sure the chart is selected, then select the Titles tab in the Chart Options dialog box.

b. Enter **Software** as the x-axis title.

c. Enter **Users** as the y-axis title.

d. Change Production in the legend to **Art**. (*Hint*: Change the text entry in the worksheet.)

e. Add a drop shadow to the chart title.

f. Save your work.

7. Annotate and draw on a chart.

a. Make sure the chart is selected, then create the text annotation **Needs More Users**.

b. Position the text annotation beneath the chart title.

c. Below the text annotation, use the Drawing toolbar to create an arrow that points to the area containing the Access data.

d. Compare your work to Figure D-22.

e. Save your work.

FIGURE D-22

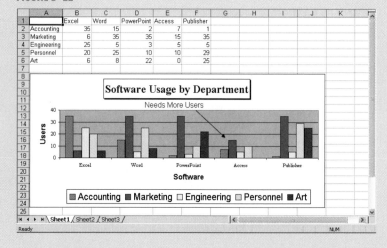

8. Preview and print a chart.

  a. In the worksheet, enter your name in cell A30.

  b. Preview the chart and data.

  c. Change the page orientation to landscape.

  d. Center the page contents horizontally and vertically on the page.

  e. Print the data and chart from the Print Preview window.

  f. Save your work.

  g. Preview only the chart, then print it.

  h. Close the workbook, then exit Excel.

▼ INDEPENDENT CHALLENGE 1

You are the operations manager for the Springfield Theater Group in Oregon. Each year the group applies to various state and federal agencies for matching funds. For this year's funding proposal, you need to create charts to document the number of productions in previous years.

  a. Sketch a sample worksheet on a piece of paper describing how you will create the charts. Which type of chart is best suited for the information you need to display? What kind of chart enhancements do you want to use? Will a 3-D effect make your chart easier to understand?

  b. Start Excel, open the Data File EX D-3.xls, then save it as **Springfield Theater Group** in the drive and folder where your Data Files are stored.

  c. Create a column chart for the data, accepting all Chart Wizard defaults.

  d. Change at least one of the colors used in a data series.

  e. Create at least two additional charts for the same data to show how different chart types display the same data. Each of these charts should be on its own chart sheet in the workbook.

  f. After creating the charts, make the appropriate enhancements. Include chart titles, legends, and value and category axis titles, using the suggestions in Table D-5.

  g. Add data labels.

  h. Enter your name in a worksheet cell.

  i. Save your work. Before printing, preview the workbook so you know what the charts look like. Adjust any items as necessary.

  j. Print the worksheet (charts and data).

  k. Close the workbook, then exit Excel.

TABLE D-5

suggested chart enhancements	
Title	Types and Number of Plays
Legend	Year 1, Year 2, Year 3, Year 4
Value axis title	Number of Plays
Category axis title	Play Types

▼ INDEPENDENT CHALLENGE 2

Beautiful You, a small beauty salon, has been using Excel for several months. One of your responsibilities at the Beautiful You salon is to re-create the company's records using Excel. Another is to convince the current staff that Excel can help them make daily operating decisions more easily and efficiently. To do this, you've decided to create charts using the previous year's operating expenses, including rent, utilities, and payroll. The manager will use these charts at the next monthly meeting.

a. Decide which data in the worksheet should be charted. Sketch two sample charts. What type of charts are best suited for the information you need to show? What kind of chart enhancements are necessary?

b. Start Excel, open the Data File EX D-4.xls from the drive and folder where your Data Files are stored, then save it as **BY Expense Charts**.

c. Create a column chart on the worksheet, containing the expense data for all four quarters.

d. Using the same data, create an area chart and one additional chart using any other appropriate chart type. (*Hint*: Move each chart to a new location on the worksheet, then deselect it before using the Wizard to create the next one.)

e. Add annotated text and arrows to the column chart that highlight any important data or trends.

f. In one chart, change the color of a data series, then in another chart, use black-and-white patterns only. (*Hint*: Use the Fill Effects button in the Format Data Series dialog box. Then display the Patterns tab. Adjust the Foreground color to black and the Background color to white, then select a pattern.)

g. Enter your name in a worksheet cell.

h. Save your work. Before printing, preview each chart so you know what the charts look like. Adjust any items as needed.

i. Print the charts.

j. Close the workbook, then exit Excel.

▼ INDEPENDENT CHALLENGE 3

You are working as an account representative at the Bright Light Ad Agency. You have been examining the expenses charged to clients of the firm. The Board of Directors wants to examine certain advertising expenses and has asked you to prepare charts that can be used in this evaluation.

a. Start Excel, open the Data File EX D-5.xls from the drive and folder where your Data Files are stored, then save it as **Bright Light**.

b. Decide what types of charts would be best suited for the data in the range A16:B24. Sketch three sample charts. What kind of chart enhancements are necessary?

c. Use the Chart Wizard to create at least three different types of charts that show the distribution of advertising expenses. (*Hint*: Move each chart to a new location on the worksheet, then deselect it before using the Wizard to create the next one.) One of the charts should be a 3-D pie chart.

d. Add annotated text and arrows highlighting important data, such as the largest expense.

e. Change the color of at least one data series.

f. Add chart titles and category and value axis titles. Format the titles with a font of your choice. Place a drop shadow around the chart title.

Advanced Challenge Exercise

- Explode a slice from the 3-D pie chart.
- Add a data label to the exploded pie slice.
- Change the alignment of labels on an axis.
- Modify the scale of the value axis in one of the charts. (*Hint*: Double-click the gridlines to open the Format Gridlines dialog box, then click the Scale tab.)

g. Enter your name in a worksheet cell.

h. Save your work. Before printing, preview the file so you know what the charts look like. Adjust any items as needed. Be sure the chart is placed appropriately on the page.

i. Print the charts, close the workbook, then exit Excel.

▼ INDEPENDENT CHALLENGE 4

Your company, Film Distribution, is headquartered in Montreal, and is considering opening a new office in the United States. Your supervisor would like you to begin investigating possible locations. You can use the Web to find and compare median pay scales in specific cities to see how relocating will affect the standard of living for those employees who move to the new office.

a. Start Excel, open a new workbook, then save it as **New Location Analysis** in the drive and folder where your Data Files are located.

b. Use your favorite search engine to find your own information sources on salary calculators, or cost-of-living calculators.

c. Determine the median incomes for Seattle, San Francisco, Dallas, Salt Lake City, Memphis, and Boston. Record this data on a sheet named **Median Income** in your workbook. See Table D-6 below for suggested data layout.

d. Format the data so it looks attractive and professional.

e. Create any type of column chart, with the data series in columns, on the same worksheet as the data. Include a descriptive title.

f. Remove the major gridlines in the Median Income chart.

g. On a blank worksheet in the current workbook, determine how much an employee would need to earn in Seattle, San Francisco, Dallas, Memphis, and Boston to maintain the same standard of living as if the company chose to relocate to Salt Lake City and pay $75,000. Name the sheet **Standard of Living**.

TABLE D-6

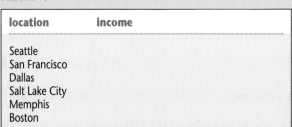

location	income
Seattle	
San Francisco	
Dallas	
Salt Lake City	
Memphis	
Boston	

h. Format the data so it looks attractive and professional.

i. Create a 3-D column chart on the same worksheet as the data. Include a descriptive title.

j. Change the color of the data series in the Standard of Living chart to bright green.

Advanced Challenge Exercise

- Format the value axis in your chart(s) so that the salary income displays a 1000 separator (comma), but no dollar sign or decimal places.
- Rotate the chart so you get a different view of the data.
- Change the alignment of the category axis labels.

k. Do not display the legends in your chart(s).

l. Enter your name in a cell in your worksheet(s).

m. Save the workbook. Preview the chart(s) and change margins as necessary.

n. Print your worksheet(s), including the data and chart(s), making setup modifications as necessary.

o. Close the workbook, then exit Excel.

▼ VISUAL WORKSHOP

Modify a worksheet, using the skills you learned in this unit and using Figure D-23 for reference. Open the Data File EX D-6.xls from the drive and folder where your Data Files are stored, then save it as **Quarterly Advertising Budget**. Create the chart, then change the chart to reflect Figure D-23. Enter your name in cell A13, save, preview, then print your results.

FIGURE D-23

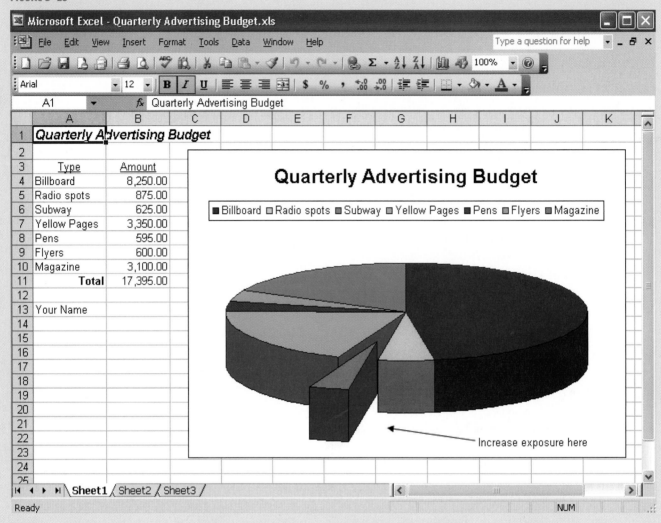

UNIT
E
Excel 2003

Working with Formulas and Functions

OBJECTIVES

Create a formula with several operators
Use names in a formula
Generate multiple totals with AutoSum
Use dates in calculations
Build a conditional formula with the IF function
Use statistical functions
Calculate payments with the PMT function
Display and print formula contents

Without formulas, Excel would simply be an electronic grid with text and numbers. Used with formulas, Excel becomes a powerful data analysis tool. As you learn how to analyze data using different types of formulas, including those containing functions, you will discover more ways to use Excel. In this unit, you will gain a further understanding of Excel formulas and learn how to use several Excel functions. Top management at MediaLoft has asked marketing director Jim Fernandez to analyze various company data. To do this, Jim creates several worksheets that require formulas and functions. Because management is considering raising salaries for store managers, Jim has asked you to create a report that compares the payroll deductions and net pay for store managers before and after a proposed raise.

Creating a Formula with Several Operators

You can create formulas that contain a combination of cell references (for example, Z100 or B2), operators (for example, * for multiplication or – for subtraction), and values (for example, 99 or 1.56). Formulas can also contain functions. You have used AutoSum to insert the SUM function into a cell. You can also create a single formula that performs several calculations. If you enter a formula with more than one operator, Excel performs the calculations in a particular sequence based on algebraic rules, called the **order of precedence** (also called the order of operations); that is, Excel performs the operation(s) within parentheses first, then calculates exponents, then any multiplication and division from left to right. Finally, it calculates addition and subtraction, from left to right. See Table E-1 for examples. ▐▞▚▞ Jim has received the gross pay and deductions for the monthly payroll and needs to complete his analysis. He has also preformatted, with the Comma style, any cells that are to contain values. He asks you to enter a formula for net pay that subtracts the payroll deductions from gross pay.

STEPS

1. **Start Excel if necessary, open the Data File EX E-1.xls from the drive and folder where your Data Files are stored, then save it as Company Data**

   The green triangles in the cells indicate that the formulas differ from the surrounding formulas. In this case, the formulas are correct, so you can ignore the triangles. The first part of the net pay formula should go in cell B11.

2. **Click Edit on the menu bar, click Go To, type B11 in the Reference box, then click OK**

   Cell B11 is now the active cell. The Go To command is especially useful when you want to select a cell in a large worksheet.

3. **Type =, click cell B6, type –, then click the Insert Function button fx on the formula bar to open the Insert Function dialog box**

   You type the equal sign (=) to indicate that a formula follows. B6 references the cell containing the gross pay, and the minus sign (–) indicates that the next entry, a sum, is subtracted from cell B6. The Insert Function dialog box allows you to choose from a list of available functions or search for a specific function. See Figure E-1.

4. **Type sum in the Search for a function text box, click Go, click SUM in the Select a function list, then click OK**

   B6:B10 appears in the Number1 text box. You want to sum the range B7:B10.

5. **With the Number1 argument selected in the Function Arguments dialog box, click the Number1 Collapse Dialog Box button ▦, select the range B7:B10 in the worksheet, click the Redisplay Dialog Box button ▦, then click OK**

   Collapsing the dialog box allows you to enter the range by selecting it. The net pay for Payroll Period 1 appears in cell B11.

6. **Copy the formula in cell B11 into cells C11:F11, then press [Ctrl][Home] to return to cell A1**

   The net pay for each column appears in row 11. See Figure E-2.

7. **Save the workbook**

FIGURE E-1: Insert Function dialog box

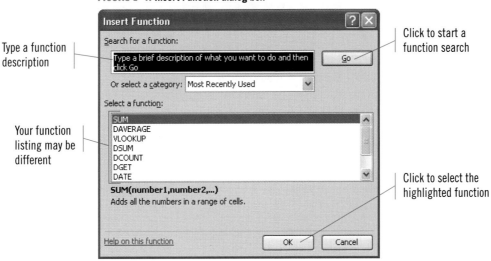

Type a function description

Click to start a function search

Your function listing may be different

Click to select the highlighted function

FIGURE E-2: Worksheet with copied formulas

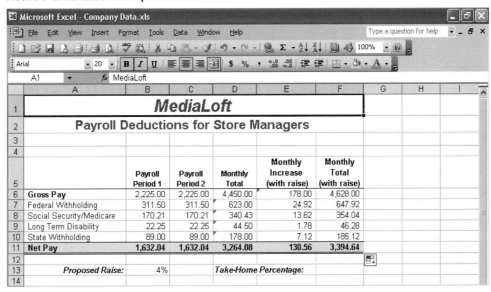

TABLE E-1: Sample formulas using parentheses and several operators

formula	order of precedence	calculated result
=10–20/10–5	Divide 20 by 10; subtract the result from 10, then subtract 5	3
=(10–20)/10–5	Subtract 20 from 10; divide that by 10; then subtract 5	–6
=(10*2)*(10+2)	Multiply 10 by 2; add 10 to 2; then multiply the results	240

Clues to Use

Using Paste Special

You can use the Paste Special command to enter formulas and values quickly or even to perform quick calculations. Click the cell(s) containing the formula or value you want to copy, click the Copy button [img] on the Standard toolbar, then right-click the cell where you want the result to appear. In the shortcut menu, click Paste Special, choose the feature you want to paste, then click OK.

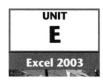

Using Names in a Formula

To reduce errors and make your worksheet easier to follow, you can assign names to cells and ranges. You can also use names in formulas to make formulas easier to build. For example, the formula Revenue-Cost is much easier to understand than the formula A2-D3. When used in formulas, names become absolute cell references by default. Names can use uppercase or lowercase letters as well as digits. After you name a cell or range, you can use the name on any sheet in the workbook. If you move a named cell or range, its name moves with it. ▰▰▰▰ Jim wants you to include a formula that calculates the percentage of monthly gross pay that the managers would actually take home (their net pay) if they received a 4% raise. You decide to name the cells that you will use in the calculation.

STEPS

QUICK TIP

You can also assign names to ranges of cells. Select the range, click the name box, then type in the range name. You can also name a range by pointing to Name on the Insert menu, then clicking Define and typing the name.

1. **Click cell F6, click the name box on the formula bar to select the active cell reference, type Gross_with_Raise, then press [Enter]**
   The name assigned to cell F6, Gross_with_Raise, appears in the name box. Note that you must type underscores instead of spaces between words. Cell F6 is now named Gross_with_Raise to refer to the monthly gross pay amount that includes the 4% raise. The name box displays as much of the name as fits (Gross_with_...). The total net pay cell needs a name.

2. **Click cell F11, click the name box, type Net_with_Raise, then press [Enter]**
   The new formula uses names instead of cell references.

QUICK TIP

You can use the Label Ranges dialog box (Insert menu, Name submenu, Label command) to designate existing column or row headings as labels. Then instead of using cell references for the column or row in formulas, you can use the labels.

3. **Click cell F13, type =, click Insert on the menu bar, point to Name, click Paste, click Net_with_Raise, then click OK**
   The name is inserted and the color of the name matches the outline around the cell reference.

4. **Type /, click Insert on the menu bar, point to Name, click Paste, click Gross_with_Raise, click OK, then click the Enter button ✔ on the formula bar**
   The formula appears in the formula bar and the result, 0.7335, appears in the cell. Cell F13 needs to be formatted in Percent style.

QUICK TIP

To replace cell references in existing formulas with the corresponding names you have added, click Insert on the menu bar, point to Name, click Apply, click the name or names, then click OK.

5. **Select cell F13 if necessary, click Format on the menu bar, click Style, click the Style name list arrow, click Percent, then click OK**
   The result shown in cell F13, 73%, is rounded to the nearest whole percent, as shown in Figure E-3. A **style** is a combination of formatting characteristics, such as bold, italic, and zero decimal places. You can use the Style dialog box instead of the Formatting toolbar to apply styles.

6. **Enter your name in cell A20, save the workbook, then preview and print the worksheet**

Clues to Use

Defining and removing styles

To define your own style (such as bold, italic, 14 point numbers with commas and zero decimal places), select a cell, format it using the Formatting toolbar, open the Style dialog box and type a name for your style, then click Add. Later, you can apply all of your formatting characteristics by applying your new style from the Style dialog box. You can also use the Style dialog box to remove styles by selecting the cell that has a style and then selecting Normal in the Style name list.

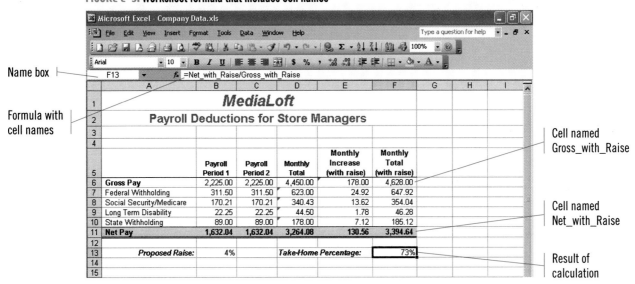

FIGURE E-3: Worksheet formula that includes cell names

Name box ⊦ — F13 — =Net_with_Raise/Gross_with_Raise

Formula with cell names

Cell named Gross_with_Raise

Cell named Net_with_Raise

Result of calculation

Clues to Use

Producing a list of names

You might want to verify the names you have assigned in a workbook and the cells they reference. To paste a list of names in a workbook, select a blank cell that has several blank cells beside and beneath it. Click Insert on the menu bar, point to Name, then click Paste. In the Paste Name dialog box, click Paste List. Excel produces a list of names that includes the sheet name followed by an exclamation point and the cell or range the name identifies. See Figure E-4.

FIGURE E-4: Worksheet with pasted list of names

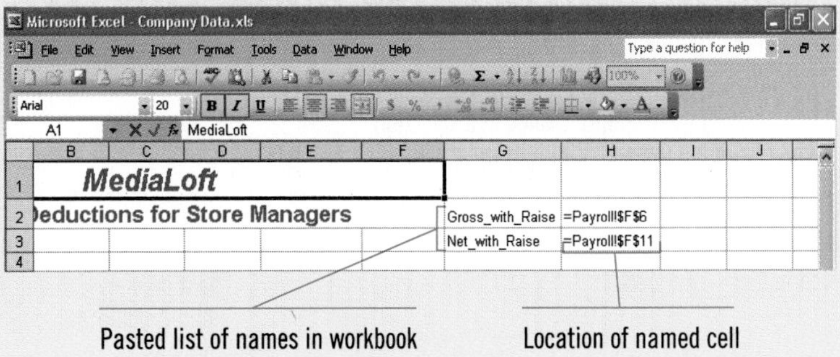

Pasted list of names in workbook   Location of named cell

Generating Multiple Totals with AutoSum

In most cases, the result of a function is a value derived from a single calculation. You have used AutoSum to produce a total of a single range of numbers; you can also use it to total multiple ranges. If you include blank cells to the right or at the bottom of a selected range, AutoSum generates several totals and enters the results in the blank cells. You can also use AutoSum to generate grand totals of worksheet subtotals. ━━━━━ Maria Abbott, MediaLoft's general sales manager, has given Jim a worksheet summarizing store sales. He asks you to complete the worksheet totals.

STEPS

TROUBLE

If you select the wrong combination of cells, click a single cell and begin again.

1. **Click the Sales sheet tab to make the Sales sheet active, select the range B5:E9, press and hold [Ctrl], then select the range B11:E15**

   To select nonadjacent cells, you must press and hold [Ctrl] while selecting the additional cells. Compare your selections with Figure E-6. Jim would like totals to appear in the last line of each selection.

2. **Click the AutoSum button Σ on the Standard toolbar**

   When the selected range you want to sum (B5:E9 and B11:E15, in this example) includes a blank cell with data values above it, AutoSum enters the total in the blank cell.

3. **Select the range B5:F17, then click Σ**

   Although Excel generates totals when you click the AutoSum button, it is a good idea to check the results.

QUICK TIP

Excel uses commas to separate multiple arguments in all functions, not just in SUM.

4. **Click cell B17**

   The formula bar reads =SUM(B15,B9). In this case, Excel ignores the data values and it totals only the sums. See Figure E-7. When generating grand totals, Excel separates the cell references with a comma.

5. **Enter your name in cell A20, save the workbook, then preview and print the worksheet**

Clues to Use

Quick calculations with AutoCalculate

To view a total quickly without entering a formula, just select the range you want to sum. The answer appears in the status bar next to SUM=. You also can perform other quick calculations, such as averaging or finding the minimum value in a selection: right-click in the status bar, and select from the list of function names. The option you select remains in effect and in the status bar until you make another selection. See Figure E-5.

FIGURE E-5: Using AutoCalculate

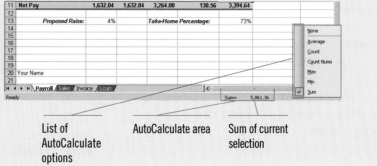

List of AutoCalculate options

AutoCalculate area

Sum of current selection

FIGURE E-6: Selecting nonadjacent ranges using [Ctrl]

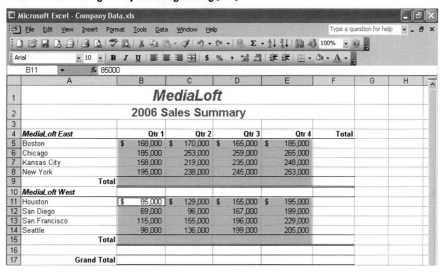

FIGURE E-7: Completed worksheet

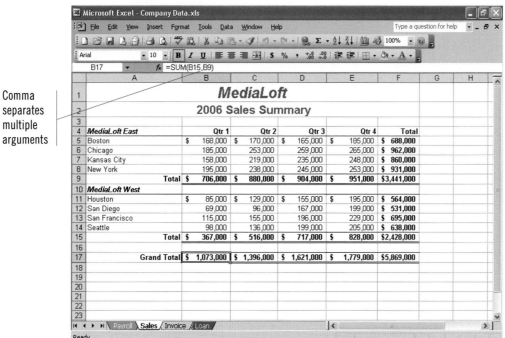

Excel 2003

Using Dates in Calculations

If you enter dates in a worksheet in a format that Excel recognizes as a date, you can sort them and perform date calculations. When you enter an Excel date format, Excel converts it to a serial number so it can be used in calculations. A date's serial number is the number of days it is from January 1, 1900. Excel assigns the serial number of "1" to January 1, 1900 and counts up from there; the serial number of January 1, 2006, for example, is 38,718. When you format the cell with the serial number using a Date format, Excel displays the serial number as a date. ▓▓▓▓▓ Jim wants you to calculate the due date and age of each invoice on his worksheet. He reminds you to enter the worksheet dates in a format that Excel recognizes, so you can use date calculations.

STEPS

1. **Click the Invoice sheet tab, click cell C4, click the Insert Function button 𝑓𝑥 on the formula bar, type date in the Search for a function text box, click Go, click DATE in the Select a function list, then click OK**

   Your calculations need to be based on a current date of 4/1/06.

TROUBLE

If the year appears with four digits instead of two, your system administrator may have set a four-digit year display. You can continue with the lesson.

2. **Enter 2006 in the Year text box, enter 4 in the Month text box, enter 1 in the Day text box, then click OK**

   The Date function uses the format DATE(year, month, day). The date appears in cell C4 as 4/1/06. Your formula in cell E7 should calculate the invoice due date, which is 30 days from the invoice date. The formula adds 30 days to the invoice date.

3. **Click cell E7, type =, click cell B7, type +30, then click the Enter button ✓ on the formula bar**

   Excel calculates the result by converting the 3/2/06 invoice date to a serial date number, adding 30 to it, then automatically formatting the result as the date 4/1/06, as shown in Figure E-8. You can use the same formula to calculate the due dates of the other invoices.

QUICK TIP

You can also perform time calculations in Excel. For example, you can enter an employee's starting and ending time, then calculate how long he or she worked. You must enter time in an Excel time format.

4. **Drag the fill handle to copy the formula in cell E7 into cells E8:E13**

   Relative cell referencing adjusts the copied formula to contain the appropriate cell references. Now you are ready to enter the formula that calculates the age of each invoice. You do this by subtracting the invoice date from the current date. Because each invoice age formula must refer to the current date, you must make cell C4, the current date cell, an absolute reference in the formula.

5. **Click cell F7, type =, click cell C4, press [F4] to add the absolute reference symbols ($), type –, click cell B7, then click ✓**

   The formula bar displays the formula $C$4–B7. The numerical result, 30, appears in cell F7 because there are 30 days between 3/2/06 and 4/1/06. You can use the same formula to calculate the age of the remaining invoices.

QUICK TIP

You can also insert the current date into a cell by using the TODAY() function. The NOW() function inserts the current date and time into a cell. If you leave the argument area within its parentheses blank, it automatically displays today's date.

6. **Drag the fill handle to copy the formula in F7 to the range F8:F13, then press [Ctrl][Home] to return to cell A1**

   The age of each invoice appears in column F, as shown in Figure E-9.

7. **Save the workbook**

FIGURE E-8: Worksheet with calculated invoice due date

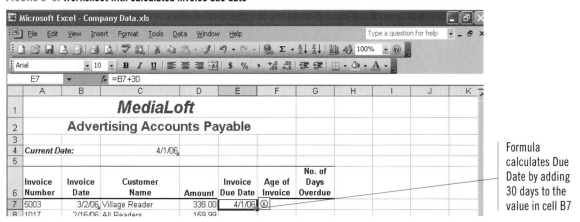

Formula calculates Due Date by adding 30 days to the value in cell B7

FIGURE E-9: Worksheet with copied formulas

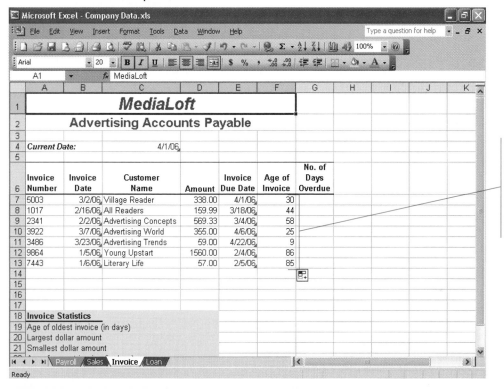

Formula calculates invoice age by subtracting invoice date from today's date

Clues to Use

Applying and creating custom number and date formats

When you use numbers and dates in worksheets or calculations, you can apply built-in Excel formats or create your own. To apply number formats, click Format on the menu bar, click Cells, then if necessary click the Number tab. In the Category list, click a category, then click the exact format in the list or scroll box to the right. To create a custom format, click Custom in the category list, then click a format that resembles the one you want. For example the value $3,789 uses the number format $#,### where # represents positive numbers. In the Type box, edit the symbols until they represent the format you want, then click OK. See Figure E-10.

FIGURE E-10: Custom formats on the Number tab in the Format Cells dialog box

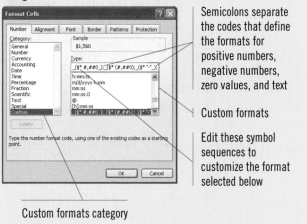

Semicolons separate the codes that define the formats for positive numbers, negative numbers, zero values, and text

Custom formats

Edit these symbol sequences to customize the format selected below

Custom formats category

Building a Conditional Formula with the IF Function

You can build a conditional formula using an IF function. A **conditional formula** is one that makes calculations based on stated conditions. For example, you can build a formula to calculate bonuses based on a person's performance rating. If a person is rated a 5 (the stated condition) on a scale of 1 to 5, with 5 being the highest rating, he or she receives an additional 10% of his or her salary as a bonus; otherwise, there is no bonus. A condition that can be answered with a true or false response is called a **logical test**. The IF function has three parts, separated by commas: a condition or logical test, an action to take if the logical test or condition is true, then an action to take if the logical test or condition is false. Another way of expressing this is: IF(test_cond,do_this,else_this). Translated into an Excel IF function, the formula to calculate bonuses would look something like this: IF(Rating=5,Salary*0.10,0). The translation would be: If the rating equals 5, multiply the salary by 0.10 (the decimal equivalent of 10%), then place the result in the selected cell; if the rating does not equal 5, place a 0 in the cell. When entering the logical test portion of an IF statement, you typically use some combination of the comparison operators listed in Table E-2. You are almost finished with the invoice worksheet. To complete it, you need to use an IF function that calculates the number of days each invoice is overdue.

STEPS

1. **Click cell G7, click the Insert Function button f_x on the formula bar, enter conditional in the Search for a function text box, click Go, click IF in the Select a function list box, then click OK**

   You want the function to calculate the number of days overdue as follows: if the age of the invoice is greater than 30, calculate the days overdue (Age of Invoice – 30), and place the result in cell G7; otherwise, place a 0 (zero) in the cell.

2. **Enter F7>30 in the Logical_test text box**

   The symbol (>) represents "greater than." So far, the formula reads: if Age of Invoice is greater than 30 (in other words, if the invoice is overdue). The next part of the function tells Excel the action to take if the invoice is over 30 days old.

3. **Enter F7–30 in the Value_if_true text box**

   This part of the formula is what you want Excel to do if the logical test is true (that is, if the age of the invoice is over 30). Continuing the translation of the formula, this part means: take the Age of Invoice value and subtract 30. The last part of the formula tells Excel the action to take if the logical test is false (that is, if the age of the invoice is 30 days or less).

4. **Enter 0 in the Value_if_false text box, then click OK**

   The function is complete, and the result, 0 (the number of days overdue), appears in cell G7. See Figure E-11.

5. **Copy the formula in cell G7 into cells G8:G13, then press [Ctrl][Home] to return to cell A1**

   Compare your results with Figure E-12.

6. **Save the workbook**

TABLE E-2: Comparison operators

operator	meaning	operator	meaning
<	Less than	<=	Less than or equal to
>	Greater than	>=	Greater than or equal to
=	Equal to	<>	Not equal to

FIGURE E-11: Worksheet with IF function

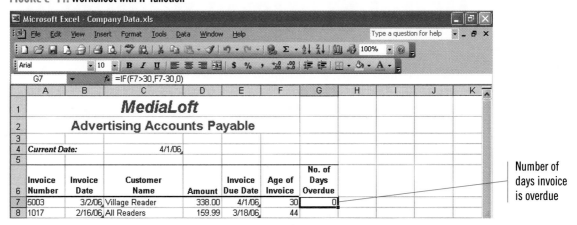

Number of days invoice is overdue

FIGURE E-12: Completed worksheet

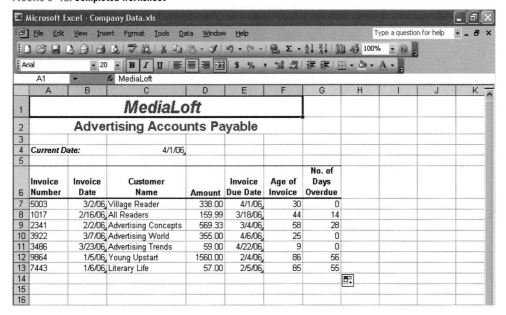

Clues to Use

Correcting circular references

A cell with a circular reference contains a formula that refers to its own cell location. If you accidentally enter a formula with a circular reference, a warning box opens alerting you to the problem. Click OK to display the Circular Reference toolbar or HELP to open a Help window explaining how to find the circular reference. In simple formulas, a circular reference is easy to spot. To correct it, edit the formula to remove any reference to the cell where the formula is located.

Using Statistical Functions

Excel offers several hundred worksheet functions. A small group of these functions calculate statistics such as averages, minimum values, and maximum values. See Table E-3 for a brief description of these commonly used functions. The AVERAGE, COUNT, MAX, and MIN functions are available in the AutoSum list as well as the Insert Function dialog box.  Jim wants to present summary information about open accounts payable, and he asks you to add some statistical functions to the worksheet. You decide to use the AutoSum list to insert these functions because it is faster and easier than typing them into the worksheet.

STEPS

1. **Click cell D19, click the AutoSum list arrow Σ ▾ and then click Max**

   The invoice age information is in cells F7:F13.

2. **Select the range F7:F13, then press [Enter]**

   The age of the oldest invoice (or maximum value in range F7:F13) is 86 days, as shown in Figure E-13. Jim needs to know the largest dollar amount among the outstanding invoices.

3. **With cell D20 selected, click Σ ▾, click Max, select the range D7:D13, then press [Enter]**

   The largest outstanding invoice, for 1560.00, is shown in cell D20. The MIN function finds the smallest dollar amount and the age of the newest invoice.

   > **QUICK TIP**
   > You can cut, copy, and paste functions from one worksheet area to another or from one workbook to another.

4. **With cell D21 selected, click Σ ▾, click Min, select the range D7:D13, then press [Enter]**

   The smallest dollar amount owed is 57.00, as shown in cell D21. Jim wants to know the age of the newest invoice.

5. **With cell D22 selected, click Σ ▾, click Min, select the range F7:F13, then press [Enter]**

   The newest invoice is 9 days old. The COUNT function calculates the number of invoices by counting the number of entries in column A.

6. **With cell D23 selected, click Σ ▾, click COUNT, select the range A7:A13, then press [Enter]**

   Cell D23 confirms that there are seven invoices. Compare your worksheet with Figure E-14.

7. **Enter your name in cell A26, save the workbook, then print the worksheet**

TABLE E-3: Commonly used statistical functions

function	worksheet action	function	worksheet action
AVERAGE	Calculates an average value	MAX	Finds the largest value
COUNT	Counts cells that contain numbers	MIN	Finds the smallest value
COUNTA	Counts cells that contain nonblank entries	MEDIAN	Finds the middle value

FIGURE E-13: Worksheet with age of oldest invoice

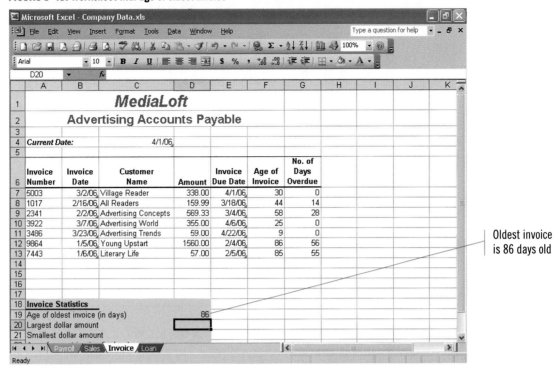

Oldest invoice is 86 days old

FIGURE E-14: Worksheet with invoice statistics

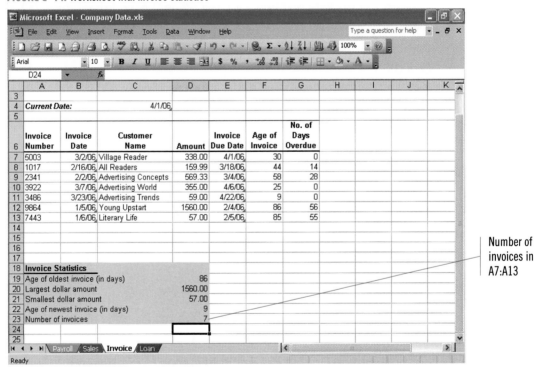

Number of invoices in A7:A13

Excel 2003

Clues to Use

Using the COUNTA function

The COUNT function counts the number of cells that contain numeric data. If the cell entries that you are trying to count contain nonnumerical data (such as invoice numbers with text entries), the COUNT function does not work and displays a count of zero. There is another function, COUNTA, that counts the number of cells that are not empty and therefore can be used to count the number of entries that contain text.

Calculating Payments with the PMT Function

PMT is a financial function that calculates the periodic payment amount for money borrowed. For example, if you want to borrow money to buy a car, and you know the principal amount, interest rate, and loan term, the PMT function can calculate your monthly payment. Say you want to borrow $15,000 at 8.5% interest and pay the loan off in five years. The Excel PMT function can tell you that your monthly payment will be $307.75 The parts of the PMT function are: PMT(rate, nper, pv, fv, type). See Figure E-15 for an illustration of a PMT function that calculates the monthly payment in the car loan example. ▓▓▓▓ For several months, MediaLoft management has been discussing the expansion of the San Diego store. Jim has obtained quotes from three different lenders on borrowing $29,000 to begin the expansion. He obtained loan quotes from a commercial bank, a venture capitalist, and an investment banker. He wants you to summarize the information, using the Excel PMT function.

STEPS

1. **Click the Loan sheet tab, click cell E5, click the Insert Function button 𝑓x on the formula bar, enter pmt in the Search for a function text box, click Go, click PMT in the Select a function list if necessary, then click OK**

2. **Move the Function Arguments dialog box so you can see row 5 of the worksheet; with the cursor in the Rate text box, click cell C5 on the worksheet, type /12, then press [Tab]**
    You must divide the annual interest by 12 because you are calculating monthly, not annual, payments.

3. **With the cursor in the Nper text box, click cell D5; click the Pv text box, click cell B5, then click OK**
    The FV and Type are optional arguments. Note that the payment of ($581.10) in cell E5 appears in red, indicating that it is a negative amount. Excel displays the result of a PMT function as a negative value to reflect the negative cash flow the loan represents to the borrower. To show the monthly payment as a positive number, you place a minus sign in front of the Pv cell reference in the function.

4. **Edit cell E5 so it reads =PMT(C5/12,D5,–B5), then click the Enter button ✓**
    A positive value of $581.10 now appears in cell E5. See Figure E-16. You can use the same formula to generate the monthly payments for the other loans.

5. **With cell E5 selected, drag the fill handle to fill the range E6:E7**
    A monthly payment of $895.44 for the venture capitalist loan appears in cell E6. A monthly payment of $1,296.43 for the investment banker loan appears in cell E7. The loans with shorter terms have much higher payments. You will not know the entire financial picture until you calculate the total payments and total interest for each lender.

6. **Click cell F5, type =, click cell E5, type *, click cell D5, then press [Tab]; in cell G5, type =, click cell F5, type –, click cell B5, then click ✓**

7. **Copy the formulas in cells F5:G5 into the range F6:G7, then return to cell A1**
    Compare your results with those in Figure E-17. You can experiment with different interest rates, loan amounts, or terms for any one of the lenders; the PMT function generates a new set of values automatically.

8. **Enter your name in cell A13, save the workbook, then preview and print the worksheet**

FIGURE E-15: Example of PMT function for car loan

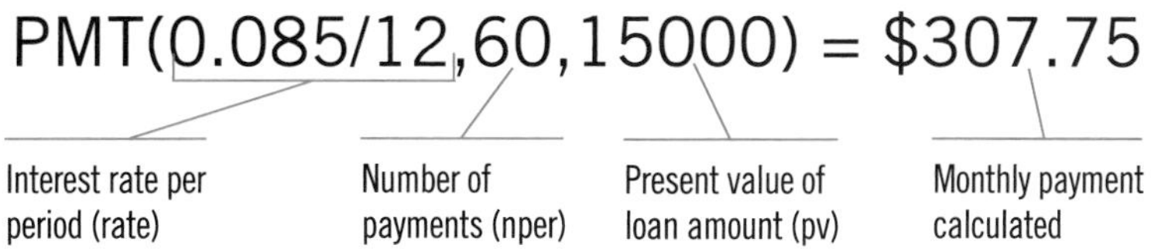

$$PMT(0.085/12, 60, 15000) = \$307.75$$

Interest rate per period (rate) | Number of payments (nper) | Present value of loan amount (pv) | Monthly payment calculated

FIGURE E-16: PMT function calculating monthly loan payment

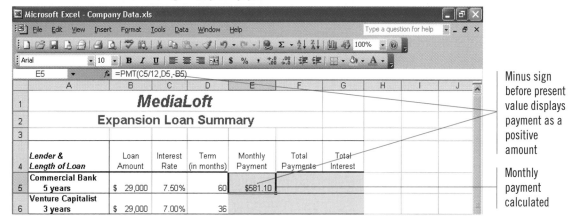

Minus sign before present value displays payment as a positive amount

Monthly payment calculated

FIGURE E-17: Completed worksheet

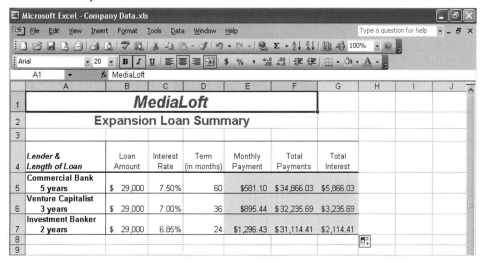

Clues to Use

Calculating future value with the FV function

You can use the FV (Future Value) function to determine the amount of money a given monthly investment will amount to, at a given interest rate after a given number of payment periods. The syntax is similar to that of the PMT function: FV(rate,nper,pmt,pv,type). For example, suppose you want to invest $1000 every month for the next 12 months into an account that pays 12% a year, and you want to know how much you will have at the end of 12 months (that is, its future value). You enter the function FV(.01,12,–1000), and Excel returns the value $12,682.50 as the future value of your investment. As with the PMT function, the units for the rate and nper must be consistent. If you made monthly payments on a three-year loan at 6% annual interest, you use the rate .06/12 and 36 periods (12*3). The arguments pv and type are optional; pv is the present value, or the total amount the series of payments is worth now. If you omit it, Excel assumes the pv is 0. The "type" argument indicates when the payments are made; 0 is the end of the period, and 1 is the beginning of the period.

Displaying and Printing Formula Contents

Excel usually displays the result of formula calculations in the worksheet area and displays formula contents for the active cell in the formula bar. However, you can instruct Excel to display the formulas directly in the worksheet cells in which they were entered. You can document worksheet formulas by first displaying the formulas, then printing them. These formula printouts are valuable paper-based worksheet documentation. Because formulas are often longer than their corresponding values, landscape orientation is the best choice for printing formulas. ▰▰▰ Jim wants you to produce a formula printout to submit with the Loan worksheet.

STEPS

1. **Click Tools on the menu bar, click Options, then click the View tab if necessary**

   The View tab of the Options dialog box appears, as shown in Figure E-18.

   QUICK TIP

   The worksheet formulas can also be displayed by selecting Formula Auditing Mode from the Formula Auditing option on the Tools menu.

2. **Under Window options, click the Formulas check box to select it, then click OK**

   The columns widen and retain their original formats. If the Formula Auditing toolbar is displayed, you can close it.

3. **Scroll horizontally to bring columns E through G into view**

   Instead of displaying formula results in the cells, Excel shows the actual formulas and automatically adjusts the column widths to accommodate them.

4. **Click the Print Preview button 🔍 on the Standard toolbar**

   The status bar reads Preview: Page 1 of 2, indicating that the worksheet will print on two pages. You want to print it on one page and include the row number and column letter headings.

   QUICK TIP

   All Page Setup options—such as Landscape orientation and Fit to scaling—apply to the active worksheet and are saved with the workbook.

5. **Click Setup in the Print Preview window, then click the Page tab if necessary**

6. **Under Orientation, click the Landscape option button; then under Scaling, click the Fit to option button and note that the wide and tall check boxes contain the number "1"**

   Selecting Landscape instructs Excel to print the worksheet sideways on the page. The Fit to option ensures that the document is printed on a single page.

   QUICK TIP

   To print row and column labels on every page of a multiple-page worksheet, click the Sheet tab, and fill in the Rows to repeat at top and the Columns to repeat at left in the Print titles section.

7. **Click the Sheet tab, in the Print section, click the Row and column headings check box to select it, click OK, then position the Zoom pointer 🔍 over column A and click**

   The worksheet formulas now appear on a single page, in landscape orientation, with row (number) and column (letter) headings. See Figure E-19.

8. **Click Print in the Print Preview window, then click OK**

   After you retrieve the printout, you want to return the worksheet to displaying formula results. You can do this easily by using a key combination.

9. **Press [Ctrl][`] to redisplay formula results**

   [Ctrl][`] (grave accent mark) toggles between displaying formula results and displaying formula contents.

10. **Save the workbook, then close it and exit Excel**

    The completed payroll worksheet is displayed in Figure E-3; the completed sales worksheet is displayed in Figure E-7; the completed invoice worksheet is shown in Figure E-14, and the completed loan worksheets are displayed in Figures E-17 and E-19.

FIGURE E-18: View tab of the Options dialog box

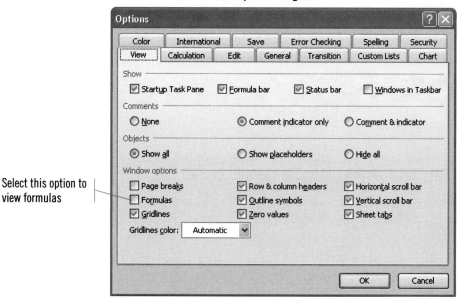

Select this option to
view formulas

FIGURE E-19: Print Preview window

Column
headings

Row headings

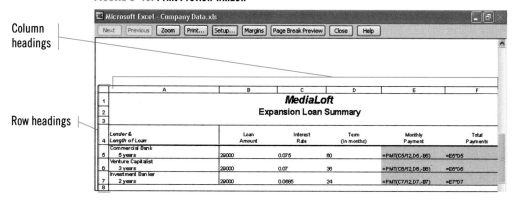

Clues to Use

Setting margins and alignment when printing part of a worksheet

You can set custom margins to print smaller sections of a worksheet. Select the range you want to print, click File on the menu bar, click Print, in the Print what section click Selection, then click Preview. In the Print Preview window, click Setup, then click the Margins tab. See Figure E-20. Double-click the margin numbers and type new ones. Use the Center on page check boxes to center the range horizontally or vertically. If you plan to print the range again, save the view after you print: click View on the menu bar, click Custom Views, click Add, then type a view name and click OK.

FIGURE E-20: Margins tab in the Page Setup dialog box

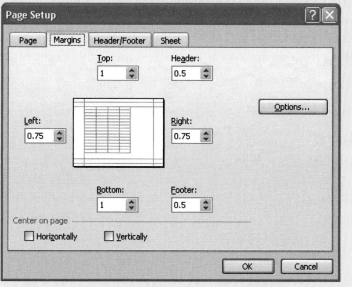

Practice

▼ CONCEPTS REVIEW

FIGURE E-21

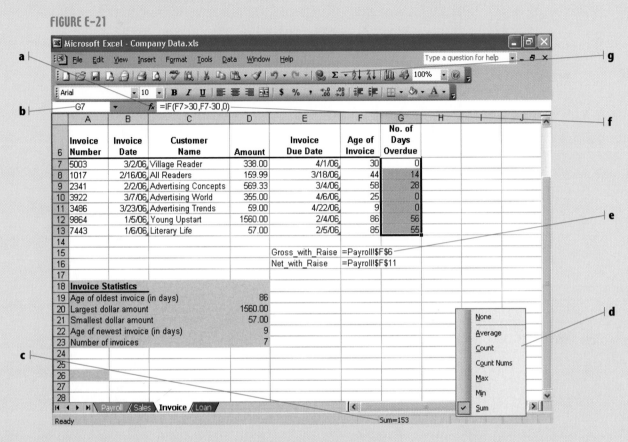

1. **Which element points to the area where a name is assigned to a cell?**
2. **Which element points to a conditional formula?**
3. **Which element points to the AutoCalculate options?**
4. **Which element points to a list of the names assigned in the worksheet?**
5. **Which element do you click to insert a function into a worksheet?**
6. **Which element points to the result of an AutoCalculate option?**
7. **Which element do you click to enter a total of adjacent values into a blank cell?**

Match each term with the statement that best describes it.

8. Style	**a.**	Function used to count the number of nonblank entries
9. COUNTA	**b.**	A combination of formatting characteristics
10. test_cond	**c.**	Part of the PMT function that represents the loan amount
11. COUNT	**d.**	Part of the IF function in which the conditions are stated
12. pv	**e.**	Function used to count the number of numerical entries

Select the best answer from the list of choices.

13. **To generate a positive payment value when using the PMT function, you must:**
    a. Enter the function arguments as positive values.
    b. Enter the function arguments as negative values.
    c. Enter the interest rate divisor as a negative value.
    d. Enter the amount being borrowed as a negative value.

14. **When you enter the rate and nper arguments in a PMT function, you must:**
    a. Be consistent in the units used.
    b. Multiply both units by 12.
    c. Divide both values by 12.
    d. Use monthly units instead of annual units.

15. **To express conditions such as less than or equal to, you can use a(n):**
    a. Statistical function.
    b. PMT function.
    c. AutoCalculate formula.
    d. Comparison operator.

16. **Which of the following statements is false?**
    a. You can use only existing number and date formats in Excel.
    b. You can create custom number and date formats in Excel.
    c. Dates are stored in Excel as serial numbers.
    d. m/d/yy is an Excel date format.

▼ SKILLS REVIEW

1. **Create a formula with several operators.**
   a. Start Excel, open the Data File EX E-2.xls from the drive and folder where your Data Files are stored, then save the workbook as **Manager Bonuses**.
   b. On the Bonuses worksheet, select cell C13 using the Go To command.
   c. Enter the formula **.2*AVERAGE(C4:C10)**.
   d. Enter the formula **.1*C13** in cell **C14**.
   e. Use the Paste Special command to paste the values and formats in B4:B10 to G4:G10, then save your work.

2. **Use names in a formula.**
   a. Name cell C13 **Dept_Bonus**.
   b. Name cell C14 **Project_Bonus**.
   c. Select the range C4:C10 and name it **Base_Pay**.
   d. In cell E4, enter the formula **Dept_Bonus*D4+Project_Bonus**.
   e. Copy the formula in cell E4 into the range E5:E10.
   f. Format range E4:E10 with the Comma style, using the Style dialog box.
   g. Select the range E4:E10, if necessary, and name it **Bonus_Total**.
   h. In cell F4, enter a formula that sums Base_Pay and Bonus_Total.
   i. Copy the formula in cell F4 into the range F5:F10.
   j. Format range F4:F10 with the Comma style, using the Style dialog box.
   k. Save your work.

3. **Generate multiple totals with AutoSum.**
   a. Select range E4:F11.
   b. Enter the totals using AutoSum.
   c. Check the formulas in cells E11:F11 to make sure they are correct.
   d. Format range E11:F11 with the Currency style, using the Style dialog box.
   e. Enter your name in cell A18, save your work, then preview and print this worksheet.

4. Use dates in calculations.

a. Make the Merit Pay sheet active.

b. In cell D6, enter the formula **B6+183**.

c. Copy the formula in cell D6 into the range D7:D14.

d. Use the NOW function to insert the date and time in cell A3.

e. In cell E18, enter the text **Last Pay Date for Year**, and in cell G18, use the Date function to enter the date **12/31/2006**.

f. Save your work.

5. Build a conditional formula with the IF function.

a. In cell F6, use the Function dialog box to enter the formula **IF(C6=5,E6*0.05,0)**.

b. Copy the formula in cell F6 into the range F7:F14.

c. Make sure the total in cell F15 is correct.

d. Apply the Comma style with no decimal places to F6:F14.

e. Save your work.

6. Use statistical functions.

a. In cell C19, enter a function to calculate the average salary in the range E6:E14.

b. In cell C20, enter a function to calculate the largest bonus in the range F6:F14.

c. In cell C21, enter a function to calculate the lowest performance rating in the range C6:C14.

d. In cell C22, enter a function to calculate the number of entries in range A6:A14.

e. Apply the Comma style with no decimal places to C19:C22. Compare your results with Figure E-22.

f. Enter your name into cell A28, then save, preview, and print the worksheet.

FIGURE E-22

18	**Department Statistics**		
19	Average Salary		30,560
20	Highest Bonus		1,825
21	Lowest Performance Rating		3
22	Number of Employees		9
23			
24			
25			
26			
27			
28			
29			
30			

◄◄ ◄ ► ►◄ \ Bonuses \ **Merit Pay** / Loan /

Ready

7. Calculate payments with the PMT function.

a. Make the Loan sheet active.

b. In cell B9, use the Insert Function dialog box to enter the formula **PMT(B5/12,B6,–B4)**.

c. In cell B10, enter the formula **B9*B6**.

d. AutoFit column B, if necessary.

e. In cell B11, enter the formula **B10–B4**.

f. Enter your name in cell A15, then save, preview, and print the worksheet.

8. Display and print formula contents.

a. Use the View tab in the Options dialog box to display formulas in the worksheet. If the Formula Auditing toolbar opens, you can close it.

b. Adjust the column widths as necessary.

c. Save, preview, and print this worksheet on one page in landscape orientation with the row and column headings.

d. Redisplay the formula results in the worksheet, then resize columns as necessary.

e. Close the workbook, then exit Excel.

▼ INDEPENDENT CHALLENGE 1

As manager of Mike's Ice Cream Parlor, you have been asked to create a worksheet that totals the monthly sales of all store products. Your monthly report should include the following:

- Sales totals for the current month for each product
- Sales totals for the last month for each product
- The percent change in sales from last month to this month

To document the report further, you decide to include a printout of the worksheet formulas.

a. Start Excel, open the Data File EX E-3.xls from the drive and folder where your Data Files are stored, then save it as **Mike's Sales**.

b. Use the TODAY function to enter today's date in cell A3.

c. Create and apply a custom format for the date entry.

d. Use AutoSum to enter totals for each week, and current month totals for each product.

e. Calculate the percent change in sales from the previous month for regular ice cream. (*Hint*: The formula in words would be (Current Month-Last Month)/Last Month.)

f. Copy the percent change formula down the column for the other products using AutoFill, then format the column with the Percent style using the Formatting toolbar.

g. Apply a Comma style with no decimal places to all weekly figures and totals, using the Formatting toolbar.

h. Enter your name into cell A15, then save, preview, and print the worksheet on a single page.

i. Display and preview the worksheet formulas, then print the formulas in landscape orientation on one page with row and column headings.

j. Close the workbook without saving the changes for displaying formulas, then exit Excel.

▼ INDEPENDENT CHALLENGE 2

You are an auditor with a certified public accounting firm. Fly Away, a manufacturer of skating products, has contacted you to audit its financial records. The management at Fly Away is considering opening a branch in Great Britain and needs its records audited to prepare the business plan. The managers at Fly Away have asked you to assist them in preparing their year-end sales summary as part of this audit. Specifically, they want to add expenses and show the percent of annual expenses that each expense category represents. They also want to show what percent of annual sales each expense category represents. You will include a formula calculating the difference between sales and expenses and another formula calculating expenses divided by sales. The expense categories and their respective dollar amounts are as follows: Building Lease $50,000; Equipment $208,000; Office $25,000; Salary $355,000; Taxes $310,000. Use these expense amounts to prepare the year-end sales and expenses summary for Fly Away.

a. Start Excel, open the Data File EX E-4.xls from the drive and folder where your Data Files are stored, then save the workbook as **Fly Away Sales**.

b. Name the cell containing the formula for total annual expenses **Annual_Expenses**. Use the name Annual_Expenses in cell C12 to create a formula calculating percent of annual expenses. Copy this formula as necessary and apply the Percent style. Add a formula that sums all the values for percent of annual expenses, which should equal 100%.

c. In cell D12, enter a formula calculating the percent of annual sales each expense category represents. Use the name **Annual_Sales** in the formula (cell B9 has been named Annual_Sales). Copy this formula as necessary and apply the Percent style. Include a formula that sums all the values for percent of annual sales.

d. Enter the formula calculating Net Profit in cell B19, using the names Annual_Sales and Annual_Expenses.

e. Enter the formula for Expenses as a percent of sales in cell B20, using the names Annual_Sales and Annual_Expenses.

f. Format cell B19 as Currency with two decimal places. Format cell B20 using the Percentage style with two decimal places. Widen the columns as necessary to display cell contents.

g. Enter your name into cell A22.

▼ INDEPENDENT CHALLENGE 2 (CONTINUED)

Advanced Challenge Exercise

- Display the Formula Auditing toolbar and check the worksheet for errors.
- Use the Formula Auditing toolbar to evaluate the formula in cell B20.
- Close the Formula Auditing toolbar.

h. Save, preview, and print the worksheet.

i. Close the workbook, then exit Excel.

▼ INDEPENDENT CHALLENGE 3

As the owner of Custom Fit, a general contracting firm specializing in home-storage projects, you are facing a business challenge at your firm. Because jobs are taking longer than expected, you decide to take out a $10,000 loan to purchase some new power tools. You check three loan sources: the Small Business Administration (SBA), your local bank, and a consortium of investors. The SBA will lend you the money at 7% interest, but you have to pay it off in three years. The local bank offers you the loan at 7.75% interest over four years. The consortium offers you a 6.75% loan, but they require you to pay it back in two years. To analyze all three loan options, you decide to build a loan summary worksheet. Using the loan terms provided, build a worksheet summarizing your options.

a. Start Excel, open a new workbook, then save it as **Custom Fit Loan Options** in the drive and folder where your Data Files are stored.

b. Enter today's date in cell A3, using the TODAY function.

c. Using Figure E-23 as a guide, enter labels and worksheet data for the three loan sources.

FIGURE E-23

Microsoft Excel - Custom Fit Loan Options.xls

File Edit View Insert Format Tools Data Window Help

A1 — Custom Fit

	A	B	C	D	E	F	G	H
1				Custom Fit				
2				Loan Options				
3	9/18/2006							
4	Loan Source	Loan Amount	Interest Rate	# Payments	Monthly Payment	Total Payments	Total Interest	
5	SBA	10,000	7.00%	36				
6	Bank	10,000	7.75%	48				
7	Investors	10,000	6.75%	24				
8								

d. Enter the monthly payment formula for your first loan source (making sure to show the payment as a positive amount), copy the formula as appropriate, then name the range containing the monthly payment formulas **Monthly_Payment**.

e. Name the cell range containing the number of payments, **Number_Payments**.

f. Enter the formula for total payments for your first loan source using the named ranges **Monthly_Payment** and **Number_Payments**, then copy the formula as necessary.

g. Name the cell range containing the formulas for Total payments, **Total_Payments**. Name the cell range containing the loan amounts, **Loan_Amount**.

h. Enter the formula for total interest for your first loan source using the named ranges **Total_Payments** and **Loan_Amount**, then copy the formula as necessary.

i. Format the worksheet using formatting appropriate to the worksheet purpose, then enter your name in cell A14.

Advanced Challenge Exercise

- Paste the range names for the worksheet starting in cell E9.
- Name the cell range C5:C7 as Interest_Rate. Name the range G5:G7 as Total_Interest.
- Delete the pasted list of names and paste the new list.

j. Save, preview, and print the worksheet on a single page. Print the worksheet formulas showing row and column headings using landscape orientation. Do not save the worksheet with the formula settings.

k. Close the workbook then exit Excel.

▼ INDEPENDENT CHALLENGE 4

You have been asked to research IRA rates for your company's human resources department. The company plans to deposit $4000 in the employees' accounts at the beginning of each year. You have been asked to research current rates at financial institutions. You will use the Web to find this information. You will use the rate information to determine the value of the deposited money after five years.

a. Open your browser, then go to the search engine of your choice and search for **IRA rates** in the search text box. Find IRA rates offered by three institutions for a $4000 deposit, then write down the institution name, the rate, and the minimum deposit in the table below.

b. Start Excel, open a new workbook, then save it as **IRA Rates** in the drive and folder where your Data Files are stored.

c. Enter the column headings, row headings, and, research results from the table below into your IRA Rates workbook.

IRA Worksheet

Institution	Rate	Minimum Deposit	Number of Years	Amount Deposited (Yearly)	Future Value
			5	4000	
			5	4000	
			5	4000	
Highest Rate					
Average Rate					
Highest Future Value					

d. Use the FV function to calculate the future value of a $4000 yearly deposit over 35 years for each institution, making sure it appears as a positive number. Assume that the payments are made at the beginning of the period, so the Type argument equals 1.

e. Use Excel functions to enter the highest rate, the average rate, and the highest future value into the workbook.

f. Enter your name in cell A15, then save, preview, and print the worksheet on a single page with one inch left and right margins.

g. Display and print the formulas for the worksheet on a single page using landscape orientation. Do not save the worksheet with the formulas displayed.

h. Close the workbook then exit Excel.

Excel 2003

▼ VISUAL WORKSHOP

Create the worksheet shown in Figure E-24. (*Hints:* Use IF formulas to enter the bonus amounts. An employee with a performance rating of seven or higher receives a bonus of $1000. If the rating is less than seven, no bonus is awarded. The summary information in cells A15:C18 uses the SUM function and statistical functions.) Enter your name in cell A20, and save the workbook as **Bonus Pay**. Preview and then print the worksheet.

FIGURE E-24

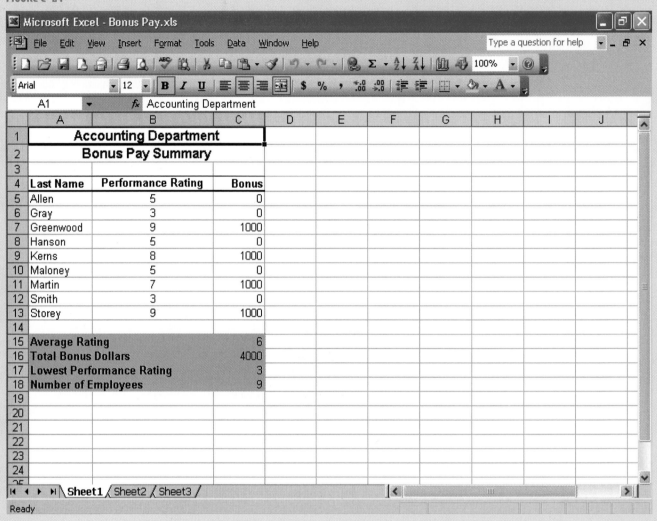

UNIT
F
Excel 2003

Managing Workbooks and Preparing Them for the Web

OBJECTIVES

Freeze columns and rows
Insert and delete worksheets
Consolidate data with 3-D references
Hide and protect worksheet areas
Save custom views of a worksheet
Control page breaks and page numbering
Create a hyperlink between Excel files
Save an Excel file as a Web page

 If you have a SAM user profile, you may have access to hands-on instruction, practice, and assessment of the skills covered in this unit. Log in to your SAM account and go to your assignments page to see what your instructor has assigned.

In this unit you will learn several Excel features to help you manage and print workbook data. You will also learn how to prepare workbooks for publication on the World Wide Web. The MediaLoft Accounting Department asks its marketing director Jim Fernandez to design a timecard summary worksheet to track salary costs for hourly workers. When the worksheet is complete, the Accounting Department will add the rest of the employees and place it on the MediaLoft intranet site for review by store managers. Jim asks you to design a worksheet using some employees from the MediaLoft Houston store. He wants you to save the worksheet as a Web page for viewing on the company's intranet site.

Freezing Columns and Rows

As rows and columns fill up with data, you might need to scroll through the worksheet to add, delete, modify, and view information, and the column or row headings may scroll out of view. Looking at information without row or column labels can be confusing. In Excel, you can temporarily freeze columns and rows, so you can keep the headings in view as you scroll. **Panes** are the columns and rows that **freeze**, or remain in place, while you scroll through your worksheet.  Jim asks you to check the total hours worked, hourly pay rate, and total pay for salespeople Paul Cristifano and Virginia Young. Because the worksheet is becoming more difficult to read as its size increases, you want to freeze the column and row labels.

STEPS

1. **Start Excel if necessary, open the Data File EX F-1.xls from the drive and folder where your Data Files are stored, then save it as** Timecard Summary

2. **Scroll through the Monday worksheet to view the data, then click cell** D6

   You select cell D6 because Excel freezes the columns to the left and the rows above the selected cell. You want to freeze columns A, B, and C as well as rows 1 through 5. By doing so, you can see each employee's last name, first name, and timecard number on the screen when you scroll to the right, and you can also read the labels in rows 1 through 5 when you scroll down.

3. **Click** Window **on the menu bar, then click** Freeze Panes

   A thin line appears along the column border to the left of the active cell, and another line appears along the row above the active cell, indicating that columns A through C and rows 1 through 5 are frozen.

4. **Scroll to the right until columns** A **through** C **and** L **through** O **are visible**

   Because columns A, B, and C are frozen, they remain on the screen; columns D through K are temporarily hidden from view. Notice that the information you are looking for in row 13 (last name, total hours, hourly pay rate, and total pay for Paul Cristifano) is readily available. Paul's data appears to be correct, but you still need to check Virginia Young's information.

5. **Scroll down until** row 26 **is visible**

   In addition to columns A through C, rows 1 through 5 remain on the screen. See Figure F-1. You are now able to verify Virginia Young's information. Even though a pane is frozen, you can click in the frozen area of the worksheet and edit the contents of the cells there, if necessary.

6. **Press** [Ctrl][Home]

   Because the panes are frozen, the cell pointer moves to cell D6, not A1.

7. **Click** Window **on the menu bar, then click** Unfreeze Panes

   The freeze lines no longer appear and the columns and rows are no longer frozen.

8. **Press** [Ctrl][Home] **to return to cell A1, then save the workbook**

Clues to Use

Viewing and arranging worksheets

In a multiple-sheet workbook, you can use the scrolling buttons to the left of the horizontal scroll bar. To scroll several tabs at once, press [Shift] while clicking one of the middle tab scrolling buttons. You can view multiple worksheets by clicking the sheet you want to view and then clicking New Window on the Window menu. Repeat this for each sheet you want to view. Each sheet becomes a button on the taskbar. To arrange the windows, click Arrange on the Window menu and choose a layout.

FIGURE F-1: Scrolled worksheet with frozen rows and columns

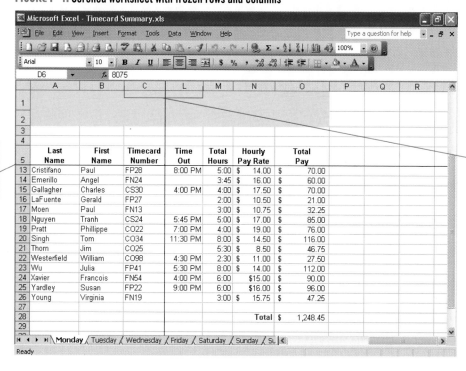

Break in row numbers due to frozen rows 1 through 5

Break in column letters due to frozen columns A through C

Clues to Use

Splitting the worksheet into multiple panes

Excel lets you split the worksheet area into vertical and/or horizontal panes, so that you can click inside any one pane and scroll to locate information in that pane while the other panes remain in place. See Figure F-2. To split a worksheet area into multiple panes, drag the split box (the small box at the top of the vertical scroll bar or at the right end of the horizontal scroll bar) in the direction you want the split to appear. To remove the split, move the pointer over the split until the pointer changes to a double-headed arrow ⬌, then double-click.

FIGURE F-2: Worksheet split into two horizontal and two vertical panes

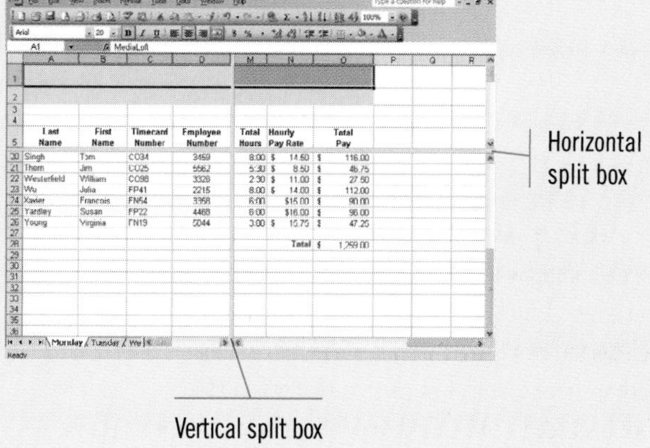

Horizontal split box

Vertical split box

Inserting and Deleting Worksheets

You can insert and delete worksheets in a workbook at any time. For example, because new workbooks open with only three sheets available (Sheet1, Sheet2, and Sheet3), you need to insert at least one more sheet if you want to have four quarterly worksheets in an annual budget workbook. You can do this by using commands on the menu bar or shortcut menu. Jim was in a hurry when he added the sheet tabs to the Timecard Summary workbook. He wants you to insert a sheet for Thursday and delete the sheet for Sunday because Houston workers do not work on Sundays.

STEPS

QUICK TIP

You can copy a selected worksheet by clicking Edit on the menu bar, then clicking Move or Copy Sheet. Choose the sheet you want the copy to precede, click the Create a copy check box, then click OK.

1. **Click the Friday sheet tab, click Insert on the menu bar, then click Worksheet**

   Excel inserts a new sheet tab labeled Sheet1 to the left of the Friday sheet.

2. **Double-click the Sheet1 tab and rename it Thursday**

   Now the tabs read Monday, Tuesday, Wednesday, Thursday, Friday, and Saturday. The tab for the Summary is not visible. You still need to delete the Sunday worksheet.

3. **Right-click the Sunday sheet tab, then click Delete on the shortcut menu shown in Figure F-3**

   The shortcut menu allows you to insert, delete, rename, move, or copy sheets; it also allows you to select all the sheets and change the tab color of a worksheet.

4. **Move the mouse pointer over any tab scrolling button, then right-click**

   Excel opens a shortcut menu of the worksheets in the active workbook. Compare your list with Figure F-4.

5. **Click Monday on the shortcut menu, then save the workbook**

Clues to Use

Grouping worksheets

You can group worksheets to work on them as a collection so that data entered into one worksheet is automatically entered into all of the selected worksheets. This is useful for data that is common to every sheet of a workbook such as headers and footers. Grouping worksheets can also be used to print multiple worksheets at one time. To group worksheets, press and hold [Ctrl] and click the tabs for the sheets you want to group. If the sheets that you want to group are adjacent, then click the first sheet and hold [Shift] while clicking the last sheet in the group.

FIGURE F-3: Worksheet shortcut menu

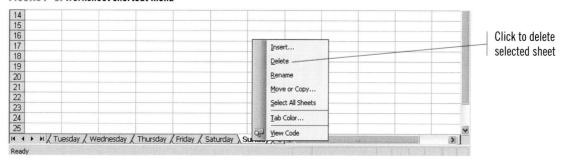

Click to delete selected sheet

FIGURE F-4: Workbook with worksheets menu

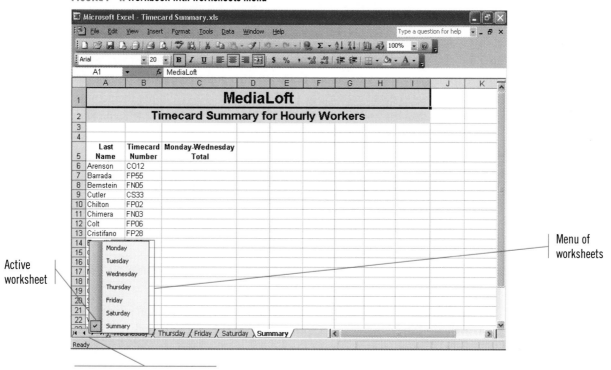

Menu of worksheets

Active worksheet

Right-click any tab scrolling button to display the menu of worksheets

Clues to Use

Specifying headers and footers

As you prepare a workbook for others to view, it is helpful to provide as much data as possible about the worksheets, such as the number of pages, who created it, and when. You can do this easily in a **header** or **footer**, which is information that prints at the top or bottom of each printed page. Headers and footers are visible on the screen only in Print Preview. To add a header, for example, click View on the menu bar, click Header and Footer, then click Custom Header. You see a dialog box similar to that in Figure F-5. Both the header and the footer are divided into three sections, and you can enter information in any or all of them. You can type information, such as your name, and click the icons to enter the page number ▣, total pages ▣, date ▣, time ▣, file path ▣, filename ▣, or sheet name ▣. You can insert a picture by clicking the Insert Picture icon ▣, and you can format the picture by clicking the Format picture icon ▣ and selecting formatting options. When you click an

icon, Excel inserts a symbol in the footer section containing an ampersand (&) and the element name in brackets. When you are finished, click OK, click the Print Preview button on the Header/Footer tab to see your header and footer, then click Close.

FIGURE F-5: Header dialog box

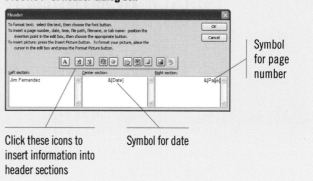

Symbol for page number

Click these icons to insert information into header sections

Symbol for date

Consolidating Data with 3-D References

When you want to summarize similar data that exists in different sheets or workbooks, you can combine and display it in one sheet. For example, you might have departmental sales figures on four different store sheets that you want to **consolidate** on one summary sheet showing total departmental sales for all stores. The best way to consolidate data is to use cell references to the various sheets on a consolidation, or summary, sheet. Because they reference other sheets that are usually behind the summary sheet, such references effectively create another dimension in the workbook and are called **3-D references**. You can reference data in other sheets and in other workbooks. Referencing cells is a better method than retyping calculated results because the data values on which calculated totals depend might change. If you reference the values, any changes to the original values are automatically reflected in the consolidation sheet. Although Jim does not have timecard data for Thursday and Friday, he wants you to use the Summary sheet to consolidate the available data. He asks you to do this by creating a formula on the Summary sheet that adds the total pay data in the Monday, Tuesday, and Wednesday sheets. You want to freeze the panes to improve the view of the worksheet before initiating the 3-D reference.

STEPS

1. **On the Monday sheet, click cell D6, click Window on the menu bar, click Freeze Panes, then scroll horizontally to bring columns L through O into view**

2. **Right-click a tab scrolling button, then click Summary**
   Because the Summary sheet (which is the consolidation sheet) will contain the reference, the cell pointer must reside there when you initiate the reference.

3. **On the Summary sheet, click cell C6, click the AutoSum button Σ on the Standard toolbar, activate the Monday sheet, press and hold [Shift] and click the Wednesday sheet tab, click cell O6, then click the Enter button ✓ on the formula bar**
   The Summary sheet becomes active, and the formula bar reads =SUM(Monday:Wednesday!O6). See Figure F-6. Monday:Wednesday references the Monday, Tuesday and Wednesday sheets. The ! (exclamation point) is an **external reference indicator**, meaning that the cells referenced are outside the active sheet; O6 is the actual cell reference in the external sheets. The result, $168.80, appears in cell C6 of the Summary sheet, showing the sum of the total pay referenced in cell O6 of the Monday, Tuesday, and Wednesday sheets.

4. **In the Summary sheet, copy cell C6 into cells C7:C26**
   Excel copies the 3-D formula in cell C6. You can test a consolidation reference by changing one cell value on which the formula is based and seeing if the formula result changes.

5. **Activate the Monday sheet, edit cell L6 to read 6:30 PM, then activate the Summary sheet**
   The sum of Beryl Arenson's pay was automatically updated in the Summary sheet. See Figure F-7.

6. **Click View on the menu bar, click Header and Footer, click Custom Footer, enter your name in the Left section text box, click OK, then click OK**

7. **Preview the worksheet, then print it**

8. **Activate the Monday sheet, unfreeze the panes, then save the workbook**

FIGURE F-6: Worksheet showing total pay

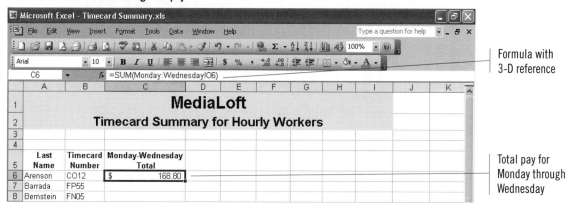

Formula with 3-D reference

Total pay for Monday through Wednesday

FIGURE F-7: Summary worksheet with updated total

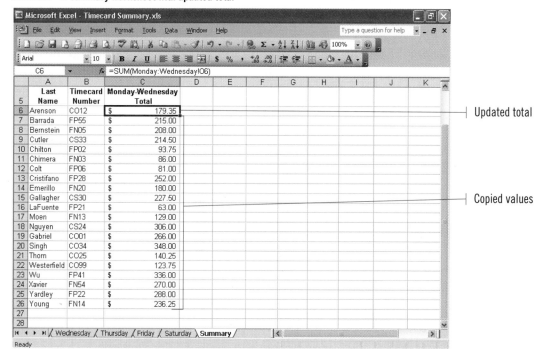

Updated total

Copied values

Clues to Use

Linking data between workbooks

Just as you can reference data between cells in a worksheet and between sheets, you can dynamically reference data between workbooks so that changes made in referenced cells in one workbook are reflected in the consolidation sheet in the other workbook. This dynamic referencing is called **linking**. To link a single cell between workbooks, open both workbooks, select the cell to receive the linked data, type = (the equal sign), select the cell in the other workbook containing the data to be linked, then press [Enter]. Excel automatically inserts the name of the referenced workbook in the cell reference. For example, if the linked data is contained in cell C7 of worksheet New in the Products workbook, the cell entry reads ='[Product.xls]New'!$C$7. To perform calculations, enter formulas on the consolidation sheet using cells in the supporting sheets. If you are linking more than one cell, you can copy the linked data to the Clipboard, select the upper-left cell in the workbook to receive the link, click Edit on the menu bar, click Paste Special, then click Paste Link.

Hiding and Protecting Worksheet Areas

Worksheets may contain sensitive information that you don't want others to view or alter. To protect such information, Excel gives you two options. You can **hide** the formulas in selected cells (or rows, columns, or entire sheets), and you can **lock** selected cells, in which case other people are able to view the data (values, numbers, labels, formulas, etc.) in those cells, but not change it. See Table F-1 for a list of options you can use to protect a worksheet. You set the lock and hide options in the Format Cells dialog box. Excel locks all cells by default, but this protection does not take effect until you activate the Excel protection feature on the Tools menu. A common worksheet protection strategy is to unlock cells in which data will be changed, sometimes referred to as the **data entry area**, and to lock cells in which the data should not be changed. Then, when you protect the worksheet, the unlocked areas can still be changed. ▰▰▰ Because Jim will assign an employee to enter the sensitive timecard information into the worksheet, he wants you to hide and lock selected areas of the worksheet.

STEPS

1. **On the Monday sheet, select the range I6:L26, click Format on the menu bar, click Cells, then click the Protection tab**

   Notice that the Locked box in the Protection tab is already checked, as shown in Figure F-8. The Locked check box is selected by default, meaning that all the cells in a new workbook start out locked. (Note, however, that cell locking is not applied unless the protection feature is also activated. The protection feature is inactive by default.) You do not want the Time In and Time Out cells to be locked when the protection feature is activated.

2. **Click the Locked check box to deselect it, then click OK**

   Excel stores time as a fraction of a 24-hour day. In the formula for total pay, hours must be multiplied by 24. This concept might be confusing to the data entry person, so you hide the formulas.

3. **Select range O6:O26, click Format on the menu bar, click Cells, click the Protection tab, click the Hidden check box to select it, then click OK**

   The data remains the same (unhidden and unlocked) until you set the protection in the next step.

4. **Click Tools on the menu bar, point to Protection, then click Protect Sheet**

   The Protect Sheet dialog box opens. The default options allow you to protect the worksheet while allowing users to select locked or unlocked cells only. You choose not to use a password.

5. **Make sure Protect worksheet and contents of locked cells is checked in the Protect Sheet dialog box, then click OK**

   You are ready to test the new worksheet protection.

6. **Click cell O6**

   The formula bar is empty because of the hidden formula setting.

7. **In cell O6, type T to confirm that locked cells cannot be changed, then click OK**

   When you attempt to change a locked cell, a message box reminds you of the protected cell's read-only status. See Figure F-9.

8. **Click cell I6, type 9, and notice that Excel allows you to begin the entry, press [Esc] to cancel the entry, then save the workbook**

   Because you unlocked the cells in columns I through L before you protected the worksheet, you can make changes to these cells. The Time In and Time Out data can be changed as necessary.

QUICK TIP

To turn off worksheet protection, click Tools on the menu bar, point to Protection, then click Unprotect Sheet. If prompted for a password, type the password, then click OK. Remember that passwords are case sensitive. If you assign the password "phone" and try to open the workbook using "Phone" or "PHONE," you will not be able to open the workbook.

FIGURE F-8: Protection tab in Format Cells dialog box

Click to remove
check mark

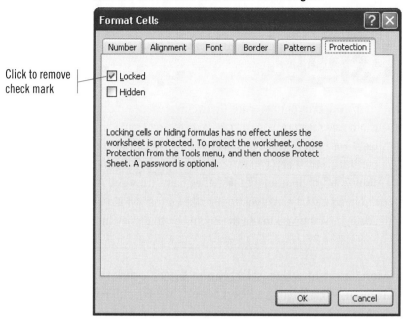

FIGURE F-9: Reminder of protected cell's read-only status

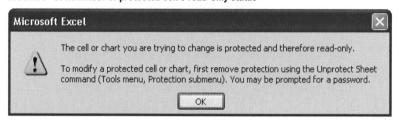

TABLE F-1: Options for hiding and protecting workbook elements

task	menu commands
Hide/Unhide a column	Format, Column, Hide or Unhide
Hide/Unhide a formula	Format, Cells, Protection tab, select/deselect Hidden check box
Hide/Unhide a row	Format, Row, Hide or Unhide
Hide/Unhide a sheet	Format, Sheet, Hide or Unhide
Hide/Unhide a workbook	Window, Hide or Unhide
Protect workbook	Tools, Protection, Protect Workbook, assign optional password
Protect worksheet	Tools, Protection, Protect Sheet, assign optional password
Unlock/Relock cells	Format, Cells, Protection tab, deselect/select Locked check box

(*Note*: Some of the hide and protect options do not take effect until protection is enabled. To enable protection, click Tools on the menu bar, point to Protection, then click Protect Sheet.)

Clues to Use

Changing workbook properties

You can also use a password to protect an entire workbook from being opened or modified by changing its file properties. Click File on the menu bar, click Save As, click Tools, then click General Options. Specify the password(s) for opening or modifying the workbook. To remove a workbook password, you can double-click the asterisks in the Password to open or Password to modify text boxes and press [Delete]. You can also use this dialog box to offer users an option to open the workbook in read-only format so that they can open, but not change it. Another way to make an entire workbook read-only is to right-click Start on the taskbar, then click Explore. Locate and right-click the filename, click Properties, click the General tab, then, in the Attributes section, select the Read-only check box.

Saving Custom Views of a Worksheet

A **view** is a set of display and/or print settings that you can name and save, then access at a later time. By using the Excel Custom Views feature, you can create several different views of a worksheet without having to create separate sheets. For example, if you often switch between portrait and landscape orientations when printing different parts of a worksheet, you can create two views with the appropriate print settings for each view. You set the display and/or print settings first, then name the view.  Because Jim wants to generate several reports from his data, he asks you to save the current print and display settings as a custom view. To better view the data, he wants you to use the Zoom box to display the entire worksheet on one screen.

STEPS

1. **With the Monday sheet active, select range A1:O28, click the Zoom list arrow on the Standard toolbar, click Selection, then press [Ctrl][Home] to return to cell A1**
   Excel adjusts the display magnification so that the selected data fits on one screen. See Figure F-10.

2. **Click View on the menu bar, then click Custom Views**
   The Custom Views dialog box opens. Any previously defined views for the active worksheet appear in the Views box. In this case, Jim has created a custom view named Generic containing default print and display settings. See Figure F-11.

3. **Click Add**
   The Add View dialog box opens, as shown in Figure F-12. Here, you enter a name for the view and decide whether to include print settings and hidden rows, columns, and filter settings. You want to include the selected options.

4. **In the Name box, type Complete Daily Worksheet, then click OK**
   After creating a custom view, you return to the worksheet. You are ready to test the two custom views. In case the views require a change to the worksheet, it's a good idea to turn off worksheet protection.

5. **Click Tools on the menu bar, point to Protection, then click Unprotect Sheet**

6. **Click View on the menu bar, then click Custom Views**
   The Custom Views dialog box opens, listing both the Complete Daily Worksheet and Generic views.

7. **Click Generic in the Views list, click Show, preview the worksheet, then close the Preview window**
   The Generic custom view returns the worksheet to the Excel default print and display settings. Now you are ready to test the new custom view.

8. **Click View on the menu bar, click Custom Views, click Complete Daily Worksheet in the Views list box if necessary, then click Show**
   The entire worksheet fits on the screen.

9. **Return to the Generic view, then save your work**

FIGURE F-10: Selected data fitted to one screen

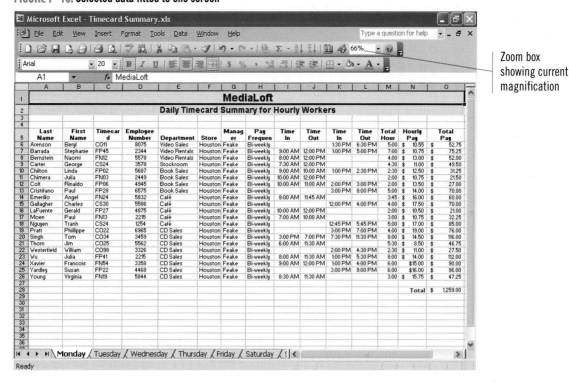

Zoom box showing current magnification

FIGURE F-11: Custom Views dialog box

Existing custom views appear here

Click to create new view

FIGURE F-12: Add View dialog box

Type name of view here

Clues to Use

Creating a workspace

If you work with several workbooks at a time, you can group them so you can open them in one step by creating a **workspace**, a file with an .xlw extension. Then, instead of opening each workbook individually, you can open the workspace. To create a workspace, open the workbooks you wish to group and position and size them as you would like them to appear. Click File on the menu bar, click Save Workspace, type a name for the workspace file, then click Save. Remember, however, that the workspace file does not contain the workbooks themselves, so you still have to save any changes you make to the original workbook files. To have the workbooks automatically open in the workspace when you start Excel, place the workspace file in your XLStart folder (C:\Program Files\Microsoft Office\Office11\XLStart).

Controlling Page Breaks and Page Numbering

The vertical and horizontal dashed lines in worksheets represent page breaks. Excel automatically inserts a page break when your worksheet data doesn't fit on one page. These page breaks are **dynamic**, which means they adjust automatically when you insert or delete rows and columns and when you change column widths or row heights. Everything to the left of the first vertical dashed line and above the first horizontal dashed line is printed on the first page. You can override the automatic breaks by choosing the Page Break command on the Insert menu. Table F-2 describes the different types of page breaks you can use. ▒▒▒▒ Jim wants another report displaying no more than half the hourly workers on each page. To accomplish this, he asks you to insert a manual page break.

STEPS

1. **Click cell A16, click Insert on the menu bar, then click Page Break**
   A dashed line appears between rows 15 and 16, indicating a horizontal page break. See Figure F-13. After you set page breaks, it's a good idea to preview each page.

2. **Preview the worksheet, then click Zoom**
   Notice that the status bar reads "Page 1 of 4" and that the data for the employees up through Charles Gallagher appears on the first page. You decide to place the date in the footer.

3. **While in the Print Preview window, click Setup, click the Header/Footer tab, click Custom Footer, click the Right section box, then click the Date button** 📅

4. **Click the Left section box, type your name, then click OK**
   Your name, the page number, and the date appear in the Footer preview area.

5. **In the Page Setup dialog box, click OK, and while still in Print Preview, check to make sure that all the pages show your name, the page numbers, and the date, click Close, save the workbook, then print the worksheet**

6. **Click View on the menu bar, click Custom Views, click Add, type Half and Half, then click OK**
   Your new custom view has the page breaks and all current print settings.

7. **Make sure cell A16 is selected, then click Insert on the menu bar and click Remove Page Break**
   Excel removes the manual page break above or to the left of the active cell.

8. **Save the workbook**

FIGURE F-13: Worksheet with horizontal page break

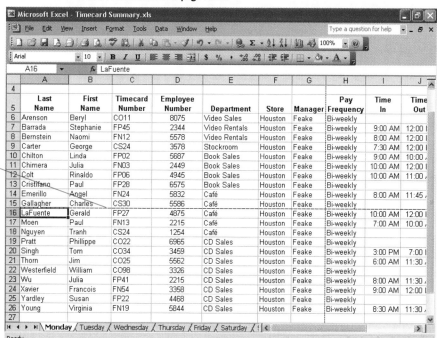

Dashed line indicates horizontal break after row 15

Clues to Use

Using Page Break Preview

You can view and change page breaks manually by clicking View on the menu bar, then clicking Page Break Preview, or clicking Page Break Preview in the Print Preview window. (If you see a Welcome to Page Break Preview dialog box, click OK to close it.) You can drag the page break lines to the desired location. See Figure F-14. If you drag a page break to the right to include more data on a page, Excel shrinks the type to fit the data on that page. To exit Page Break Preview, click View on the menu bar, then click Normal.

TABLE F-2: Page break options

type of page break	where to position cell pointer
Both horizontal and vertical page breaks	Select the cell below and to the right of the gridline where you want the breaks to occur
Only a horizontal page break	Select the cell in column A that is directly below the gridline where you want the page to break
Only a vertical page break	Select a cell in row 1 that is to the right of the gridline where you want the page to break

FIGURE F-14: Page Break Preview window

Drag page break lines to change page breaks

Creating a Hyperlink Between Excel Files

As you manage the content and appearance of your workbooks, you may want the workbook user to view information in another location. It might be nonessential information or data that is too detailed to place in the workbook itself. In these cases, you can create a **hyperlink**, an object (a filename, a word, a phrase, or a graphic) in a worksheet that, when you click it, displays, or "jumps to," another worksheet, called the **target**. The target can also be a document or a site on the World Wide Web. Hyperlinks are navigational tools between worksheets and are not used to exchange information. For example, in a worksheet that lists customer invoices, at each customer's name, you might create a hyperlink to an Excel file containing payment terms for each customer. Jim wants managers who view the Timecard Summary workbook to be able to view the pay categories for MediaLoft store employees. He asks you to create a hyperlink at the Hourly Pay Rate column heading. Users can click the hyperlink to view the Pay Rate worksheet.

STEPS

1. **Click cell N5 (the cell containing the text Hourly Pay Rate) on the Monday worksheet**

2. **Click the** Insert Hyperlink button **on the Standard toolbar, then click** Existing File or Web Page, **if it is not already selected**

   The Insert Hyperlink dialog box opens. See Figure F-15. The icons under Link to on the left side of the dialog box let you specify the type of location you want the link to jump to: an existing file or Web page, a place in the same document, a new document, or an e-mail address. Because you want the link to display a document that has been created, the first icon, Existing File or Web Page, is correct.

3. **Click the** Look in list arrow, **navigate to the location where your Data Files are stored if necessary, then click** Pay Rate Classifications.xls **in the file list**

   The filename you selected appears in the Address text box. This is the document users see when they click this hyperlink. You can also specify the ScreenTip that users see when they hold the pointer over the hyperlink.

4. **Click** ScreenTip, **type** Click here to see MediaLoft pay rate classifications, **click** OK, **edit the** Text to display **text box to show** Hourly Pay Rate, **then click** OK **again**

   Cell N5 now contains underlined blue text, indicating that it is a hyperlink. After you create a hyperlink, you should check it to make sure that it jumps to the correct destination.

5. **Move the pointer over the** Hourly Pay Rate text, **view the ScreenTip, then click once**

   Notice that when you move the pointer over the text, the pointer changes to , indicating that it is a hyperlink, and the ScreenTip appears. After you click, the Pay Rate Classifications worksheet appears. See Figure F-16. The Web toolbar appears beneath the Standard and Formatting toolbars.

6. **Click the** Back button **on the Web toolbar, save the workbook, then print the worksheet**

Clues to Use

Finding and replacing data and formats

You can easily change worksheet data by using the Find and Replace feature. Click Edit on the menu bar, click Replace, enter the text you want to find, press [Tab], then enter the text with which you want to replace it. Use the Find Next, Find All, Replace, and

Replace All buttons to find and replace any or all occurrences of the specified text. You can specify a data format for your search criteria by clicking the Options button, clicking the Format list arrow, and selecting a format.

FIGURE F-15: Insert Hyperlink dialog box

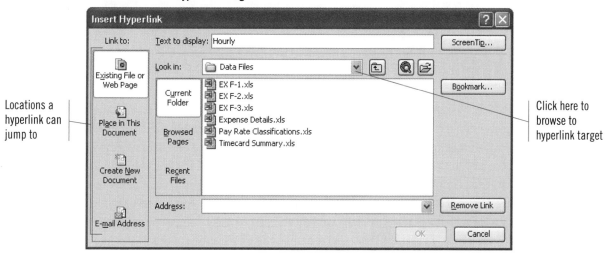

Locations a hyperlink can jump to

Click here to browse to hyperlink target

FIGURE F-16: Target document

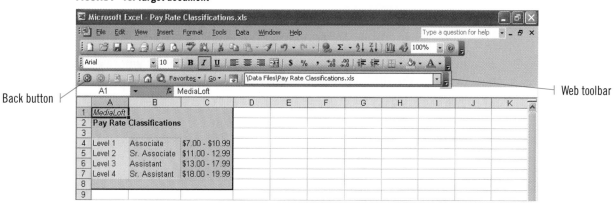

Back button

Web toolbar

Clues to Use

Using research services

You can access resources online and locally on your computer using the Research task pane. To open the Research task pane, click Tools on the menu bar, then click Research. The Search for text box allows you to specify a research topic. The task pane also has a drop-down list of the resources available to search for your topic. You can insert the information you find into your worksheet by moving your cursor over the information you want to insert, clicking the list arrow on the right, then clicking Insert, Copy, or Look Up. The research services feature will expand as more companies develop databases that are specifically designed for use in the Research task pane.

Saving an Excel File as a Web Page

One way to share Excel data is to place, or **publish**, the data on a network or on the Web so that others can access it using their Web browsers. The network can be an **intranet**, which is an internal network site used by a particular group of people who work together. If you post an entire workbook, users can click worksheet tabs to view each sheet. You can make the workbook interactive, meaning that users can enter, format, and perform data calculations. To publish an Excel document to an intranet or the Web, you must first save it in an **HTML (Hypertext Markup Language)** format. You can save your Excel file as a **single file Web page** that integrates all of the worksheets and graphical elements from the workbook into a single file. This file format is called MHTML. Incorporating the HTML and supporting files into one file makes it easier to publish your Excel file to the Web. Users who have IE 4.0 or higher can open a Web page saved in MHTML format. ▄▄▄▄ Jim asks you to save the entire Timecard Summary workbook in MHT format so he can publish it on the MediaLoft intranet for managers to view.

STEPS

1. **Click File on the menu bar, then click Save as Web Page**
   The Save As dialog box opens. By default, the Entire Workbook option button is selected. You want the title bar of the Web page to be more descriptive than the filename.

2. **Click Change Title**
   The Set Page Title dialog box opens.

3. **Type MediaLoft Houston Timecard Summary, then click OK**
   The new title appears in the Page title area.

QUICK TIP
To avoid problems when publishing your pages to a Web server, it is best to use lowercase characters, omit special characters and spaces, and limit your filename to eight characters.

4. **Click the Save in list arrow to navigate to the drive and folder where your Data Files are stored, change the filename to timesum, then click the Save as type list arrow and click Single File Web Page**
   The Save as type list box indicates that the workbook is to be saved as a Single File Web Page, which is in MHTML or MHT format. See Figure F-17.

5. **Click Save**
   A dialog box appears, indicating that the custom views you saved earlier will not be part of the HTML file.

6. **Click Yes**
   Excel saves the workbook as an MHT file in the folder location you specified in the Save As dialog box. The MHT file is open on your screen.

7. **Click File on the menu bar, click Web Page Preview, then if necessary maximize the browser window**
   The workbook opens in your default Web browser, showing you what it would look like if you opened the workbook on an intranet or on the Web. See Figure F-18.

8. **Click the Summary Sheet tab, then print the worksheet using your browser**

9. **Close the Web browser window, then close the timesum.mht workbook and the Pay Rate Classifications.xls workbook**

Clues to Use

Converting Excel files to other file types

You can use the Save As option on the File menu to save a workbook in a format that can be opened in earlier versions of Excel or in other spreadsheet programs. You can also use the Save As option to convert an Excel file to other file types such as XML, TXT (text file type), and CSV (comma-delimited file type).

FIGURE F-17: Save As dialog box

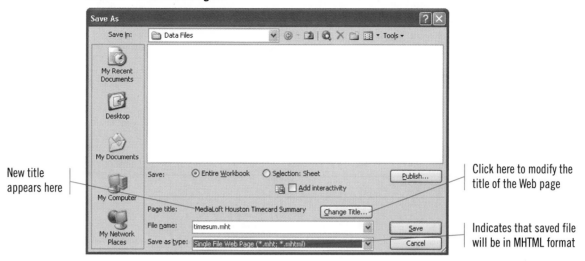

New title appears here

Click here to modify the title of the Web page

Indicates that saved file will be in MHTML format

FIGURE F-18: Workbook in Web page preview

Your screen will differ if you are using a different browser

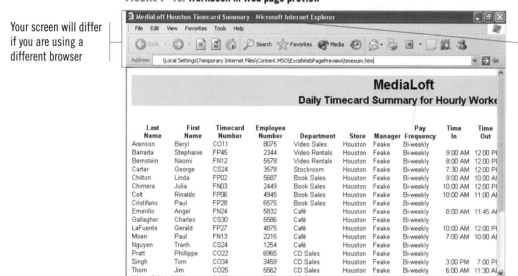

New title appears in the title bar

Sheet tabs allow users to view other sheets in their browser

Clues to Use

Holding Web discussions

You can attach a discussion comment to an Excel worksheet that you are going to save as an HTML document. This allows people viewing your worksheet on the Web to review and reply to your comments. To insert a discussion comment in Excel, click Tools on the menu bar, point to Online Collaboration, then click Web Discussions. This displays the Web Discussions toolbar. See Figure F-19. You can add comments that others can view on the Web by clicking the Insert Discussion about the Workbook button 🗗 on the Web Discussions Toolbar. Your comments, which are stored on a discussion server, appear with the worksheet when it is saved and published as a Web document. People viewing your worksheet on the Web can reply by clicking the Discuss button 🗔 on the Standard Buttons toolbar

in Internet Explorer to display the Discussions toolbar. Then they can click the Insert Discussion about the Workbook button 🗗. (*Note*: You must specify a discussion server to use this feature.)

FIGURE F-19: Web Discussion toolbar

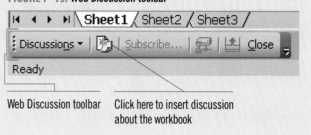

Web Discussion toolbar

Click here to insert discussion about the workbook

Practice

▼ CONCEPTS REVIEW

FIGURE F-20

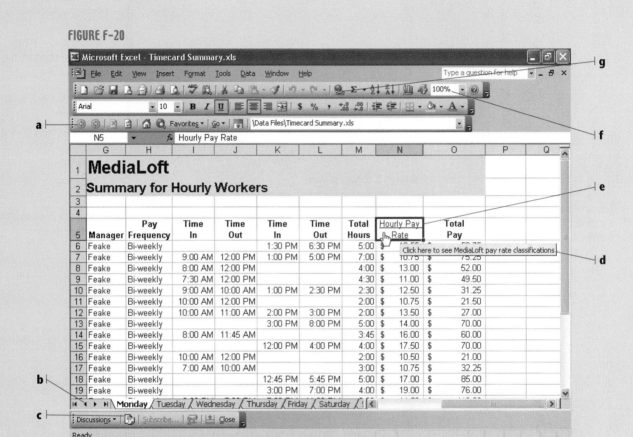

1. Which element points to a ScreenTip for a hyperlink?
2. Which element points to the Zoom box?
3. Which element points to a hyperlink?
4. Which element points to the Back button of the Web toolbar?
5. Which element do you click to insert a hyperlink into a worksheet?
6. Which element do you right-click to get a menu of the worksheets?
7. Which element do you click to insert a comment that can be viewed by others on the Web?

Match each term with the statement that best describes it.

8. Dashed line
9. Hyperlink
10. 3-D reference
11.
12.

a. Inserts a picture into header or footer
b. A navigational tool for use between worksheets or workbooks
c. Indicates a page break
d. Formats a picture in a header or footer
e. Uses values from different worksheets or workbooks

Select the best answer from the list of choices.

13. You can save frequently used display and print settings by using the _____ feature.

   a. HTML

   b. Custom Views

   c. View menu

   d. Save command

14. You can group several workbooks in a _____ so they can be opened together rather than individually.

   a. Workgroup

   b. Consolidated workbook

   c. Workspace

   d. Work unit

15. You can specify data formats in the Find and Replace dialog box by clicking the _____ button.

   a. Options

   b. Format

   c. Data

   d. Tools

16. You can group worksheets by pressing and holding _____ while clicking the sheet tabs that you want to group.

   a. [Alt]

   b. [Spacebar]

   c. [Ctrl]

   d. [F6]

▼ SKILLS REVIEW

1. Freeze columns and rows.

   a. Start Excel, open the Data File EX F-2.xls from the drive and folder where your Data Files are stored, then save it as **San Francisco Budget**.

   b. Activate the 2005 sheet if necessary, then freeze columns A and B and rows 1 through 3 for improved viewing. (*Hint*: Click cell C4 prior to issuing the Freeze Panes command.)

   c. Scroll until columns A and B and F through H are visible.

   d. Press **[Ctrl][Home]** to return to cell C4.

   e. Unfreeze the panes.

   f. Split the 2005 sheet into two horizontal panes. (*Hint*: Drag the Horizontal split box.) Remove the split by double-clicking over the split, then save your work.

2. Insert and delete worksheets.

   a. With the 2005 sheet active, use the sheet shortcut menu to insert a new sheet to its left.

   b. Delete the 2004 sheet, rename the new sheet 2007, and position it to the right of the 2006 sheet.

   c. Add a custom footer to the 2005 sheet with your name on the left side and the page number on the right side.

   d. Add a custom header with the worksheet name on the left side.

   e. Save and preview the 2005 sheet, compare your results to Figure F-21, then print it.

3. Consolidate data with 3-D references.

   a. In cell C22, enter a reference to cell G7.

   b. In cell C23, enter a reference to cell G18.

   c. Activate the 2006 worksheet.

   d. In cell C4, enter a reference to cell C4 on the 2005 worksheet.

   e. In the 2006 worksheet, copy the contents of cell C4 into cells C5:C6.

   f. Preview the 2006 worksheet, then use the Setup button to add your name to the left side of the footer.

   g. Print the 2006 worksheet, then save your work.

FIGURE F-21

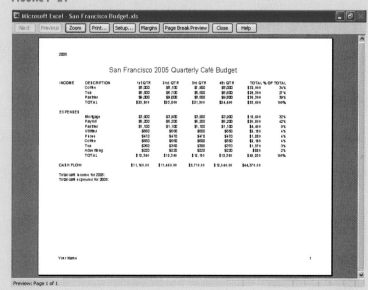

▼ SKILLS REVIEW (CONTINUED)

4. **Hide and protect worksheet areas.**

   a. On the 2005 sheet, unlock the expense data in the range C10:F17.

   b. On the 2005 sheet, hide the percent of total formulas in the range H4:H18 and the cash flow formulas in the range C20:G20.

   c. Protect the sheet without using a password.

   d. To make sure the other cells are locked, attempt to make an entry in cell D4. You should see the error message displayed in Figure F-22.

FIGURE F-22

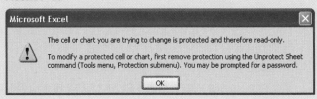

   e. Change the first quarter mortgage expense to $4000.

   f. Verify the formulas in column H and row 20 are hidden.

   g. Unprotect the worksheet.

   h. Save the workbook.

5. **Save custom views of a worksheet.**

   a. Set the zoom on the 2005 worksheet to fit the worksheet data to the screen.

   b. Make this a new view called **Entire 2005 Budget**.

   c. Use the Zoom box to change the magnification percentage of the worksheet to 200%. Save the worksheet at 200% as a new view called **200**.

   d. Use the Custom Views dialog box to delete the 200 view.

   e. Use the Custom Views dialog box to return to Generic view.

   f. Save the workbook.

6. **Control page breaks and page numbering.**

   a. Insert a page break above cell A9.

   b. Save the view as **Halves**.

   c. View the worksheet in Page Break Preview and modify the page break so it occurs after row ten. (*Hint*: Drag the page break line.)

   d. Return to the Halves view.

   e. Save the workbook.

7. **Create a hyperlink between Excel files.**

   a. On the 2005 worksheet, make cell A9 a hyperlink to the file **Expense Details.xls**.

   b. Test the link, then print the Expense Details worksheet.

   c. Edit the hyperlink in cell A9, adding a ScreenTip that reads **Expense Assumptions**.

   d. On the 2006 worksheet, enter the text **Based on 2005 budget** in cell A2.

   e. Make the text in cell A2 a hyperlink to cell A1 in the 2005 worksheet. (*Hint*: Use the Place in This Document button and note the cell reference in the Type the cell reference text box.)

   f. Test the hyperlink.

   g. Save the workbook and protect it with the password **pass**. (*Hint*: Use lowercase letters for the password.)

   h. Close and reopen the workbook to test the password. (*Hint*: If you cannot open the workbook, check that you are using lowercase letters.)

   i. Remove the password and save the workbook again.

8. **Save an Excel file as a Web page.**

   a. If you have access to a Web discussion server, attach a discussion comment to the 2005 worksheet with your name and the date you reviewed the budget. (If you don't have access to a discussion server, proceed to Step b.)

   b. Save the entire budget workbook as a Web page in MHT format with a title that reads **Our Budget** and the file named **sfbudget**.

   c. Preview the Web page in your browser. If your browser doesn't open automatically, check your taskbar.

   d. Test the worksheet tabs in the browser to make sure they work.

   e. Print the 2005 worksheet from your browser.

   f. Close your browser.

   g. Return to Excel, close the .mht document and the Expense Details.xls workbook, then exit Excel.

▼ INDEPENDENT CHALLENGE 1

As a new employee at SoftSales, a computer software retailer, you are responsible for tracking the sales of different product lines and determining which computer operating system generates the most software sales each month. Although sales figures vary from month to month, the format in which data is entered does not. You decide to create a worksheet tracking sales across platforms by month. Use a separate worksheet for each month and create data for three months. Use your own data for the number of software packages sold in the Windows and Macintosh columns for each product.

a. Start Excel, create a new workbook, then save it as **Software Sales Summary.xls** in the drive and folder where your Data Files are stored.

b. Add a fourth sheet by clicking Insert on the menu bar, then clicking Worksheet.

c. Drag the fourth sheet to the right of Sheet3.

d. Group the worksheets by clicking Sheet1, then press and hold [Shift] while clicking Sheet4.

e. With the worksheets grouped, use Table F-3 as a guide to enter the row and column labels that need to appear on each of the four sheets.

f. Rename Sheet1 to **January** by right-clicking the sheet name and entering the new name. Rename Sheet2 to **February**, Sheet3 to **March**, and Sheet4 to **Summary**.

g. Enter your own data, and formulas for the totals in the January, February, and March sheets.

h. Use the AutoSum function on the Summary sheet to total the information in all three monthly sheets.

i. Hide the Summary worksheet. (*Hint*: Select the Sheet command on the Format menu and choose Hide.)

j. Unhide the Summary worksheet. (*Hint*: Select the Sheet command on the Format menu and choose Unhide, then click OK.)

TABLE F-3

	Windows	Macintosh	Total
Games Software			
Combat Flight Simulator			
Safari			
NASCAR Racing			
Total			
Business Software			
Word Processing			
Spreadsheet			
Presentation			
Graphics			
Page Layout			
Total			
Utilities Products			
Antivirus			
File Recovery			
Total			

k. Group the worksheets again by clicking the January sheet then pressing and holding [Shift] while clicking the Summary sheet. Add headers to all four worksheets that include your name on the left, the sheet name in the center, and the date on the right.

l. Format the worksheet appropriately.

m. Save the workbook, preview and print the four worksheets, then exit Excel.

▼ INDEPENDENT CHALLENGE 2

You own PC Assist, a software training company located in Montreal, Canada. You have added several new entries to the August check register and are ready to enter September's check activity. Because the sheet for August includes much of the same information you need for September, you decide to copy it. Then you edit the new sheet to fit your needs for the September check activity. You use sheet referencing to enter the beginning balance and beginning check number. Using your own data, you complete five checks for the September register.

a. Start Excel, open the file EX F-3.xls from the drive and folder where your Data Files are stored, then save it as **Update to Check Register**. The expense amounts in the worksheet includes all taxes.

b. Delete Sheet2 and Sheet3, then create a worksheet for September by copying the August sheet and renaming it. If necessary, move the September sheet before the August sheet.

c. With the September sheet active, delete the data in the range A6:E24.

▼ INDEPENDENT CHALLENGE 2 (CONTINUED)

d. To update the balance at the beginning of the month, use sheet referencing from the last balance entry in the August sheet.

e. Generate the first check number. (*Hint*: Use a formula that references the last check number in August and adds one.)

f. Enter data for five checks using September 2006 dates. For the check number, use the number above it and add 1. Delete the balances in the range F11:F24.

g. Use the Find and Replace dialog box to change the beginning balance for August from **22000** to **27000**, formatted as a number with two decimal places. (*Hint*: The Options >> button allows you to change the data format.)

Advanced Challenge Exercise

■ Add a new worksheet to the workbook and name it **Statistics**.

■ Enter labels for August and September statistics into the Statistics worksheet using the table below as a guide.

August Statistics	
Number of Checks	
Average Check Amount	
Number of Classroom Expenses	
September Statistics	
Number of Checks	
Average Check Amount	
Number of Classroom Expenses	

■ Use 3-D references and the appropriate statistical functions to enter the number of checks, average check amount, and the number of classroom expenses for the months of August and September. (*Hint*: Use the Insert Function dialog box to enter the COUNT function for the number of checks, the AVERAGE function for the check averages, and the COUNTIF function with the criteria **Classroom** for the number of classroom expenses.)

■ Format the statistical information appropriately, add your name to the statistics worksheet footer, save the workbook, preview the worksheet, then print it in landscape orientation on a single page.

h. Add your name to the September sheet footer. Save the workbook, then preview and print the September worksheet. Close the workbook and exit Excel.

▼ INDEPENDENT CHALLENGE 3

You have decided to create a spreadsheet to track the long-distance phone calls made by you and your two roommates each month. You create a workbook with a separate sheet for each person and track the following information for each long-distance call: date of call, time of call, call minutes, city called, state called, area code, phone number, and call charge. Then you total the charges for each person and create a summary sheet of all three roommates' charges for the month. You are not sure what programs your roommates will be using to view the information so you also save the summary information in a text format.

a. Start Excel, create a new workbook, then save it as **Monthly Long Distance** in the drive and folder where your Data Files are stored.

b. Create a sheet for the first roommate. Enter column headings to track each call, then create two copies of the sheet and label the tabs.

c. Use your own data, entering at least three long-distance calls for each roommate.

d. Group the worksheets and create totals for minutes and charges on each roommate's sheet.

e. Create a summary sheet that shows each name and uses cell references to display the total minutes and total charges for each person.

f. On the summary sheet, create a hyperlink from each person's name to cell A1 of their respective worksheet. Enter your name on all worksheet footers, save the workbook, then print the four worksheets.

g. Create a workbook with the same type of information for the two people in the apartment next door. Save it as **Next Door.xls**. Enter your name on all worksheet footers, save the workbook, then print the three worksheets.

h. Arrange the two open workbooks in a tiled display on your screen. (*Hint*: Select the Arrange option on the Window menu.)

▼ INDEPENDENT CHALLENGE 3 (CONTINUED)

i. Use linking to create a 3-D reference that displays the neighbors' totals on your summary sheet so your roommates can compare their expenses with the neighbors'.

j. Create a workspace that includes the workbooks Monthly Long Distance and Next Door in the tiled layout. Name the workspace **Phonebill.xlw**. (*Hint*: Save Workspace is an option on the File menu.)

k. Hide the Next Door.xls workbook. (*Hint*: Hide is an option on the Window menu.)

l. Unhide the Next Door.xls workbook. (*Hint*: Unhide is an option on the Window menu.)

m. Change the workbook properties of the Next Door.xls workbook to Read-only.

n. Save the Summary sheet as a text file named Monthly Long Distance.txt. (*Hint*: Use the Save As command on the File menu.)

o. Close any open files and exit Excel.

▼ INDEPENDENT CHALLENGE 4

The creative director at WebProductions, a Web design company, is considering purchasing digital cameras for the New York and Montreal offices. You have been asked to research this purchase by comparing features and current prices in U.S. and Canadian currencies. You investigate online vendors and prepare a worksheet containing the following information about each camera: Manufacturer, Model, Zoom Lens Magnification, Megapixel Rating, Max Resolution, and Price in both U.S. and Canadian currencies. Your worksheet information will be protected but, because currency rates flucuate, the Canadian prices are unlocked. You use an online currency converter to calculate the price information in Canadian currency.

a. Find features and pricing (in U.S. dollars) for five digital cameras using the search engine of your choice. Also, search for a currency converter site, then convert the U.S. prices you found from the online vendors into Canadian currency.

b. Start Excel, create a new workbook, then save it as **Camera Research** in the drive and folder where your Data Files are stored, then enter the column headings shown in the table below.

Manufacturer	Model	Zoom Lens Magnification	Megapixel Rating	Max Resolution	Price $USD	Price $CAD

c. Enter the information you found on the Web into the worksheet. Some of the entries may include ranges of values.

d. Enter the information from the table into your Camera Research workbook. Name the worksheet **Online Vendors.**

e. Add a custom header that displays the sheet name centered on the printout.

f. Add a custom footer that includes your name on the left side of the printout.

g. Make the cells in the Manufacturer column hyperlinks to the manufacturer's Web site.

h. Use the Research task pane and the English (U.S. or Canada) thesaurus to find a synonym for **manufacturer**. Use the insert option in the Research task pane to replace the Manufacturer label in your worksheet with one of the listed synonyms.

i. Unlock the price information in the Canadian price column. Protect the worksheet without using a password. Save the workbook.

j. Save the workbook with the name **camera** in MHTML format for management's use and preview it in your Web browser.

k. Print the worksheet from your browser.

l. Exit your browser and return to the workbook in MHTML format.

Advanced Challenge Exercise

- Unprotect the worksheet, insert the company name, **WebProductions**, in cell A10 and create an e-mail link to it using your e-mail address.
- Insert a subject of **Digital Cameras** in the subject area.
- Add a ScreenTip of **Contact Us**.
- Preview the worksheet, then print it in landscape orientation on one page.

m. Close the workbook and exit Excel.

Excel 2003

▼ VISUAL WORKSHOP

Create the worksheet shown in Figure F-23, then save it as **Martinez**. Enter your name in the footer, save the workbook and print the worksheet. Save the workbook as a Single File Web page (MHTML) using the name **martinez**. Preview the worksheet in your Web browser, then print the sheet from the browser. Notice that the text in cell A1 is a hyperlink to the Our History worksheet; the graphic is from the Clip Gallery. If you don't have this graphic, substitute a graphic of your choice.

FIGURE F-23

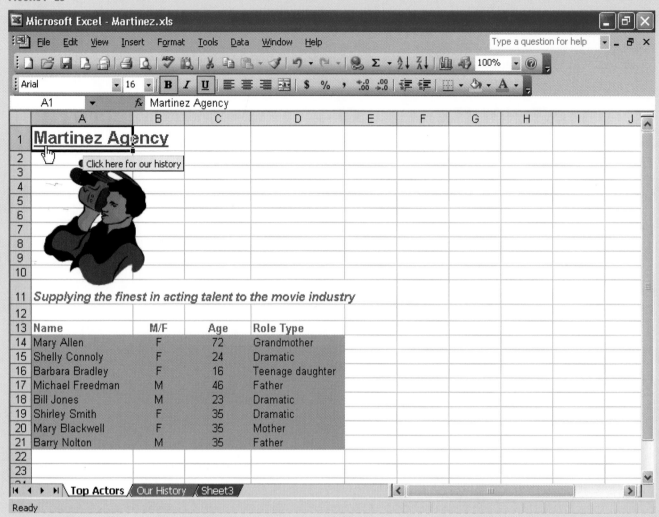

Automating Worksheet Tasks

OBJECTIVES

Plan a macro
Record a macro
Run a macro
Edit a macro
Use shortcut keys with macros
Use the Personal Macro Workbook
Add a macro as a menu item
Create a toolbar for macros

If you have a SAM user profile, you may have access to hands-on instruction, practice, and assessment of the skills covered in this unit. Log in to your SAM account and go to your assignments page to see what your instructor has assigned.

A **macro** is a set of instructions that performs tasks in the order you specify. You create macros to automate frequently performed Excel tasks. For example, if you usually enter your name and date in a worksheet footer, you can record the keystrokes in an Excel macro that enters the text and inserts the current date automatically when you run the macro. In this unit, you will plan and design a simple macro, then record and run it. Then you will edit the macro and explore ways to make it more easily available as you work.  Jim Fernandez, the office manager for MediaLoft, wants you to create a macro for the Accounting Department. The macro needs to automatically insert text that identifies the worksheet as an Accounting Department document.

Planning a Macro

You create macros for tasks that you perform frequently. For example, you can create a macro to enter and format text or to save and print a worksheet. To create a macro, you record the series of actions or write the instructions in a special programming language. Because the sequence of actions is important, you need to plan the macro carefully before you record it. ▰▰▰▰ Jim wants you to create a macro for the Accounting Department that inserts the text "Accounting Department" in the upper-left corner of any worksheet. You work with him to plan the macro using the following guidelines:

DETAILS

- **Assign the macro a descriptive name.**

  The first character of a macro name must be a letter; the remaining characters can be letters, numbers, or underscores. Spaces are not allowed in macro names; use underscores in place of spaces. (Press [Shift][–] to enter an underscore character.) Jim wants you to name the macro "DeptStamp." See Table G-1 for a list of macros Jim might create to automate other tasks.

- **Write out the steps the macro will perform.**

  This planning helps eliminate careless errors. Jim writes a description of the macro he wants, as shown in Figure G-1.

- **Decide how you will perform the actions you want to record.**

  You can use the mouse, the keyboard, or a combination of the two. Jim wants you to use both the mouse and the keyboard.

- **Practice the steps you want Excel to record, and write them down.**

  Jim has written down the sequence of actions he wants you to include in the macro.

- **Decide where to store the description of the macro and the macro itself.**

  Macros can be stored in an active workbook, in a new workbook, or in the Personal Macro Workbook, a special workbook used only for macro storage. Jim asks you to store the macro in a new workbook.

TABLE G-1: Possible macros and their descriptive names

description of macro	descriptive name
Enter a frequently used proper name, such as Jim Fernandez	JimFernandez
Enter a frequently used company name, such as MediaLoft	Company_Name
Print the active worksheet on a single page, in landscape orientation	FitToLand
Add a footer to a worksheet	FooterStamp
Show a generic view of a worksheet using the default print and display settings	GenericView

Macro to create stamp with the department name

Name:	DeptStamp
Description:	Adds a stamp to the top left of the worksheet, identifying it as an Accounting Department worksheet
Steps:	1. Position the cell pointer in cell A1.
	2. Type Accounting Department, then click the Enter button.
	3. Click Format on the menu bar, then click Cells.
	4. Click the Font tab, under Font style, click Bold, under Underline, click Single, and under Color, click Red, then click OK.

Clues to Use

Macros and viruses

When you open an Excel workbook that has macros, you may see a message asking you if you want to enable or disable them. If you know your workbook came from a trusted source, click Enable macros. If you are not sure of the workbook's source, click Disable macros, because a macro may contain a **virus**, a destructive software program that can damage your computer files. If you disable the macros in a workbook, you will not be able to use them. For more information about macro security and security levels, type "About macro security" in the Type a question for help text box.

Recording a Macro

The easiest way to create a macro is to record it using the Excel Macro Recorder. You turn the Macro Recorder on, name the macro, enter the keystrokes and select the commands you want the macro to perform, then stop the recorder. As you record the macro, Excel automatically translates each action into program code you can later view and modify. You can take as long as you want to record the macro; a recorded macro contains only your actions, not the amount of time you took to record it. ▰▰▰ Jim wants you to create a macro that enters a department "stamp" in cell A1 of the active worksheet. You create this macro by recording your actions.

STEPS

1. **Start Excel, save the new blank workbook as My Excel Macros in the drive and folder where your Data Files are stored**

   You are ready to start recording the macro.

2. **Click Tools on the menu bar, point to Macro, then click Record New Macro**

   The Record Macro dialog box opens. See Figure G-2. The default name Macro1 is selected. You can either assign this name or enter a new name. This dialog box also lets you assign a shortcut key for running the macro and assign a storage location for the macro.

3. **Type DeptStamp in the Macro name text box**

4. **If the Store macro in list box does not display This Workbook, click the list arrow and select This Workbook**

5. **If the Description text box does not contain your name, select the existing name, type your own name, then click OK**

   The dialog box closes. A small Stop Recording toolbar appears containing the Stop Recording button ▣, and the word "Recording" appears on the status bar. Take your time performing the steps below. Excel records every keystroke, menu selection, and mouse action that you make.

   > **TROUBLE**
   >
   > If the Stop Recording toolbar is not displayed, click View, point to Toolbars, then click Stop Recording.

6. **Press [Ctrl][Home]**

   When you begin an Excel session, macros record absolute cell references. By beginning the recording in cell A1, you ensure that the macro includes the instruction to select cell A1 as the first step, in cases where A1 is not already selected.

7. **Type Accounting Department in cell A1, then click the Enter button ✔ on the formula bar**

8. **Click Format on the menu bar, then click Cells**

9. **Click the Font tab, in the Font style list box click Bold, click the Underline list arrow and click Single, then click the Color list arrow and click the red color (third row, first color on the left)**

   See Figure G-3.

   > **TROUBLE**
   >
   > If your results differ from Figure G-4, clear the contents of cell A1, then slowly and carefully repeat Steps 2 through 10. When prompted to replace the existing macro at the end of Step 5, click Yes.

10. **Click OK, click ▣ on the Stop Recording toolbar, click cell D1 to deselect cell A1, then save the workbook**

    Compare your results with Figure G-4.

FIGURE G-2: Record Macro dialog box

Type macro name here

Reflects the computer user's name and the system date

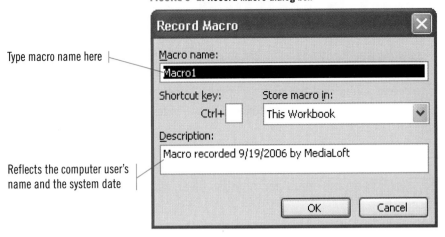

FIGURE G-3: Font tab of the Format Cells dialog box

Stop recording toolbar

Macro will apply these formatting attributes to the text

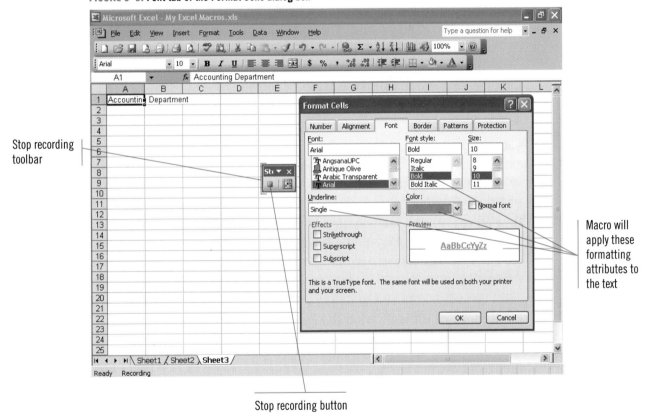

Stop recording button

FIGURE G-4: Accounting Department stamp

Running a Macro

Once you record a macro, you should test it to make sure that the actions it performs are correct. To test a macro, you **run,** or play, it. One way to run a macro is to select the macro in the Macros dialog box, then click Run. ▀▓▓▓▓ Jim asks you to clear the contents of cell A1 and then test the DeptStamp macro. After you run the macro in the My Excel Macros workbook, he asks you to test the macro once more from a newly opened workbook.

STEPS

1. **Click cell A1, click Edit on the menu bar, point to Clear, click All, then click any other cell to deselect cell A1**

   When you delete only the contents of a cell, any formatting still remains in the cell. By using the Clear All option on the Edit menu, you can be sure that the cell is free of contents and formatting.

2. **Click Tools on the menu bar, point to Macro, then click Macros**

   The Macro dialog box, shown in Figure G-5, lists all the macros contained in the open workbooks. If other people have used your computer, other macros may be listed.

3. **Make sure DeptStamp is selected, click Run, then deselect cell A1**

   Watch your screen as the macro quickly plays back the steps you recorded in the previous lesson. When the macro is finished, your screen should look like Figure G-6. As long as the workbook containing the macro remains open, you can run the macro in any open workbook.

4. **Click the New button ☐ on the Standard toolbar**

   Because the new workbook automatically fills the screen, it is difficult to be sure that the My Excel Macros.xls workbook is still open.

5. **Click Window on the menu bar**

   A list of open workbooks appears underneath the menu options. The active workbook name (in this case, Book2) appears with a check mark to its left. The My Excel Macros.xls workbook appears on the menu, so you know it's open. See Figure G-7.

6. **Deselect cell A1, click Tools on the menu bar, point to Macro, click Macros, make sure 'My Excel Macros.xls'!DeptStamp is selected, click Run, then deselect cell A1**

   When multiple workbooks are open, the macro name in the Macro dialog box includes the workbook name between single quotation marks, followed by an exclamation point, indicating that the macro is outside the active workbook. Because you only used this workbook to test the macro, you don't need to save it.

7. **Close Book2.xls without saving changes**

   The My Excel Macros.xls workbook reappears.

Clues to Use

Setting macro security levels

If you get a security error message when attempting to open a workbook containing a macro, the security level may be set too high. You can enable macros by changing the security level for workbooks. Click the Tools menu, point to the Macro option, click Security, then set the security level to Medium. You must save, then close and reopen the workbook to activate the new security level.

FIGURE G-5: Macro dialog box

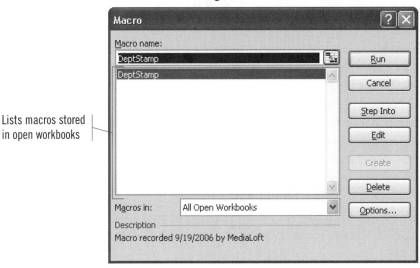

Lists macros stored in open workbooks

FIGURE G-6: Result of running DeptStamp macro

DeptStamp macro inserts formatted text in cell A1

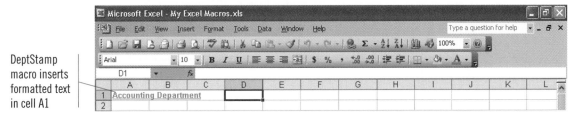

FIGURE G-7: Window menu listing open workbooks

Check mark indicates active workbook

Indicates this workbook is still open

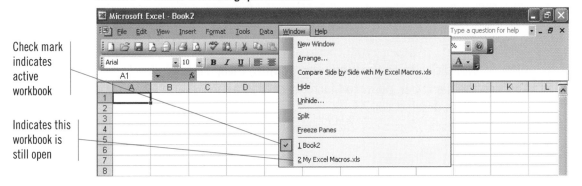

Clues to Use

Adding a digital signature to a macro

If the macro security level in Excel is set to High, only macros that are digitally signed from trusted sources can run. To sign a macro with a trusted digital signature, you need a valid certificate issued by a certificate authority. To digitally sign a macro with a certificate you have obtained, make sure the workbook containing it is open, then click the Tools menu, point to Macro, click Visual Basic Editor, select the macro in the module you want to sign in the Project Explorer (it will be in Module 1 unless you named the module), click the Tools menu, click Digital Signature, click Choose, select the certificate, then click OK twice.

Editing a Macro

When you use the Macro Recorder to create a macro, the program instructions, called **program code**, are recorded automatically in the **Visual Basic for Applications (VBA)** programming language. Each macro is stored as a **module**, or program code container, attached to the workbook. After you record a macro, you might need to change it. If you have a lot of changes to make, it might be best to rerecord the macro. But if you need to make only minor adjustments, you can edit the macro code directly using the **Visual Basic Editor**, a program that lets you display and edit your macro code. Jim wants you to modify his macro to change the point size of the department stamp to 14.

STEPS

1. **Make sure the My Excel Macros.xls workbook is open, click** Tools **on the menu bar, point to** Macro, **click** Macros, **make sure** DeptStamp **is selected, then click** Edit

   The Visual Basic Editor starts, showing the DeptStamp macro steps in a numbered module window (in this case, Module1).

2. **If necessary, maximize the window titled** My Excel Macros.xls – [Module1(Code)], **then examine the steps in the macro, comparing your screen to Figure G-8**

   The name of the macro and the date it was recorded appear at the top of the module window. Below that, Excel has translated your keystrokes and commands into macro code. When you open and make selections in a dialog box during macro recording, Excel automatically stores all the dialog box settings in the macro code. For example, the line .FontStyle = "Bold" was generated when you clicked Bold in the Format Cells dialog box. You also see lines of code that you didn't generate directly while recording the DeptStamp macro; for example, .Name = "Arial".

3. **In the line .Size = 10, double-click** 10 **to select it, then type** 14

   Because Module1 is attached to the workbook and not stored as a separate file, any changes to the module are saved automatically when you save the workbook.

4. **In the Visual Basic Editor, click** File **on the menu bar, click** Print, **click** OK **to print the module, then review the printout**

5. **Click** File **on the menu bar, then click** Close and Return to Microsoft Excel

   You want to rerun the DeptStamp macro to make sure the macro reflects the change you made using the Visual Basic Editor.

6. **Click cell** A1, **click** Edit **on the menu bar, point to** Clear, **click** All, **deselect cell** A1, **click** Tools **on the menu bar, point to** Macro, **click** Macros, **make sure** DeptStamp **is selected, click** Run, **then deselect cell** A1

   Compare your results to Figure G-9. The department stamp is now in 14-point type.

7. **Save the workbook**

FIGURE G-8: Visual Basic Editor showing Module1

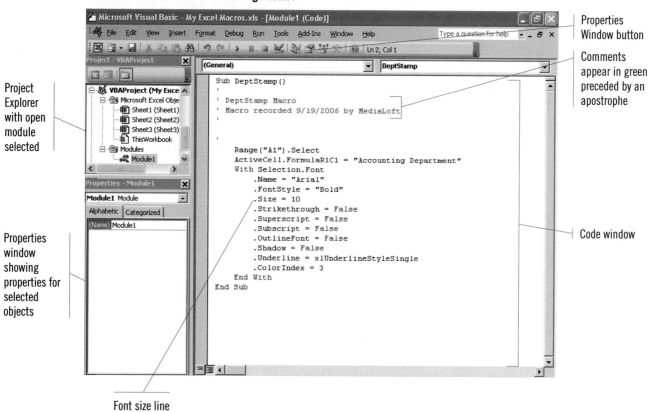

Properties Window button

Comments appear in green preceded by an apostrophe

Project Explorer with open module selected

Properties window showing properties for selected objects

Code window

Font size line

FIGURE G-9: Result of running edited DeptStamp macro

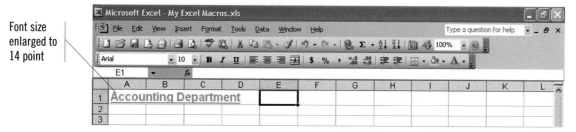

Font size enlarged to 14 point

Clues to Use

Adding comments to Visual Basic code

With practice, you will be able to interpret the lines of macro code. Others who use your macro, however, might want to know the function of a particular line. You can explain the code by adding comments to the macro. **Comments** are explanatory text added to the lines of code. When you enter a comment, you must type an apostrophe (') before the comment text. Otherwise, the program tries to interpret it as a command. On the screen, comments appear in green after you press [Enter], as shown in Figure G-8. You also can insert blank lines as comments in the macro code to make the code more readable. To do this, type an apostrophe, then press [Enter].

Using Shortcut Keys with Macros

In addition to running a macro from the Macro dialog box, you can run a macro by using a shortcut key combination you assign to it. Using shortcut keys reduces the number of actions you need to take to run a macro. You assign shortcut key combinations in the Record Macro dialog box. ▰▰▰▰▰ Jim also wants you to create a macro called CompanyName to enter the company name into a worksheet. You will assign a shortcut key combination to run the macro.

STEPS

1. **Click cell B2**

   You will record the macro in cell B2. You want the macro to enter the company name anywhere in a worksheet. Therefore, you do not begin the macro with an instruction to position the cell pointer, as you did in the DeptStamp macro.

2. **Click Tools on the menu bar, point to Macro, then click Record New Macro**

   The Record Macro dialog box opens. Notice the option Shortcut key: Ctrl+ followed by a blank box. You can type a letter (A–Z) in the Shortcut key text box to assign the key combination of [Ctrl] plus that letter to run the macro. You use the key combination [Ctrl][Shift] plus a letter to avoid overriding any of the Excel [Ctrl] [letter] shortcut keys, such as [Ctrl][C] for Copy.

3. **With the default macro name selected, type CompanyName, click the Shortcut key text box, press and hold [Shift], type C, then, if necessary, replace the name in the Description box with your name**

   Compare your screen with Figure G-10. You are ready to record the CompanyName macro.

4. **Click OK to close the dialog box**

   By default, Excel records absolute cell references in macros. Beginning the macro in cell B2 causes the macro code to begin with a statement to select cell B2. Because you want to be able to run this macro in any active cell, you need to instruct Excel to record relative cell references while recording the macro.

5. **Click the Relative Reference button 🔲 on the Stop Recording toolbar**

   The Relative Reference button is now selected. See Figure G-11. This button is a toggle and retains the relative reference setting until you click it again to turn it off or you exit Excel.

6. **Type MediaLoft in cell B2, click the Enter button ✅ on the formula bar, press [Ctrl][I] to italicize the text, click the Stop Recording button 🔲 on the Stop Recording toolbar, then deselect cell B2**

   MediaLoft appears in italics in cell B2. You are ready to run the macro in cell A5 using the shortcut key combination.

7. **Click cell A5, press and hold [Ctrl][Shift], type C, then deselect the cell**

   The company name appears in cell A5. See Figure G-12. Because the macro played back in the selected cell (A5) instead of the cell where it was recorded (B2), you know that the macro recorded relative cell references.

8. **Save the workbook**

FIGURE G-10: Record Macro dialog box with shortcut key assigned

Shortcut to run macro

FIGURE G-11: Stop Recording toolbar with Relative Reference button selected

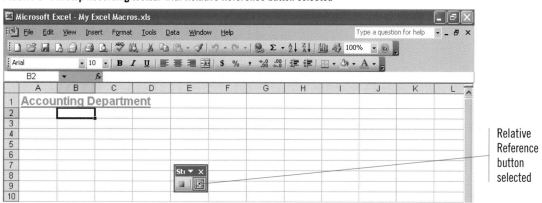

Relative Reference button selected

FIGURE G-12: Result of running the CompanyName macro

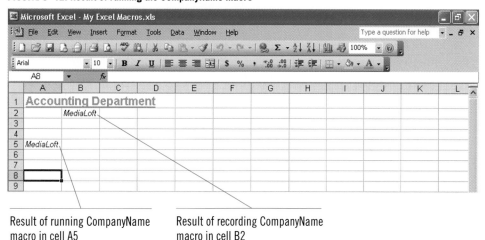

Result of running CompanyName macro in cell A5

Result of recording CompanyName macro in cell B2

Clues to Use

Running a macro from a hotspot on your worksheet

You can create a **hotspot** on your worksheet that runs a macro when you click it. To create a hotspot, first add an AutoShape to the worksheet: click AutoShapes on the Drawing toolbar, point to a shape category, and then click a shape. Drag across a worksheet area to create a shape, then type to add a label to the button, such as "Click to run Name macro." Right-click the button and click Assign Macro on the shortcut menu to choose the macro the button runs.

Excel 2003

Using the Personal Macro Workbook

You can store commonly used macros in a **Personal Macro Workbook**. The Personal Macro Workbook is always available, unless you specify otherwise, and gives you access to all the macros it contains, regardless of which workbooks are open. The Personal Macro Workbook file is automatically created the first time you choose to store a macro in it. You can add additional macros to the Personal Macro Workbook by saving them there. By default, the Personal.xls workbook opens each time you start Excel, but you don't see it because Excel designates it as a hidden file. Jim often likes to add a footer to his worksheets identifying his department, the workbook name, the worksheet name, his name, and the current date. He wants you to create a macro that automatically inserts this footer. Because he wants to use this macro in future worksheets, he asks you to store this macro in the Personal Macro Workbook.

STEPS

1. **From any cell in the active worksheet, click Tools on the menu bar, point to Macro, then click Record New Macro**

   The Record Macro dialog box opens.

2. **Type FooterStamp in the Macro name text box, click the Shortcut key text box, press and hold [Shift], type F, then click the Store macro in list arrow**

   You have named the macro FooterStamp and assigned it the shortcut combination [Ctrl][Shift][F]. Notice that This Workbook is selected by default, indicating that Excel automatically stores macros in the active workbook. See Figure G-13. You also can choose to store the macro in a new workbook or in the Personal Macro Workbook.

3. **Click Personal Macro Workbook, replace the existing name in the Description text box with your own name, if necessary, then click OK**

   The recorder is on, and you are ready to record the macro keystrokes. If you are prompted to replace an existing macro named FooterStamp, click Yes.

4. **Click File on the menu bar, click Page Setup, click the Header/Footer tab (make sure to do this even if it is already active), click Custom Footer, in the Left section box, type Accounting; click the Center section box, click the File Name button 🔳, press [Spacebar], type /, press [Spacebar], click the Tab Name button 🔳 to insert the sheet name; click the Right section box, type your name followed by a comma, press [Spacebar], click the Date button 🔳, then click OK to return to the Header/Footer tab**

   The footer stamp is set up, as shown in Figure G-14.

5. **Click OK to return to the worksheet, then click the Stop Recording button 🔳 on the Stop Recording toolbar**

   You want to ensure that the macro can set the footer stamp in any active worksheet.

6. **Activate Sheet2, in cell A1 type FooterStamp macro test, press [Enter], press and hold [Ctrl][Shift], then type F**

   The FooterStamp macro plays back the sequence of commands.

7. **Preview the worksheet to verify that the new footer is inserted, then close the Preview window**

8. **Save the workbook, then print the worksheet**

FIGURE G-13: Record Macro dialog box showing macro storage options

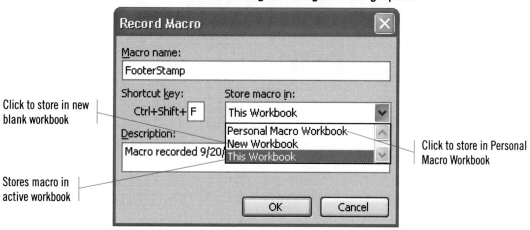

Click to store in new blank workbook

Stores macro in active workbook

Click to store in Personal Macro Workbook

FIGURE G-14: Header/Footer tab showing custom footer settings

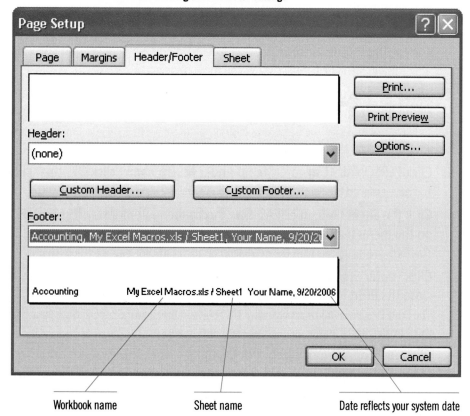

Workbook name

Sheet name

Date reflects your system date

Clues to Use

Working with the Personal Macro Workbook

Once you use the Personal Macro Workbook, it opens automatically each time you start Excel so you can add macros to it. By default, the Personal Macro Workbook is hidden as a precautionary measure so you don't accidentally delete anything from it. If you need to delete a macro from the Personal Macro Workbook, click Unhide on the Window menu, click PERSONAL.XLS, then click OK. To hide the Personal Macro Workbook, click Hide on the Window menu when the workbook is active.

Adding a Macro as a Menu Item

In addition to storing macros in the Personal Macro Workbook so that they are always available, you can add macros as items on any Excel menu available from the menu bar, just under the title bar. To increase the availability of the FooterStamp macro, Jim decides to add it as an item on the Tools menu. He wants you to add a custom menu item to the Tools menu and assign the macro to that menu item.

STEPS

QUICK TIP

You may need to reposition the Customize dialog box to make the Tools option on the Worksheet menu bar visible.

1. **With Sheet2 active, click Tools on the menu bar, click Customize, click the Commands tab, then under Categories, click Macros**

   See Figure G-15.

2. **Click Custom Menu Item under Commands, drag the selection over Tools on the menu bar (the menu opens), then point just under the last menu option, but do not release the mouse button**

   Compare your screen to Figure G-16.

3. **Release the mouse button**

   Now, Custom Menu Item is the last item on the Tools menu.

4. **With the Tools menu still open, right-click Custom Menu Item, select the text in the Name box (&Custom Menu Item), type Footer Stamp, then click Assign Macro**

   Unlike a macro name, the name of a custom menu item can have spaces between words like all standard menu items. The Assign Macro dialog box opens.

5. **Click PERSONAL.XLS!FooterStamp under Macro name, click OK, then click Close**

   You have assigned the FooterStamp macro to the new menu command.

6. **Click the Sheet3 tab, in cell A1 type macro menu item test, press [Enter], then click Tools on the menu bar**

   The Tools menu appears with the new menu option at the bottom. See Figure G-17.

7. **Click Footer Stamp, preview the worksheet to verify that the footer was inserted, then close the Print Preview window**

   The Print Preview window appears with the footer stamp. Because others using your computer might be confused by the macro on the menu, it's a good idea to remove it.

8. **Click Tools on the menu bar, click Customize, click the Toolbars tab, click Worksheet Menu Bar to highlight it, click Reset, click OK to confirm, click Close, click Tools on the menu bar to make sure that the custom item has been deleted, then save the workbook**

Clues to Use

Adding a custom menu

You can create a custom menu on an existing toolbar and assign macros to it. To do this, click Tools on the menu bar, click Customize, click the Commands tab, click New Menu in the Categories list, then drag the New Menu from the Commands box to the toolbar. To name the new menu, right-click, then enter a name in the Name box. You can drag Custom Menu Items from the Commands tab of the Customize dialog box to the menu and then right-click each menu item to assign macros to them.

FIGURE G-15: Commands tab of the Customize dialog box

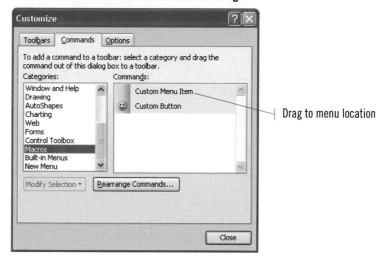

Drag to menu location

FIGURE G-16: Tools menu showing placement of the Custom Menu Item

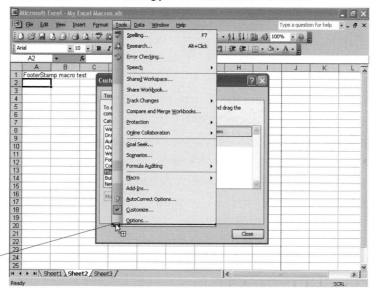

Pointer and line showing location at which to drop menu item

FIGURE G-17: Tools menu with new Footer Stamp item

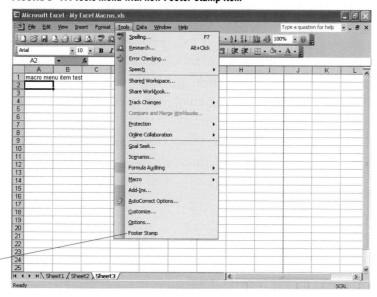

Added menu item

Creating a Toolbar for Macros

Toolbars contain buttons that let you single-click to issue commands you use frequently. You can create your own custom toolbars to organize commands so that you can find and use them quickly. Once you create a toolbar, you can add buttons to it so you can run macros by simply clicking the buttons. ▰▰▰▰▰ Jim asks you to create a custom toolbar called Macros that contains buttons to run two of his macros.

STEPS

1. **With Sheet3 active, click Tools on the menu bar, click Customize, click the Toolbars tab, then click New**

   The New Toolbar dialog box opens, as shown in Figure G-18. Under Toolbar name, a default name of Custom 1 is selected.

2. **Type Macros, then click OK**

   Excel adds the new toolbar named Macros to the bottom of the Toolbars list, and a small, empty toolbar named Macros opens. See Figure G-19. You cannot see the entire toolbar name. A new toolbar starts out small and expands to fit the buttons you assign to it.

3. **Click the Commands tab in the Customize dialog box, click Macros in the Categories list, then drag the Custom button ☺ over the new Macros toolbar and release the mouse button**

   The Macros toolbar now contains one button. You want the toolbar to contain two macros, so you need to add one more button.

4. **Drag the ☺ button over the Macros toolbar again**

   With the two buttons in place, you are ready to customize the buttons and assign macros to them.

5. **Right-click the left button ☺ on the Macros toolbar, select &Custom Button in the Name box, type Department Stamp, click Assign Macro, click DeptStamp, then click OK**

   With the first toolbar button customized, you are ready to customize the second button.

6. **With the Customize dialog box open, right-click the right button ☺ on the Macros toolbar, edit the name to read Company Name, click Change Button Image, click the 👤 image (seventh row, first column), right-click 👤, click Assign Macro, click CompanyName to select it, click OK, then click Close to close the Customize dialog box**

   The Macros toolbar appears with the two customized macro buttons.

7. **Move the mouse pointer over ☺ on the Macros toolbar to display the macro name (Department Stamp), then click to run the macro, click cell B2, move the mouse pointer over 👤 on the Macros toolbar to display the macro name (Company Name), click to run that macro, then deselect the cell**

   Compare your screen with Figure G-20. The DeptStamp macro automatically replaces the contents of cell A1. Because others using your computer might be confused by the new toolbar, it's a good idea to remove it.

8. **Click Tools on the menu bar, click Customize, click the Toolbars tab if necessary, in the Toolbars window click Macros to highlight it, click Delete, click OK to confirm the deletion, then click Close**

9. **Save the workbook, print Sheet3, close the workbook, save changes to the Personal Macro Workbook if prompted, then exit Excel**

   The completed figure for Sheet1 is shown in Figure G-12.

FIGURE G-18: New Toolbar dialog box

Type toolbar name here

FIGURE G-19: Customize dialog box with new Macros toolbar

Your list may differ

Check marks indicate toolbars in view

New Macros toolbar

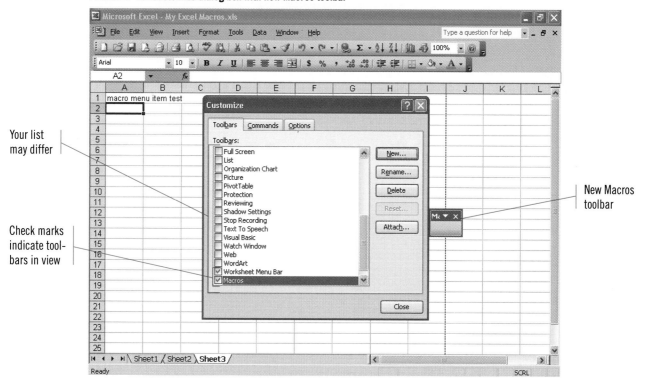

FIGURE G-20: Worksheet showing Macros toolbar with two customized buttons

Click to run DeptStamp macro

Click to run CompanyName macro

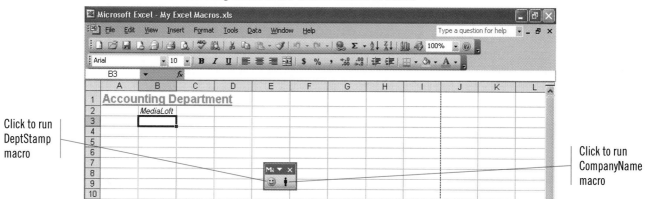

Clues to Use

Organizing macros

You can organize your workbooks containing macros by placing them in folders with names that describe the macro tasks. To rename a folder, right-click the folder, click Rename on the shortcut menu, then enter the new name.

Excel 2003

Practice

▼ CONCEPTS REVIEW

FIGURE G-21

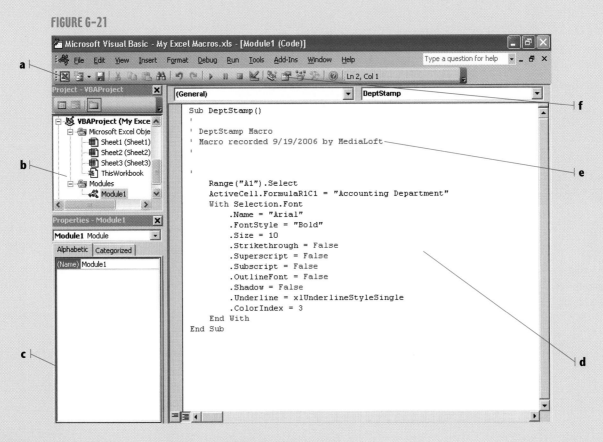

1. Which element points to a comment in the Visual Basic code?
2. Which element points to the Code window?
3. Which element points to the Properties Window button?
4. Which element points to the Project Explorer?
5. Which element points to the Properties window?
6. Which element do you click to return to Excel without closing the module?

Match each term or button with the statement that best describes it.

7. Visual Basic Editor

8. Macro comments

9. Personal Macro Workbook

10. ☺

11. ▦

a. Used to add a custom button on a macros toolbar code

b. Used to store commonly used macros

c. Used to record relative cell references

d. Used to make changes to macro code

e. Statements that appear in green explaining the macro

Select the best answer from the list of choices.

12. **Which of the following is the best candidate for a macro?**
    a. One-button or one-keystroke commands.
    b. Nonsequential tasks.
    c. Seldom-used commands or tasks.
    d. Often-used sequences of commands or actions.

13. **You can open the Visual Basic Editor by clicking the _____ button in the Macro dialog box.**
    a. Edit
    b. Visual Basic Editor
    c. Modules
    d. Programs

14. **Commonly used macros should be stored in:**
    a. The Common Macro Workbook.
    b. The Personal Macro Workbook.
    c. The Master Macro Workbook.
    d. The Custom Macro Workbook.

15. **Which of the following is *not* true about editing a macro?**
    a. A macro cannot be edited and must be recorded again.
    b. You edit macros using the Visual Basic Editor.
    c. You can type changes directly in the existing program code.
    d. You can make more than one editing change in a macro.

16. **Why is it important to plan a macro?**
    a. Macros won't be stored if they contain errors.
    b. Macros can't be deleted.
    c. It is impossible to edit a macro.
    d. Planning helps prevent careless errors from being introduced into the macro.

17. **Macros are recorded with relative references:**
    a. Only if relative references are chosen while recording the macro.
    b. In all cases.
    c. Only if the Relative Reference button is selected.
    d. Only if the Absolute Reference button is not selected.

18. **You can run macros:**
    a. From the Macro dialog box.
    b. From shortcut key combinations.
    c. From custom menu commands.
    d. Using all of the above.

19. **To change the security level for workbooks on your computer you must:**
    a. Click Tools, then click Security.
    b. Click Edit, then click Security.
    c. Click Edit, point to Tools, then click Security.
    d. Click Tools, point to Macros, then click Security.

▼ SKILLS REVIEW

1. **Plan a macro.**
    a. You need to plan a macro that enters and formats your name, address, and telephone number in a worksheet.
    b. Write out the steps the macro will perform.
    c. Write out how the macro could be used in a workbook.

2. Record a macro.

    a. Start Excel, open a new workbook, then save it as **Macros** in the drive and folder where your Data Files are stored. You want to record a macro that enters and formats your name, address, and telephone number in a worksheet.

    b. Name the macro **MyAddress**, store it in the current workbook, and make sure your name appears as the person who recorded the macro.

    c. Record the macro, entering your name in cell A1, your street address in cell A2, your city, state, and ZIP code in cell A3, and your telephone number in cell A4.

    d. Format the information in 12-point Arial bold.

    e. Resize column A to fit the information entirely in that column.

    f. Add a border and make the text blue.

    g. Stop the recorder and save the workbook.

3. Run a macro.

    a. Clear cell entries and formats in the range affected by the macro.

    b. Check the security level for workbooks on your computer. (*Hint*: Click the Tools menu, point to Macro, then click Security.)

    c. Run the MyAddress macro to place your name and address information in cell A1.

    d. On the worksheet, clear all the cell entries and formats generated by running the MyAddress macro.

    e. Save the workbook.

4. Edit a macro.

    a. Open the MyAddress macro in the Visual Basic Editor.

    b. Locate the line of code that defines the font size, then change the size to 16 point.

    c. Edit an existing comment line to describe this macro's function.

    d. Save and print the module, then use the Close and Return to Microsoft Excel option on the File menu to return to Excel.

    e. Test the macro on Sheet1.

    f. Save the workbook.

5. Use shortcut keys with macros.

    a. Record a macro called **NameStamp** in the current workbook that enters your full name in italics in the selected cell of a worksheet. (*Hint*: You need to record a relative cell reference).

    b. Assign your macro the shortcut key combination [Ctrl][Shift][N] and store it in the current workbook, using your name as the creator.

    c. After you record the macro, clear the cell containing your name that you used to record the macro.

    d. Use the shortcut key combination to run the MyName macro.

    e. Save the workbook.

6. Use the Personal Macro Workbook.

    a. Using Sheet1, record a new macro called **FitToLand** and store it in the Personal Macro workbook. The macro should set the print orientation to landscape, with content scaled to fit on one page. If you are prompted to replace the existing FitToLand macro, click Yes.

    b. After you record the macro, activate Sheet2, and enter test data in row 1 that exceeds one page width.

    c. In the Page Setup dialog box, make sure the orientation is set to portrait and the scaling is 100% of normal size.

    d. Run the macro.

    e. Preview Sheet2 and verify that it's in Landscape view and that the test data fits on one page.

    f. Save the workbook.

7. Add a macro as a menu item.

    a. On the Commands tab in the Customize dialog box, specify that you want to use the Macros category to create a Custom Menu Item placing the Custom Menu Item at the bottom of the Tools menu.

    b. Rename the Custom Menu Item **Fit to Landscape**.

    c. Assign the macro PERSONAL.XLS!FitToLand to the command.

    d. Go to Sheet3 and make sure the orientation is set to portrait and the scaling is 100% of normal size. Enter test data in column A that exceeds one page in length.

    e. Run the Fit to Landscape macro from the Tools menu.

    f. Preview the worksheet and verify that it is in landscape view and that the test data fits on one page.

    g. Reset the Worksheet Menu bar.

    h. Verify that the Fit to Landscape command has been removed from the Tools menu.

    i. Save the workbook.

8. Create a toolbar for macros.

    a. With the Macros.xls workbook still open, use the Toolbars tab of the Customize dialog box to create a new custom toolbar, titled **My Info**.

    b. Display the Macros category on the Commands tab of the Customize dialog box, then drag the Custom Button to the My Info toolbar.

    c. Drag the Custom Button to the My Info toolbar a second time to create another button.

    d. Rename the first button **My Address**, and assign the MyAddress macro to it.

    e. Rename the second button **My Name**, and assign the NameStamp macro to it.

    f. Change the second button image to one of your choice.

    g. On Sheet3, clear the existing cell data. Test the first macro button on the My Info toolbar. Select cell A7 and test the second macro button on the My Info toolbar.

    h. Use the Toolbars tab of the Customize dialog box to delete the toolbar named My Info.

    i. Save the workbook, print Sheet3, close the workbook, then exit Excel.

▼ INDEPENDENT CHALLENGE 1

As a computer-support employee of Boston Accounting Solutions, you need to develop ways to help your fellow employees work more efficiently. Employees have asked for Excel macros that can do the following:

- Delete the current row and insert a blank row.
- Delete the current column and insert a blank column.
- Place the department name of Accounting in a 12-point font in red in cell A1 (the width of A1 should be increased if necessary).

    a. Plan and write the steps necessary for each macro.

    b. Start Excel, save a blank workbook as **Excel Utility Macros** in the drive and folder where your Data Files are stored.

    c. Create a macro for each employee request described above, name them DeleteRow, DeleteColumn, and DepartmentName, then save them in the Excel Utility Macros.xls workbook.

    d. Add comment lines to each macro containing your name and describing the function of the macro, then return to Excel.

    e. Use the Commands tab of the Customize dialog box to add three Custom Menu items to the Tools menu. Right-click each Custom Menu item to name the new menu items DeleteRow, DeleteColumn, and DepartmentName. Assign the macros you created in Step c to the new menu items.

    f. Use the Toolbars tab of the Customize dialog box to create a new toolbar called **Helpers**.

    g. Use the Commands tab of the Customize dialog box to drag three Custom buttons to the Helpers toolbar.

    h. Right-click each toolbar button to name them DeleteRow, DeleteColumn, and DepartmentName. Assign the macros created in step c to the new toolbar buttons.

    i. Right-click each toolbar button to change the button images.

    j. Test each macro by using the Run command, the menu command, and the new toolbar button.

    k. Delete the new toolbar, then reset the Worksheet Menu Bar on the toolbars tab of the Customize dialog box.

    l. Save the workbook, print the module containing the program code for all three macros, then close the workbook and exit Excel.

▼ INDEPENDENT CHALLENGE 2

You are an analyst in the Atlantic Bank Loan Department. Every quarter, you produce a number of single-page quarterly budget worksheets. Your manager has informed you that certain worksheets need to contain a footer stamp indicating that the worksheet was produced in the loan department. The footer should also show the current page number out of the total number of pages, (for example, 1 of 5) and the workbook filename. It's tedious to add the footer stamp to the numerous worksheets you produce. You want to record a macro to do this.

    a. Plan and write the steps to create the macro described above.

    b. Start Excel, save a blank workbook as **Footer Stamp** in the drive and folder where your Data Files are stored.

    c. Create the macro using the plan from Step a, name it **footerstamp**, assign it the shortcut key combination [Ctrl][Shift][H], and store it in the current workbook.

    d. Edit the macro to add a descriptive comment line with your name.

    e. Add the footerstamp macro to the Tools menu.

    f. Create a toolbar titled **Stamp**, then add a button to the toolbar to run the macro.

    g. Enter the text **Testing Footer** in cell A1. Test the macro using the shortcut key combination, then delete the footer. Test the macro using the menu command on the Tools menu, then delete the footer again. Test the new button on the Stamp toolbar.

    h. Delete the new toolbar, then reset the Worksheet Menu Bar.

    i. Save the workbook, print the module for the macro, close the module and the workbook, then exit Excel.

    j. Create a folder named **Macros** in the drive and folder where your Data Files are stored then drag a copy of the Footer Stamp.xls file into the Macros folder.

    k. Rename the folder **Footer Macros**.

    l. Close the workbook, then exit Excel.

▼ INDEPENDENT CHALLENGE 3

You are an administrative assistant at the Sydney, Australia, branch of Computers Inc. A major part of your job is to create spreadsheets that project sales results in different markets. It seems that you are constantly changing the print settings so that workbooks print in landscape orientation and are scaled to fit on one page. You have decided that it's time to create a macro to streamline this process.

    a. Plan and write the steps necessary to create the macro.

    b. Start Excel, create a new workbook, then save it as **Computers Inc Macro** in the drive and folder where your Data Files are stored.

    c. Create a macro that changes the page orientation to landscape and scales the worksheet to fit on one page. Name the macro **LandFit**, assign it the shortcut key combination [Ctrl][Shift][L], and store it in the current workbook.

    d. Add the macro to the Tools menu.

    e. Go to Sheet2 and enter the text **Testing Macro** in cell A1 and enter your name in cell A2. Enter test data in column A that exceeds one page in length. Test the macro using the new menu command.

FIGURE G-22

```
ters Inc Macro.xls - [Module1 (Code)]
at  Debug  Run  Tools  Add-Ins  Window  Help
 C  ▶  II  ⬛  ⬛                      Ln 29, Col 43
General)                              ▼  LandFit

  Sub LandFit()
  '
  ' LandFit Macro
  ' Macro recorded 9/20/2006 by Your Name
  '
  ' Keyboard Shortcut: Ctrl+Shift+L
  'Your Name

      With ActiveSheet.PageSetup
          .PrintTitleRows = ""
          .PrintTitleColumns = ""
      End With
      ActiveSheet.PageSetup.PrintArea = ""
      With ActiveSheet.PageSetup
          .LeftHeader = ""
          .CenterHeader = "Computers Inc"
          .RightHeader = ""
          .LeftFooter = ""
          .CenterFooter = ""
          .RightFooter = ""
```

    f. Reset the Worksheet Menu Bar and go to Sheet3.

    g. Edit the macro to include the company name, **Computers Inc**, in the center header and add your name as a comment. Use Figure G-22 as a guide. Enter test data in row 1 that exceeds one page in width. Test the macro using the shortcut key combination, making sure the header was added.

    h. Add a custom menu to the standard toolbar and name it **Macros**. Add a custom menu item to the new Macros menu, name the menu option **Page Orientation**, and assign the LandFit macro to it.

    i. On Sheet3, delete the header and change the page orientation to portrait, then test the macro using the new menu.

▼ INDEPENDENT CHALLENGE 3 (CONTINUED)

j. Reset the standard toolbar.

k. Print the module for the macro.

Advanced Challenge Exercise

- Use the Help feature in Excel to research how digital certificates, used to sign a macro, are obtained and copy your findings into Sheet1.
- Use the Help feature to find the difference between class 2 and class 3 digital certificates and copy your findings into Sheet1.
- Use the Help feature to find the steps to digitally sign a file and copy the steps into Sheet1. Print Sheet1.

l. Save and close the workbook, then exit Excel.

▼ INDEPENDENT CHALLENGE 4

PC Assist, a software training company, has decided to begin purchasing its branch office supplies through online vendors. One of the products the company needs to purchase is toner for the Hewlett-Packard LaserJet 3100 printers in the offices. You have been asked to research vendors and prices on the Web. You want to create a workbook to hold office supply vendor information that you can use for various products. You want to add a macro to this workbook to find the lowest price of the product, format the information, and add a descriptive footer to the worksheet.

Using the search engine of your choice, find three online suppliers of toner for the company's printers and note their prices.

a. Start Excel, create a new workbook, then save it as **Office Supplies**.

b. Complete the table below with three online suppliers of office products you found in your search.

c. Enter three vendors and their prices from your table into your worksheet. Enter the Product name **Toner** in the cell next to Office Product.

d. Create a macro named **Toner** in the Office Supplies.xls workbook that can be activated by the [Ctrl][Shift][T] key combination. The macro should do the following:

Office Product	
Vendor	Price
Lowest Price	

- Find the lowest price for the office product and insert it to the right of the Lowest Price label.
- Boldface the Lowest Price text and the cell to its right that will contain the lowest value.
- Place a thick box border around all the information.
- Fill the information area with a light turquoise color.
- Add a footer with the company name **PC Assist** on the left and the workbook name on the right.

e. Clear all the formatting, the footer, and the lowest price from the worksheet.

f. Test the macro using the key combination [Ctrl][Shift][T].

g. Enter your name in cell A15, save your workbook, then print the results of the macro. Open the macro in the Visual Basic Editor, enter your name as a comment, then print the macro code.

Advanced Challenge Exercise

- Return to Excel and create a macro named **Toner_Average** that does the following:
  - Inserts a label **Average Price** under the Lowest Price label.
  - Finds the average toner price, inserts it under the lowest price, and formats it as a number with two decimal places.
  - Boldfaces the Average Price label and the average toner price.
- Delete the average toner price that was inserted by recording the Toner_Average macro. Do not delete the Average Price label.
- Make the Average Price label a hotspot that runs the macro when clicked. Run the Toner_Average macro using the hotspot.
- In the Visual Basic code for the Toner_Average macro, enter your name as a comment, then print the macro code.

h. Print the worksheet. Save and close the workbook, then exit Excel.

▼ VISUAL WORKSHOP

Create the macro shown in Figure G-23. (*Hint*: Enter the months using the default font size, then change the size to the size shown.) Test the macro, save the workbook as **Accounting Macro**, and then print the module.

FIGURE G-23

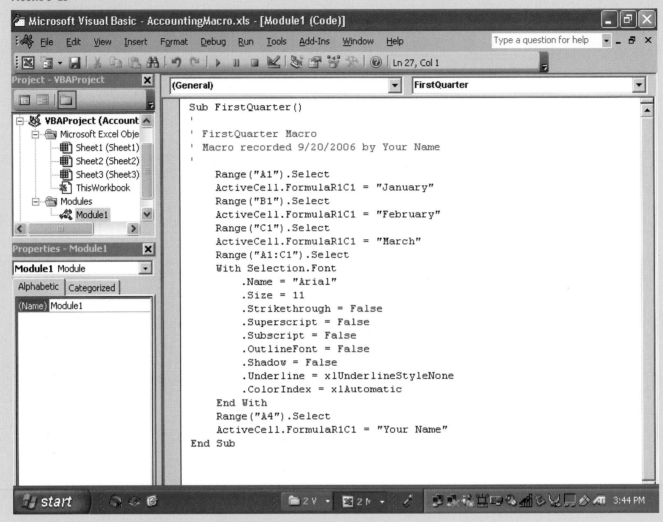

Using Lists

OBJECTIVES

Plan a list
Create a list
Add records with the data form
Find records
Delete records
Sort a list on one field
Sort a list on multiple fields
Print a list

If you have a SAM user profile, you may have access to hands-on instruction, practice, and assessment of the skills covered in this unit. Log in to your SAM account and go to your assignments page to see what your instructor has assigned.

In addition to using Excel's spreadsheet features, you can also use Excel as a database. A **database** is an organized collection of related information, such as a telephone book, a card catalog, or a roster of company employees. A worksheet used as a database contains rows and columns of similarly structured data and is called a **list**. Using an Excel list, you can organize and manage worksheet information so that you can quickly find data for projects, reports, and charts. In this unit, you'll learn how to plan and create a list; add, change, find, and delete information in a list; and then sort and print a list. MediaLoft uses lists to analyze new customer information. MediaLoft marketing director Jim Fernandez has asked you to help him build and manage a list of new customers as part of the ongoing strategy to focus on the company's advertising expenses.

Planning a List

When planning a list, consider what information the list needs to contain and how you want to work with the data, now and in the future. As you plan a list, you should understand its most important components. A list is organized into rows called records. A **record** contains data about an object or person. Records are composed of fields. **Fields** are columns in the list; each field describes a characteristic about the record, such as a customer's last name or street address. Each field has a **field name**, a column label that describes the field. To plan your list, use the steps below. See Table H-1 for additional planning guidelines. If your list contains more records than can fit on one worksheet (that is, more than 65,536 records), you should consider using database software rather than spreadsheet software.  Jim has asked you to compile a list of new customers. Before entering the data into an Excel worksheet, you plan the list using the following guidelines.

DETAILS

- **Identify the purpose of the list**

  Determine the kind of information the list should contain. Jim wants to use the list to identify how new customers found out about MediaLoft.

- **Plan the structure of the list**

  Determine the fields that make up a record. Jim has customer cards that contain information about each new customer. Figure H-1 shows a typical card. Each record will contain data for one customer. The fields in each record correspond to the descriptive information on the cards.

- **Write down the names of the fields**

  Field names appear in the first row of a list. Field names can be up to 255 characters long (the maximum column width), although shorter names are easier to see in the cells. Field names describe each piece of information. Jim's list will contain nine field names, each one corresponding to the nine pieces of information on each card.

- **Determine any special number formatting required in the list**

  Most lists contain both text and numbers. When planning a list, consider whether any fields require specific number formatting. For example, some zip codes begin with zero. Because Excel automatically drops a leading zero when entering numeric data, you must format zip code fields using a special format to display the full zip code. Jim's list includes a zip code field that needs this format.

FIGURE H-1: Customer record and corresponding field names

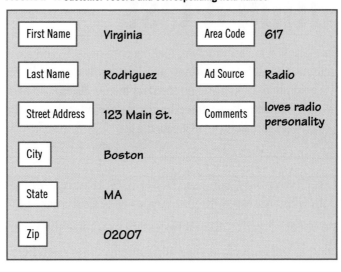

TABLE H-1: Guidelines for planning a list

worksheet structure guidelines	row and column content guidelines
Lists can be created from any contiguous range of cells on your worksheet	Plan and design your list so that all rows have similar items in the same column
A list should not have any blank rows or columns	Do not insert extra spaces at the beginning of a cell because that can affect sorting and searching
Data defined by your list can be used independently of data outside of the list on the worksheet	Instead of blank rows or columns between your labels and your data, use formatting to make column labels stand out from the data
Data can be organized on a worksheet using multiple lists to define sets of related data	Use the same format for all cells below the field name in a column

Creating a List

Once you have planned the list structure, the sequence of fields, and any appropriate formatting, you are ready to create the list. Table H-2 provides guidelines for naming fields. You then select the range and tell Excel that it is a list using a command on the Data menu. Jim asks you to build a list with his customer information. You begin by entering the field names. After entering the field names, you enter the corresponding customer information, then create the list.

STEPS

1. **Start Excel if necessary, open the Data File EX H-1.xls from the drive and folder where your Data Files are stored, then save it as** New Customer List

2. **Rename Sheet1** Practice, **then if necessary maximize the Excel window**

3. **Beginning in cell A1 and moving horizontally, enter each field name in a separate cell, as shown in Figure H-2**

   Field names are usually in the first row of the list. Don't worry if your field names are wider than the cells; you will fix this later.

4. **Select the field headings in range A1:I1, then click the Bold button** B **on the Formatting toolbar; with range A1:I1 still selected, click the Borders list arrow, then click the Thick Bottom Border (second column, second row)**

5. **Enter the information from Figure H-3 in the rows immediately below the field names, without leaving any blank rows**

   The data appears in columns organized by field name. The leading zeroes are dropped in the zip code column.

6. **Select column F, click Format on the menu bar, click Cells, on the Number tab under Category click Special, from the Type list click Zip Code, then click OK**

   The zip codes now have leading zeroes.

7. **Select the range A1:I4, click Format on the menu bar, point to Column, then click AutoFit Selection**

   Resizing the column widths this way is faster than double-clicking the column divider lines between each pair of columns.

8. **With A1:I4 selected, click Data on the menu bar, point to List, click Create List, make sure My list has headers is checked, click OK, then press [Ctrl][Home] to return to cell A1**

   The List toolbar appears and the list now has a blue border. See Figure H-4. **AutoFilter list arrows**, which let you display portions of your data, appear next to each column header. The blank last row of the list is the insert row, ready for new list data to be added.

TABLE H-2: Guidelines for naming fields

guideline	explanation
Use text to name fields	Numbers can be interpreted as parts of formulas
Do not use duplicate field names	Duplicate field names can cause Excel to enter and sort information incorrectly
Use descriptive names	Avoid names that might be confused with cell addresses, such as Q4

FIGURE H-2: Field names entered and formatted in row 1

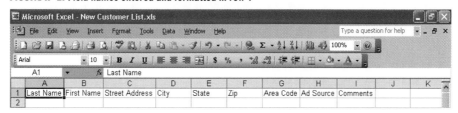

FIGURE H-3: Cards with customer information

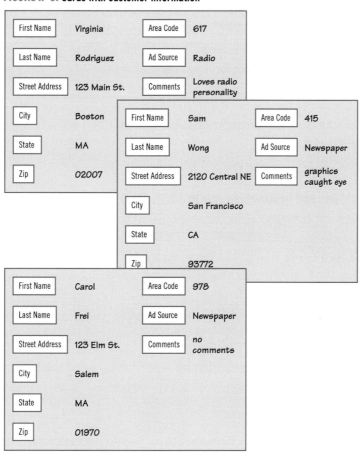

FIGURE H-4: List with three records

AutoFilter drop-
down arrow

Blue border
defines the list

Insert row

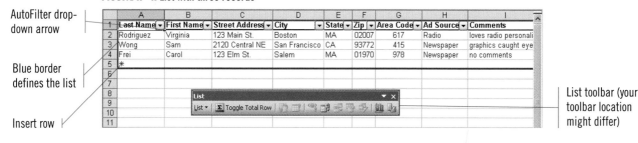

List toolbar (your
toolbar location
might differ)

Clues to Use

Filtering lists using AutoFilter

You can filter a list to show only the rows that meet specific criteria. For example, you might want to display only the records of customers in a certain zip code, or only residents of California. The AutoFilter list arrows, which automatically appear when you create a list, provide an easy way to apply a filter. The list arrows allow you to specify certain criteria for a field. For example, if you specify MA as the criteria in a State field, Excel displays only the records where MA is entered as the state. The AutoFilter options also include Sort Ascending and Sort Descending, which can be used to arrange your list data in increasing or decreasing order. Remember that a **filter** displays particular records, while a **sort** changes the order of records.

Adding Records with the Data Form

You can add records to a list by typing data directly into the last row of the list, which is called the **insert row**. Typing information in this row automatically adds the data to the list and expands the list's boundaries. You can also use a data form as a quick, easy method of data entry. A **data form** is a dialog box that displays one record at a time. ▄▄▄▄▄ You have entered all the customer records Jim had on his cards, but he receives the names of two additional customers. You decide to add the new customer information to the list using both methods: the data form and the insert row.

STEPS

1. **Make sure the New Customer List file is open, then activate Sheet2 and rename it Working List**

   Working List contains the nearly completed customer list.

   QUICK TIP
   You can also open a data form by clicking List on the List toolbar and then clicking Form.

2. **Select any cell in the customer list, click Data on the menu bar, then click Form**

   A data form containing the first record appears, as shown in Figure H-5.

3. **Click New**

   A blank data form appears with the insertion point in the first field.

   TROUBLE
   If you accidentally press [↑] or [↓] while in a data form and find that you displayed the wrong record, press [↑] or [↓] until you return to the desired record.

4. **Type Chavez in the Last Name box, then press [Tab]**

   The insertion point moves to the next field.

5. **Enter the rest of the information for Jane Chavez, using the information shown in Figure H-6**

   Press [Tab] to move the insertion point to the next field, or click in the next field box to move the insertion point there.

6. **Click Close to add Jane Chavez's record, then if necessary scroll down to view the end of the list**

   The record that you added with the data form appears at the end of the list.

   QUICK TIP
   Excel automatically extends formatting and formulas in lists.

7. **Click cell A47, enter Ross, press [Tab], then enter the rest of the information for Cathy Ross in the insert row using the information shown in Figure H-6**

8. **Return to cell A1, then save the workbook**

FIGURE H-5: Data form showing first record in the list

Current record number

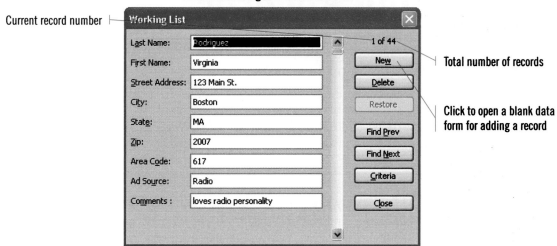

Total number of records

Click to open a blank data
form for adding a record

FIGURE H-6: Information for two new records

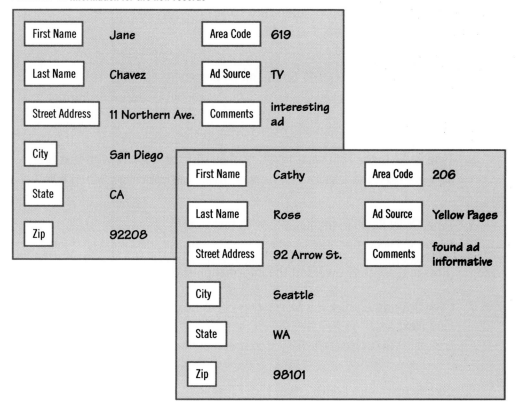

Finding Records

From time to time, you need to locate specific records in your list. You can use the Excel Find command on the Edit menu or the data form to search your list. You can also use the Replace command on the Edit menu to locate and replace existing entries or portions of entries with specified information.  Jim wants to be more specific about the radio ad source, so he asks you to replace "Radio" with "KWIN Radio." He also wants to know how many of the new customers originated from the company's TV ads. You begin by searching for those records with the ad source "TV."

STEPS

TROUBLE

If you receive the message "No range was found that could be filtered," select cell A1, then repeat Step 1.

1. **Click cell A1 if necessary, click Data on the menu bar, click Form, then click Criteria**

   The data form changes so that all fields are blank and "Criteria" appears in the upper-right corner. See Figure H-7. In this dialog box, you enter criteria that specify the records you want to find. You want to search for records whose Ad Source field contains the label "TV."

2. **Click in the Ad Source text box, type TV, then click Find Next**

   Excel displays the first record for a customer who learned about the company through its TV ads. See Figure H-8.

QUICK TIP

You can also use comparison operators when searching using the data form. For example, you could specify >s in a Last Name field box to display those records with customer last names starting with the letter "s" or later in the alphabet. To display customers who live in a particular area of the country, you could enter >90000 in the Zip Code field box.

3. **Click Find Next and examine the Ad Source field for each found record until no more matching records appear, then click Close**

   There are six customers whose ad source is TV.

4. **Return to cell A1, click Edit on the menu bar, then click Replace**

   The Find and Replace dialog box opens with the Replace tab selected and the insertion point in the Find what box. See Figure H-9.

5. **Type Radio in the Find what text box, then click the Replace with text box**

   Jim wants you to search for entries containing "Radio" and replace them with "KWIN Radio."

6. **Type KWIN Radio in the Replace with text box**

   Because you notice that there are other list entries containing the word "radio" with a lowercase "r" (in the Comments column), you need to make sure that only capitalized instances of the word are replaced.

QUICK TIP

Be sure to clear this option for future searches in which you may not want to use it.

7. **Click Options >>, click the Match case check box to select it, click Options <<, then click Find Next**

   Excel moves the cell pointer to the first occurrence of "Radio."

8. **Click Replace All, click OK, then click Close**

   The dialog box closes. Excel made seven replacements. Note that in the Comments column, each instance of the word "radio" remains unchanged.

9. **Make sure there are no entries in the Ad Source column that read "Radio," then save the workbook**

FIGURE H-7: Criteria data form

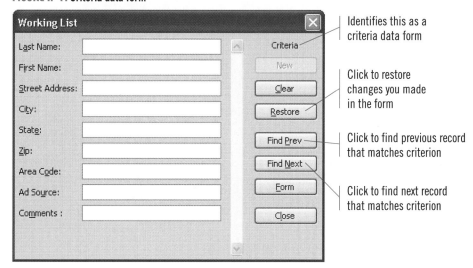

Identifies this as a criteria data form

Click to restore changes you made in the form

Click to find previous record that matches criterion

Click to find next record that matches criterion

FIGURE H-8: Finding a record using the data form

Record number of the displayed record

FIGURE H-9: Find and Replace dialog box

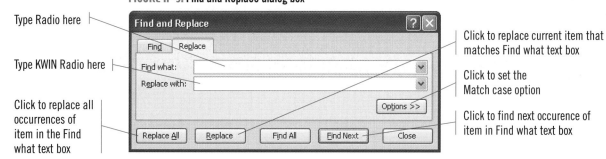

Type Radio here

Type KWIN Radio here

Click to replace all occurrences of item in the Find what text box

Click to replace current item that matches Find what text box

Click to set the Match case option

Click to find next occurence of item in Find what text box

Clues to Use

Using wildcards to fine-tune your search

You can use special symbols called **wildcards** when defining search criteria in the data form or Replace dialog box. The question mark (?) wildcard stands for any single character. For example, if you do not know whether a customer's last name is Paulsen or Paulson, you can specify Pauls?n as the search criteria to locate both options. The asterisk (*) wildcard stands for any group of characters. For example, if you specify Jan* as the search criteria in the First Name field, Excel locates all records with first names beginning with Jan (for instance, Jan, Janet, and Janice).

Deleting Records

You need to keep your list up to date by removing obsolete records. One way to remove records is to use the Delete button on the data form. You can also delete all records that share something in common—that is, records that meet certain criteria. For example, you can specify a criterion for Excel to find the next record containing zip code 01879, then remove the record by using the Delete button. If specifying one criterion does not meet your needs, you can set multiple criteria. Jim notices two entries for Carolyn Smith, and wants you to check the list for additional duplicate entries. You use the data form to delete the duplicate record.

STEPS

1. **Click Data on the menu bar, click Form, then click Criteria**
   The Criteria data form opens.

2. **Type Smith in the Last Name text box, press [Tab] to move the insertion point to the First Name text box, type Carolyn, then click Find Next**
   Excel displays the first record for a customer whose name is Carolyn Smith. You decide to leave the initial entry for Carolyn Smith (record 5 of 46) and delete the second one, once you confirm that it is a duplicate.

3. **Click Find Next**
   The duplicate record for Carolyn Smith, number 40, appears as shown in Figure H-10. You are ready to delete the duplicate entry.

4. **Click Delete, then click OK to confirm the deletion**
   The duplicate record for Carolyn Smith is deleted, and all the other records move up one row. The data form now shows the record for Manuel Julio.

5. **Click Close to return to the worksheet, if necessary scroll down until rows 41–46 are visible, then read the entry in row 41**
   Notice that the duplicate entry for Carolyn Smith is gone and that Manuel Julio moved up a row and is now in row 41. You also notice a record for K. C. Splint in row 43, which is a duplicate entry.

6. **Return to cell A1, and read the record information for K. C. Splint in row 8**
   After confirming the duplicate entry, you decide to delete the row.

7. **Click cell A8, click List on the List toolbar, then point to Delete**
   The delete options are displayed. See Figure H-11.

8. **Click Row**
   The duplicate record for K. C. Splint is deleted and the other records move up to fill in the gap.

9. **Save the workbook**

FIGURE H-10: Data form showing duplicate record for Carolyn Smith

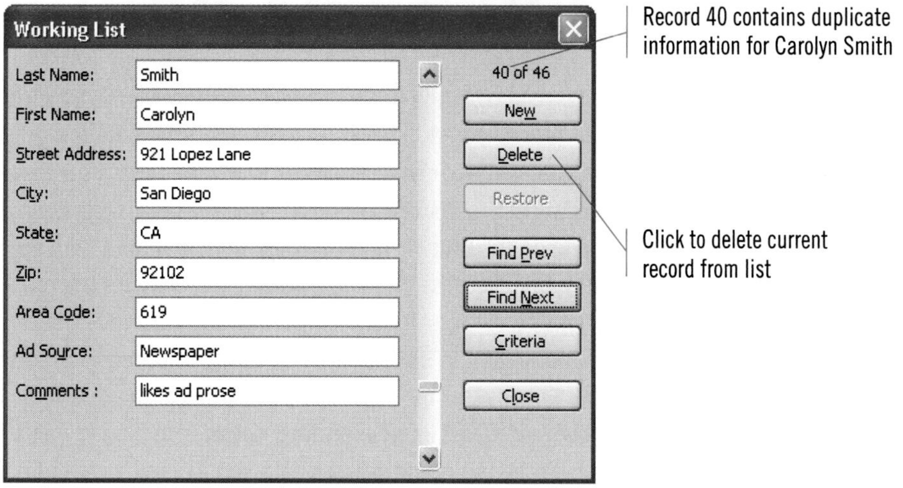

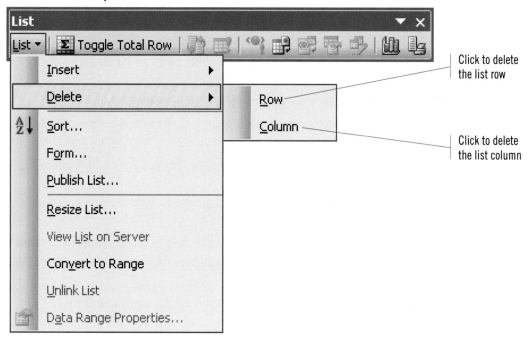

Record 40 contains duplicate information for Carolyn Smith

Click to delete current record from list

FIGURE H-11: Delete options

Click to delete the list row

Click to delete the list column

Clues to Use

Deleting records using the worksheet

When you delete a record using the data form, you cannot undo your deletion. When you delete a record by deleting its row in the worksheet, however, you can immediately retrieve it. To do so, you can either use the Undo command on the Edit menu, click the Undo button on the Standard toolbar, or press [Ctrl][Z].

Sorting a List on One Field

Usually, you enter records in the order in which you receive the information, rather than in alphabetical or numerical order. When you add records to a list using the data form, Excel adds the records to the end of the list. You can change the order of the records any time using the Excel **sort** feature. You can use the sort buttons on the Standard toolbar to sort records by one field, such as zip code or last name. You can also use the Sort command on the Data menu to sort on more than one field, such as zip code and then, within each zip code, by last name. Because the data is a list, Excel changes the order of the records while keeping each record, or row of information, together. You can sort an entire list or any portion of a list, and you can arrange sorted information in ascending or descending order. In **ascending order**, the lowest value (the beginning of the alphabet, or the earliest date) appears at the top of the list. In a field containing labels and numbers, numbers come first. In **descending order**, the highest value (the end of the alphabet or the latest date) appears at the top of the list. In a field containing labels and numbers, labels come first. Table H-3 provides examples of ascending and descending sorts. Because Jim wants to be able to return the records to their original order following any sorts, he wants you to create a new field called Entry Order. You then perform several single field sorts on the list.

STEPS

1. **Click cell J1, enter the column heading Entry Order, then format cell J1 with a thick bottom border**

   The AutoCorrect options button appears after you enter the label because the list is expanded to include the new column.

2. **Type 1 in cell J2, press [Enter], type 2 in cell J3, press [Enter], select cells J2:J3, then drag the fill handle to cell J45**

3. **Return to cell A1, then scroll to bring column J into view**

   The records are numbered as shown in Figure H-12. You are now ready to sort the list in ascending order by last name. You must position the cell pointer within the column you want to sort before issuing the sort command.

4. **Return to cell A1 if necessary, then click the Sort Ascending button ⬇ on the Standard toolbar**

   Excel rearranges the records in ascending order by last name, as shown in Figure H-13. You can also sort the list in descending order by any field.

5. **Click cell G5, then click the Sort Descending button ⬇ on the Standard toolbar**

   Excel sorts the list, placing those records with higher-digit area codes at the top. You are now ready to return the list to its original entry order.

6. **Click cell J1, click ⬇ on the Standard toolbar, then save the workbook**

   The list returns to its original order.

TABLE H-3: Sort order options and examples

option	alphabetic	numeric	date	alphanumeric
Ascending	A, B, C	7, 8, 9	1/1, 2/1, 3/1	12A, 99B, DX8, QT7
Descending	C, B, A	9, 8, 7	3/1, 2/1, 1/1	QT7, DX8, 99B, 12A

FIGURE H-12: List with Entry Order field added

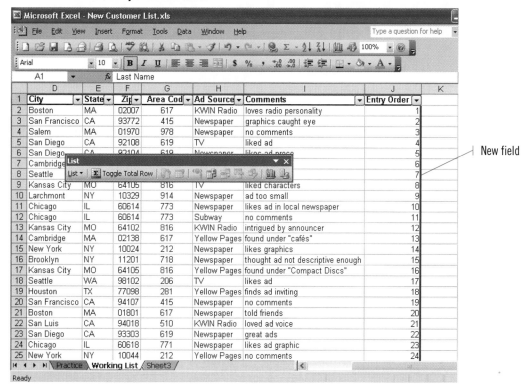

New field

FIGURE H-13: List sorted alphabetically by Last Name field

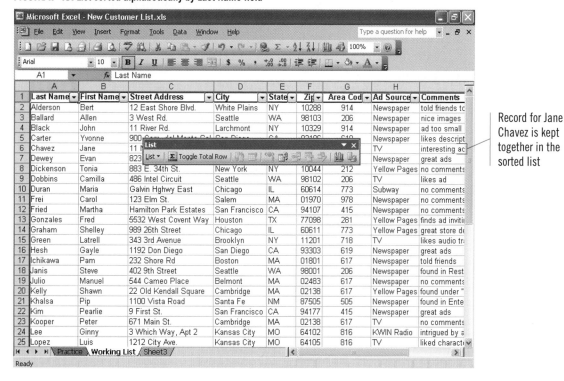

Record for Jane Chavez is kept together in the sorted list

Clues to Use

Sorting records using the AutoFilter

You can sort a list in ascending or descending order on one field using the AutoFilter list arrows next to the field name. Click the AutoFilter list arrow, then click Sort Ascending or Sort Descending to sort the list in the desired order. You may need to scroll up to the top of the list to see the sort commands.

Sorting a List on Multiple Fields

You can sort lists by as many as three fields by specifying **sort keys**, the criteria on which the sort is based. For example, you could sort first on the Ad Source field to reorder the records according to ad source, and then specify Last Name as a second sort key. The records would be sorted by Ad Source, and then within each ad source, by last name. You can enter up to three column headings in the Sort dialog box to specify the sort keys. It doesn't matter which cell is selected when you sort using the Sort dialog box. ▰▰▰▰ Jim wants you to sort the records alphabetically by state first, then within the state by zip code.

STEPS

QUICK TIP
You can include capitalization as a sort criterion by clicking Options in the Sort dialog box, then selecting the Case sensitive box. When you choose this option, lowercase entries precede uppercase entries.

1. **Click List on the List toolbar, then click Sort**
   The Sort dialog box opens, as shown in Figure H-14. You want to sort the list by state and then by zip code.

2. **Click the Sort by list arrow, click State, then click the Ascending option button to select it, if necessary**
   The list will be sorted alphabetically in ascending order (A–Z) by the State field. A second sort criterion will sort the entries within each state grouping.

3. **Click the top Then by list arrow, click Zip, then click the Descending option button**
   You could also sort by a third key by selecting a field in the bottom Then by list box.

4. **Click OK to perform the sort, return to cell A1, then scroll through the list to see the result of the sort**
   The list is sorted alphabetically by state in ascending order, then within each state by zip code in descending order. Compare your results with Figure H-15.

5. **Save the workbook**

FIGURE H-14: Sort dialog box

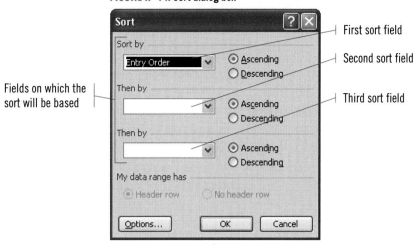

Fields on which the sort will be based

First sort field

Second sort field

Third sort field

FIGURE H-15: List sorted by two fields

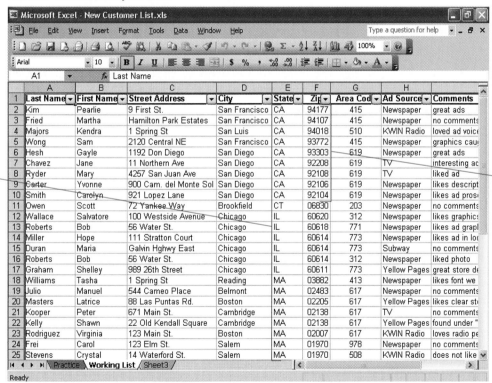

First sort by state in ascending order

Second sort by zip code in descending order

Clues to Use

Specifying a custom sort order

You can identify a custom sort order for the field selected in the Sort by box. Click Options in the Sort dialog box, click the First key sort order list arrow, then click the desired custom order. Commonly used custom sort orders are days of the week (Sun, Mon, Tues, Wed, etc.) and months (Jan, Feb, Mar, etc.); alphabetic sorts do not sort these items properly.

UNIT
H

Excel 2003

Printing a List

If a list is small enough to fit on one page, you can print it as you would any other Excel worksheet. If you have more columns than can fit on a portrait-oriented page, you can set the page orientation to landscape. Because lists often have more rows than can fit on a page, you can define the first row of the list (containing the field names) as the **print title**, which prints at the top of every page. Most lists do not have any descriptive information above the field names on the worksheet. To augment the information contained in the field names, you can use headers and footers to add identifying text, such as the list title or report date. If you want to exclude any fields from your list report, you can hide the selected columns from view so that they do not print. ▨▨▨▨ Jim has finished updating his list and would like you to print it. You begin by previewing the list.

STEPS

1. **Click the Print Preview button 🔍 on the Standard toolbar**

   The status bar reads Preview: Page 1 of 2. You want all the field names in the list to fit on a single page, but you need two pages to fit all the data.

2. **In the Print Preview window, click Setup, click the Page tab if necessary, click the Landscape option button under Orientation, click the Fit to option button under Scaling, double-click the tall box and type 2, click OK, then click Next**

   The list still does not fit on a single page. Because the records on page 2 appear without column headings, you want to set up the first row of the list, which contains the field names, as a repeating print title.

> **QUICK TIP**
>
> If you open the Page Setup dialog box from the Print Preview window, you cannot set print titles. You must choose Page Setup from the File menu to assign print titles.

3. **Click Close to close the Print Preview window, click File on the menu bar, click Page Setup, click the Sheet tab, click the Rows to repeat at top text box under Print titles, click any cell in row 1, compare your Page Setup dialog box to Figure H-16, then click OK**

   When you select row 1 as a print title, Excel automatically inserts an absolute reference to a beginning row to repeat at the top of each page—in this case, the print title to repeat beginning and ending with row 1.

4. **Click 🔍, click Next to view the second page, then click Zoom**

   Setting up a print title to repeat row 1 causes the field names to appear at the top of each printed page.

5. **Click Setup, click the Header/Footer tab, click Custom Header, click the Left section box and enter your name, then click the Center section box and enter MediaLoft -, press [Spacebar], then click the Filename button 📄**

6. **Select the header information in the Center section box, click the Font button 🅰, change the font size to 14 and the style to Bold, click OK, click OK again to return to the Header/Footer tab, click OK to preview the list, then click Close**

> **QUICK TIP**
>
> To print more than one worksheet, select each sheet tab while holding down [Shift] or [Ctrl], then click the Print button 🖨.

7. **Save the workbook, print the worksheet, close the workbook, then exit Excel**

   Compare your printed worksheet with Figure H-17.

FIGURE H-16: Sheet tab of the Page Setup dialog box

Indicates that row 1 will appear at the top of each printed page

Turns gridline display on or off

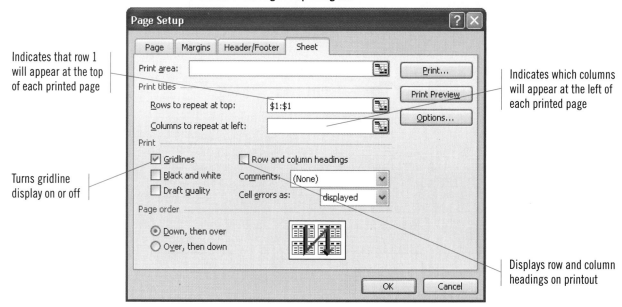

Indicates which columns will appear at the left of each printed page

Displays row and column headings on printout

FIGURE H-17: Completed list

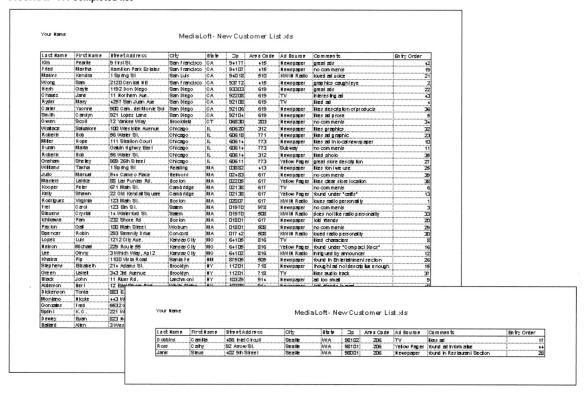

Clues to Use

Setting a print area

There are times when you want to print only part of a worksheet. To do this, select any worksheet range, then click File on the menu bar and click Print. In the Print dialog box, choose Selection under Print what, then click OK. If you want to print a selected area repeatedly, it's best to define a **print area**, which prints when you click the Print button on the Standard toolbar. To set a print area, click View on the menu bar, then click Page Break Preview. In the preview window, select the area you want to print. (If you see a Welcome dialog box,

click OK.) Right-click the area, then select Set Print Area. The print area becomes outlined in a blue border. You can drag the border to extend the print area or add nonadjacent cells to it by selecting them, right-clicking them, then selecting Add to Print Area. When printing a print area that is part of a list, you must select Active sheet, rather than List, in the Print what section of the Print dialog box. To clear a print area, click File on the menu bar, point to Print Area, then click Clear Print Area.

Practice

▼ CONCEPTS REVIEW

FIGURE H-18

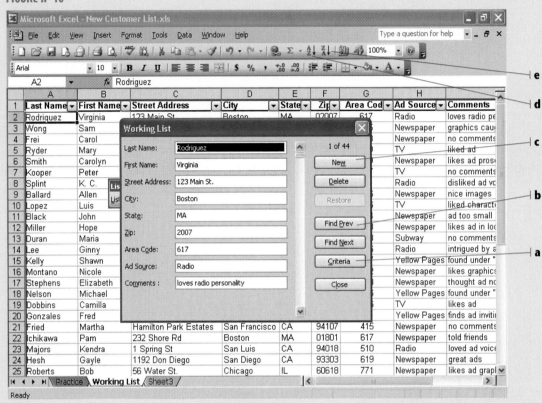

1. Which element do you click to sort a list in ascending order?
2. Which element do you click to sort a list in descending order?
3. Which element do you click to open a blank data form?
4. Which element do you click to search for records by specifying data in a field?
5. Which element do you click to find an earlier occurrence of a record that matches specified criteria?

Match each term with the statement that best describes it.

6. Data form
7. Record
8. List
9. Field name
10. Sort

a. Arrange records in a particular sequence
b. Organized collection of related information in Excel
c. Row in an Excel list
d. Used for entering data into a list
e. Label positioned at the top of the column identifying data

Select the best answer from the list of choices.

11. Which of the following Excel sorting options do you use to sort a list of employee names in order from Z to A?
    a. Absolute
    b. Ascending
    c. Alphabetic
    d. Descending

12. Which of the following series appears in descending order?
    a. 4, 5, 6, A, B, C
    b. 8, 6, 4, C, B, A
    c. 8, 7, 6, 5, 6, 7
    d. C, B, A, 6, 5, 4

13. What color is the border that encloses a list on a worksheet?
    a. Red
    b. Blue
    c. Green
    d. Yellow

14. When printing a list on multiple pages, you can define a print title containing repeating row(s) to:
    a. Include appropriate fields in the printout.
    b. Include the header in list reports.
    c. Include field names at the top of each printed page.
    d. Exclude from the printout all rows under the first row.

▼ SKILLS REVIEW

1. **Create a list.**
   a. Create a new workbook, then save it as **Employee List** in the drive and folder where your Data Files are stored.
   b. Enter the field names and records shown in the following table:
   c. Apply bold formatting to the field names and center the field names in the columns.
   d. Adjust the column widths to make the data readable.

Last Name	First Name	Years Employed	Position	Full/Part Time	Training?
Lenon	Sarah	5	Video Sales	F	Y
Marino	Donato	3	CD Sales	P	N
Khederian	Jay	4	Video Sales	F	Y
Jones	Cathy	1	Video Sales	F	N
Rabinowicz	Miriam	2	CD Sales	P	Y

   e. Select the field names and the records, then create a list from the selected range. Adjust the column widths, if necessary, to display the field names.
   f. Enter your name in the worksheet footer, then save and print the list.

2. **Add records with the data form.**
   a. Click any record in the list.
   b. Open the data form and add a new record for **Danielle Gitano**, a one-year employee in book sales. Danielle works full time and has not completed training.
   c. Use the insert row to add a new record for **George Worthen**. George works full time, has worked at the company five years in book sales, and has completed training.
   d. Use the insert row to add a new record for **Valerie Atkins**. Valerie works full time, has worked at the company three years in video sales, and has completed training.
   e. Save the file.

3. Find and delete records.

   a. Use the Find command to find the record for **Cathy Jones**.

   b. Delete the record.

   c. Use the Find command to find the record for **Valerie Atkins**.

   d. Delete the record.

   e. Save the file.

4. Sort a list on one field.

   a. Sort the list in descending order by years employed.

   b. Sort the list alphabetically in descending order by training.

   c. Sort the list alphabetically in ascending order by position.

   d. Sort the list alphabetically in ascending order by last name.

   e. Save the file.

5. Sort a list on multiple fields.

   a. Sort the list first in ascending order by years employed and then alphabetically in descending order by last name.

   b. Check the list to make sure the records appear in the correct order.

   c. Sort the list alphabetically in ascending order, first by whether or not the employees have completed training and then by last name.

   d. Check the list to make sure the records appear in the correct order.

   e. Save the file.

6. Print a list.

   a. Add a header that reads **Employee Information** in the center, then format the header in bold.

   b. Add the file name to the center section of the footer.

   c. Use the Margins tab in the Page Setup dialog box to add top and bottom margins of one inch.

   d. Select all of the information in the worksheet and change the font size to 16.

   e. Use the Sheet tab of the Page Setup dialog box to add column A as a print title that repeats at the left of each printed page.

   f. Save the workbook, then print the list.

   g. Close the workbook, then exit Excel.

▼ INDEPENDENT CHALLENGE 1

You own Personalize IT, an advertising firm located in New Zealand. The firm sells specialty items imprinted with the customer's name and/or logo such as hats, pens, mugs, and T-shirts. Plan and build a list of order information with eight records using the items sold. Your list should contain at least five different customers. (Some customers may place more than one order.)

   a. Prepare a list plan that states your goal, outlines the data you need, and identifies the list elements.

   b. Sketch a sample list on a piece of paper, indicating how the list should be built. Which of the data fields should be formatted as labels? As values?

   c. Start Excel, create a new workbook, then save it as **Personalize IT** in the drive and folder where your Data Files are stored. Build the list by first entering **Personalize IT** as the worksheet title in cell A1, then enter the following field names in the designated cells:

   d. Enter eight data records using your own data.

   e. Select the range A2:E10 and create a list. Adjust the column widths as necessary.

   f. Enter **Subtotal** in cell F2, **Total** in cell G2, **Tax** in cell H2, and **.125** in cell I2 (the 12.5% Goods and Services tax). Make sure the new items are added to the list range.

   g. Enter formulas to calculate the subtotal (Quantity*Cost) in cell F3 and the total (including tax) in cell G3. Copy the formulas down the columns.

   h. Format the Cost, Subtotal, and Total columns as currency. Adjust the column widths as necessary.

   i. Add a new record to your list using the data form. Add another record using the insert row.

Cell	Field name
A2	**Customer Last**
B2	**Customer First**
C2	**Item**
D2	**Quantity**
E2	**Cost**

▼ INDEPENDENT CHALLENGE 1 (CONTINUED)

j. Sort the list in ascending order by Item using the Sort Ascending button on the Standard toolbar.

k. Enter your name in the worksheet footer, then save the workbook.

l. Preview the worksheet, print the worksheet on one page, close the workbook, then exit Excel.

▼ INDEPENDENT CHALLENGE 2

You are taking a class titled Television Shows: Past and Present at a local community college. The instructor has given you an Excel list of television programs from the '60s and '70s. She has included fields tracking the following information: the number of years the show was a favorite, favorite character, the show's length in minutes, least favorite character, and comments about the show. The instructor has included data for each show in the list. She has asked you to add a field (column label) and one record (a show of your choosing) to the list. Because the list should cover only 30-minute shows, you need to delete any records for shows longer than 30 minutes. Also, your instructor wants you to sort and format the list as needed before printing. Feel free to change any of the list data to suit your tastes and opinions.

a. Start Excel, open the file EX H-2.xls from the drive and folder where your Data Files are stored, then save it as **Television Shows of the Past**.

b. Add a field called **Rating** in column G. The list formatting should be extended to include the new column and your worksheet should look like Figure H-19. Complete the Rating field for each record with a value of 1–5 with 5 being the highest, that reflects the rating you would give the television show.

FIGURE H-19

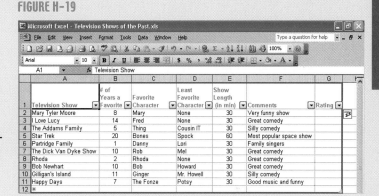

c. Use the data form to add one record for a 30-minute show to the list. Make sure to enter information in every field.

d. Use the data form to delete any records having show lengths other than 30. (*Hint*: Use the comparison operator <> in the Show Length field to find records not equal to 30.)

e. Make any formatting changes to the list as needed and save the list.

f. Sort the list in ascending order by show name.

g. Enter your name in the worksheet footer, save the workbook, then print the list.

h. Sort the list again, this time in descending order by the number of years the show was a favorite.

i. Add a centered header that reads **Television Shows of the Past: '60s and '70s**.

j. Save the workbook, preview it, then print the list.

Advanced Challenge Exercise

■ Use the Page Break Preview view to create a print area that prints only the first two columns, Television Show, and # of Years a Favorite. Print the print area. (*Hint*: You must change the "Print what" setting in the Print dialog box from List to Active sheet.)

■ Add the third column, Favorite Character, to the print area using the shortcut menu option, then print the print area.

k. Save the workbook, close the workbook, then exit Excel.

▼ INDEPENDENT CHALLENGE 3

You are the assistant manager at Nite Owl Video in Brisbane, Australia. You have assembled an Excel list of the most popular Australian films your store rents, along with information about the Australian Film Institute (AFI) award they won, the release dates, and the film genres. Your customers have suggested that you prepare an in-store handout listing the films with the information sorted in different ways.

a. Start Excel, open the file EX H-3.xls from the drive and folder where your Data Files are stored, then save it as **Best Films**.

b. Sort the list in ascending order by Genre. Sort the list again in ascending order by Film Name.

FIGURE H-20

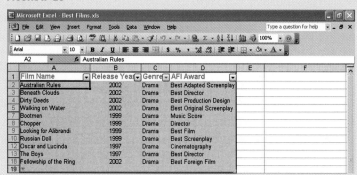

c. Sort the list again using two fields, this time in descending order by Release Year, then in ascending order by Genre.

d. Enter your name in the worksheet footer, then save the workbook.

e. Use the data form to add a record to the list with the following information: Film Name: Fellowship of the Ring; Release Year: 2002; Genre: Drama; AFI Award: Best Foreign Film.

f. Use the data form to find and delete the record for the film *Passion*.

g. Use AutoFilter to display only dramas. (*Hint*: Click the AutoFilter list arrow in the Genre column and select Drama.) Compare your list to Figure H-20.

h. Redisplay all films. (*Hint*: Click the AutoFilter list arrow in the Genre column and select All.)

Advanced Challenge Exercise

■ Create your own sort order of: Drama, Comedy, Thriller, Suspense for the Genre column. (*Hint*: You must create a custom list using Options on the Tools menu and the Custom Lists tab.)

■ Sort the list in ascending order on the Genre field using your custom sort order. You need to clear all sort fields except the first key sort field in the Sort dialog box.

i. Save the workbook, print the list, close the workbook, then exit Excel.

▼ INDEPENDENT CHALLENGE 4

Your local newspaper has decided to start publishing the top-selling MP3 titles. They want to list the best-selling titles in the genres of Pop, Hip Hop, Country, and Classical. You have been asked to research the bestselling MP3 music along with price information. You create a list to hold the information about the top two titles for each genre. Using AutoFilter, you then display titles by the type of music and sort the list.

a. Go to the search engine of your choice and research the top selling MP3 titles in the categories of Pop, Country, Hip Hop, and Classical.

b. Complete the table below with the MP3 title information you found in your search.

Title	Artist	Genre	Price

c. Start Excel, enter your name in the worksheet footer of the new workbook, then save the workbook as **MP3 Titles**.

d. Use your table to enter the top two titles for each of the four music categories, along with the artist and price information, into your Excel worksheet. Save the workbook.

e. Create a list that contains the MP3 information.

f. Use AutoFilter to display only the Pop titles. (*Hint*: Click the AutoFilter arrow in the Genre column and select Pop.)

g. Use AutoFilter to display all the records. (*Hint*: Click the AutoFilter arrow in the Genre column and select All.)

h. Use the data form to delete both Pop records.

i. Use the AutoFilter to sort the list in ascending order by price. (*Hint*: Click the AutoFilter arrow in the Price column and select Sort Ascending.)

j. Save the workbook, print the list, close the workbook, then exit Excel.

▼ VISUAL WORKSHOP

Create the worksheet shown in Figure H-21. Save the workbook as **Famous Jazz Performers** in the drive and folder where your Data Files are stored. Once you've entered the field names and records, sort the list using two fields. The first sort should be in ascending order by Contribution to Jazz, and the second sort should be in ascending order by Last Name. Change the page setup so that the list is printed in landscape orientation on one page and centered on the page horizontally. Add a header that is centered, formatted in bold with a size of 16, and reads Famous Jazz Performers. Enter your name in the worksheet footer. Save the workbook, preview and print the list, close the workbook, then exit Excel.

FIGURE H-21

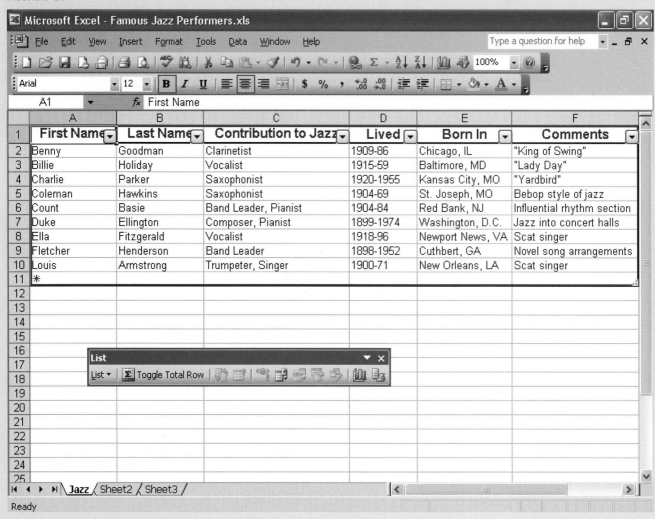

Glossary

3-D reference A reference that uses values on other sheets or workbooks, effectively creating another dimension to a workbook.

Absolute cell reference A cell reference that contains a dollar sign before the column letter and/or row number to indicate the absolute, or fixed, contents of specific cells. For example, the formula $A$1+$B$1 calculates only the sum of these specific cells no matter where the formula is copied in the workbook.

Active cell The current location of the cell pointer.

Alignment The placement of cell contents; for example, left, center, or right.

Area chart A line chart in which each area is given a solid color or pattern to emphasize the relationship between the pieces of charted information.

Argument Information that a function needs to calculate an answer. In an expression, multiple arguments are separated by commas. All of the arguments are enclosed in parentheses; for example, =SUM(A1:B1).

Argument ScreenTip The yellow box that appears as you build a function. As you build the function using different elements, the box displays these elements. You can click each element to display its online help.

Arithmetic operator A symbol used in a formula (such as + or -, / or *) to perform mathematical operations.

Ascending order In sorting worksheet records, the order that begins with the letter A or the number 1.

Attribute The styling features such as bold, italics, and underlining that can be applied to cell contents.

AutoCalculate value Value displayed in the status bar that represents the sum of values in the selected range.

AutoComplete A feature that automatically completes entries based on other entries in the same column.

AutoFill A feature that creates a series of text entries or numbers when a range is selected using the fill handle.

AutoFill Options button Allows you to specify what you want to fill and whether or not you want to include formatting.

AutoFilter An Excel list feature that lets you click a list arrow and select criteria by which to display certain types of records.

AutoFilter list arrows Small triangles that appear next to field names in an Excel list; used to display portions of your data.

AutoFit A feature that automatically adjusts the width of a column to accommodate its widest entry when the boundary to the right of the column selector is double-clicked.

AutoFormat Preset schemes that can be applied to format a range instantly. Excel comes with 16 AutoFormats that include colors, fonts, and numeric formatting.

AutoSum A feature that automatically creates totals using the SUM function when you click the AutoSum button.

Background color The color applied to the background of a cell.

Bar chart A chart that shows information as a series of horizontal bars.

Border The edge of a cell, an area of a worksheet, or a selected object; you can change its color or line style.

Category axis Also known as the x-axis in a 2-dimensional chart.

Cell The intersection of a column and row in a worksheet, datasheet, or table.

Cell address The location of a cell expressed by the column and row coordinates; the cell address of the cell in column A, row 1, is A1.

Cell pointer A highlighted rectangle around a cell that indicates the active cell.

Cell reference The address or name that identifies a cell's position in a worksheet; it consists of a letter that identifies the cell's column and a number that identifies its row; for example, cell B3. Cell references in worksheets can be used in formulas and are relative or absolute.

Chart A graphic representation of worksheet information. Types include 2-D and 3-D column, bar, pie, area, and line charts.

Chart sheet A separate sheet that contains only a chart linked to worksheet data.

Chart Wizard A series of dialog boxes that helps you create or modify a chart.

Clip An individual media file, such as art, sound, animation, or a movie.

Clip art An image such as a corporate logo, a picture, or a photo.

Clipboard A temporary storage area for cut or copied items that are available for pasting. *See* Office Clipboard.

Clipboard task pane A task pane that shows the contents of the Office Clipboard; contains options for copying and pasting items.

Code *See* Program Code.

Comments In a Visual Basic procedure, notes that explain the purpose of the macro or procedure; they are preceded by a single apostrophe and appear in green on a color monitor.

Column chart The default chart type in Excel, which displays information as a series of vertical columns.

Column heading The gray box containing the letter above the column in a worksheet.

Combination chart Combines a column and line chart to compare data requiring different scales of measure.

Complex formula An equation that uses more than one type of arithmetic operator.

Conditional format A cell format that is based on the cell's value or the outcome of a formula.

Conditional formula A formula that makes calculations based on stated conditions, such as calculating a rebate based on a particular purchase amount.

Consolidate To combine data on multiple worksheets and display the result on another worksheet.

Control menu box A box in the upper-left corner of a window used to resize or close a window.

Data entry area The unlocked portion of a worksheet where users are able to enter and change data.

Data form In an Excel list (or database), a dialog box that displays one record at a time.

Data marker A graphical representation of a data point, such as a bar or column.

Data point Individual piece of data plotted in a chart.

Data series The selected range in a worksheet that Excel converts into a graphic and displays as a chart.

Database An organized collection of related information. In Excel, a database is called a list.

Descending order In sorting an Excel list, the order that begins with the letter Z or the highest number in a list.

Drag-and-drop technique Method in which you drag the contents of selected cells to a new location.

Dummy column/row Blank column or row included at the end of a range that enables a formula to adjust when columns or rows are added or deleted.

Dynamic page breaks In a larger workbook, horizontal or vertical dashed lines that represent the place where pages print separately. They also adjust automatically when you insert or delete rows or columns, or change column widths or row heights.

Electronic spreadsheet A computer program that performs calculations on data and organizes information into worksheets. A worksheet is divided into columns and rows, which form individual cells.

Embedded chart A chart displayed as an object in a worksheet.

Exploding pie slice A slice of a pie chart that has been pulled away from the whole pie to add emphasis.

External reference indicator The exclamation point (!) used in a formula to indicate that a referenced cell is outside the active sheet.

Field In a list (an Excel database), a column that describes a characteristic about records, such as first name or city.

Field name A column label that describes a field.

Fill color The cell background color.

Fill handle A small square in the lower-right corner of the active cell used to copy cell contents.

Filter To display data in an Excel list that meet specified criteria.

Font The typeface or design of a set of characters.

Font size The size of characters, measured in units called points (pts).

Footer Information that prints at the bottom of each printed page; on screen, a footer is visible only in Print Preview.

Format The appearance of text and numbers, including color, font, attributes, borders, and shading. *See also* Number format.

Format Painter A feature used to copy the formatting applied to one set of text or in one cell to another.

Formatting toolbar A toolbar that contains buttons for frequently used formatting commands.

Formula A set of instructions used to perform numeric calculations (adding, multiplying, averaging, etc.).

Formula bar The area below the menu bar and above the Excel workspace where you enter and edit data in a worksheet cell. The formula bar becomes active when you start typing or editing cell data. It includes the Enter button and the Cancel button.

Formula prefix An arithmetic symbol, such as the equal sign (=), used to start a formula.

Freeze To hold in place selected columns or rows when scrolling in a worksheet that is divided in panes. *See also* panes.

Function A special, predefined formula that provides a shortcut for a commonly used calculation; for example, AVERAGE.

Getting Started task pane Lets you quickly open new or existing workbooks.

Gridlines Horizontal and/or vertical lines within a chart that make the chart easier to read.

Header Information that prints at the top of each printed page; on screen, a header is visible only in Print Preview.

Help system A utility that gives you immediate access to definitions, steps, explanations, and useful tips.

Hide To make rows, columns, formulas, or sheets invisible to workbook users.

Hotspot An object that, when clicked, will run a macro or open a file.

HTML Hypertext Markup Language, the format of pages that a Web browser such as Internet Explorer or Netscape Navigator can read.

Hyperlink An object (a filename, a word, a phrase, or a graphic) in a worksheet that, when you click it, will display another worksheet or a Web page called the target.

Input Information that produces desired results, or output, in a worksheet.

Insert row The last row in an Excel list, where a record can be entered.

Insertion point The blinking vertical line that appears in the formula bar or in a cell during editing in Excel.

Intranet An internal network site used by a particular group of people who work together.

Keyword A representative word on which the Help system can search to find information on your area of interest.

Label Descriptive text or other information that identifies the rows and columns of a worksheet. Labels are not included in calculations.

Label prefix A character, such as the apostrophe, that identifies an entry as a label and controls the way it appears in the cell.

Landscape orientation A print setting that positions the worksheet on the page so the page is wider than it is tall.

Legend A key explaining how information is represented by colors or patterns in a chart.

Line chart A graph of data that is mapped by a series of lines. Line charts show changes in data or categories of data over time and can be used to document trends.

Linking The dynamic referencing of data in other workbooks, so that when data in the other workbooks is changed, the references in the current workbook are automatically updated.

List The Excel term for a database, an organized collection of related information.

Lock To secure a row, column, or sheet so that data in that location cannot be changed.

Logical test The first part of an IF function; if the logical test is true, then the second part of the function is applied, and if it is false, then the third part of the function is applied.

Macro A set of instructions recorded or written in the Visual Basic programming language used to automate worksheet tasks.

Menu bar The bar beneath the title bar that contains the names of menus, that when clicked, open menus from which you choose program commands.

Minor gridlines Gridlines that show the values between the tick marks.

Mixed reference A formula containing both a relative and absolute reference.

Mode indicator A box located in the lower-left corner of the status bar that informs you of a program's status. For example, when Excel is performing a task, the word "Wait" appears.

Module In Visual Basic, a module is stored in a workbook and contains macro procedures.

Moving border The dashed line that appears around a cell or range that is copied to the Clipboard.

Name box The left-most area in the formula bar that shows the cell reference or name of the active cell. For example, A1 refers to cell A1 of the active worksheet. You can also display a list of names in a workbook using the Name list arrow.

Named range A range of cells given a meaningful name; it retains its name when moved and can be referenced in a formula.

Number format A format applied to values to express numeric concepts, such as currency, date, and percentage.

Object A chart or graphic image that can be moved and resized and that contains handles when selected.

Office Clipboard A temporary storage area shared by all Office programs that can be used to cut, copy and paste multiple items within and between Office programs. The Office Clipboard can hold up to 24 items collected from any Office program. *See also* Clipboard task pane.

Order of precedence The order in which Excel calculates parts of a formula: (1) exponents, (2) multiplication and division, and (3) addition and subtraction.

Output The end result of a worksheet.

Panes Sections into which you can divide a worksheet when you want to work on separate parts of the worksheet at the same time; one pane freezes, or remains in place, while you scroll in another pane until you see the desired information.

Paste Function A series of dialog boxes that helps you build functions; it lists and describes all Excel functions.

Personal macro workbook A workbook that can contain macros that are available to any open workbook. By default, the personal macro workbook is hidden.

Pie chart A circular chart that represents data as slices of a pie. A pie chart is useful for showing the relationship of parts to a whole; pie slices can be extracted for emphasis. *See also* Exploding pie slice.

Plot area The area inside the horizontal and vertical chart axes.

Point A unit of measure used for fonts and row height. One inch equals 72 points, or a point is equal to 1/72 of an inch.

Pointing method Specifying formula cell references by selecting the desired cell with the mouse instead of typing its cell reference; it eliminates typing errors. Also known as Pointing.

Portrait orientation A print setting that positions the worksheet on the page so the page is taller than it is wide.

Preview A view of the worksheet exactly as it will appear on paper.

Print area A portion of a worksheet that you can define using the Print Area command on the File menu; after you define a print area, clicking the Print icon on the Standard toolbar prints only that worksheet area.

Print title In a list that spans more than one page, the field names that print at the top of every printed page.

Program code Macro instructions, written in the Visual Basic for Applications programming language.

Publish To place an Excel workbook or worksheet on a Web site or an intranet in HTML format so that others can access it using their Web browsers.

Range A selected group of adjacent cells.

Range finder A feature that outlines an equation's arguments in blue and green.

Record In a list (an Excel database), data about an object or a person.

Relative cell reference A type of cell reference used to indicate a relative position in the worksheet. It allows you to copy and move formulas from one area to another of the same dimensions. Excel automatically changes the column and row numbers to reflect the new position. Also known as Relative reference.

Research services Reference information available through the Research task pane that can be inserted into your document.

Row height The vertical dimension of a cell.

Row heading The gray box containing the row number to the left of the row.

Run To play, as a macro.

Series of labels Preprogrammed series, such as days of the week and months of the year. They are formed by typing the first word of the series, then dragging the fill handle to select and fill the desired range of cells.

Sheet A term used for a worksheet.

Sheet tab A description at the bottom of each worksheet that identifies it in a workbook. In an open workbook, move to a worksheet by clicking its sheet tab. Also known as Worksheet tab.

Sheet tab scrolling buttons Buttons that enable you to move among sheets within a workbook.

Single-file Web page A Web page that integrates all of the worksheets and graphical elements from a workbook into a single file in the MHTML file format, making it easier to publish to the Web. Users who have IE 4.0 or higher can open a Web page saved in MHTML format.

Sizing handles Small boxes appearing along the corners and sides of charts and graphic images that are used for moving and resizing.

Sort To change the order of records in a list according to one or more fields, such as Last Name.

Sort keys Criteria on which a sort, or a reordering of data, is based.

Standard toolbar A toolbar that contains buttons for frequently used operating and editing commands.

Status bar The bar at the bottom of the Excel window that provides information about various keys, commands, and processes.

Style A named combination of formatting characteristics, such as bold, italic, and zero decimal places.

SUM The most frequently used function, this adds columns or rows of cells.

Target The location that a hyperlink displays after you click it.

Task pane A window area to the right of the worksheet that provides worksheet options, such as creating a new workbook, conducting a search, inserting Clip Art, and using the Office Clipboard.

Task pane list arrow Lets you switch between 11 different task panes.

Template An Excel file saved with a special format that lets you open a new file based on an existing workbook's design and/or content.

Text annotations Labels added to a chart to draw attention to a particular area.

Text color The color applied to text in a cell or on a chart.

Tick marks Notations of a scale of measure on a chart axis.

Title bar The bar at the top of the program window that indicates the program name and the name of the current file.

Toggle button A button that turns a feature on and off.

Toolbar A bar that contains buttons that you can click to perform commands.

Toolbar Options button A button you click on a toolbar to view toolbar buttons not currently visible.

Truncate To shorten the display of cell information because a cell is too wide.

Type a question for help box Area on the menu bar in which you can query the Excel help system by typing a question.

Value   A number, formula, or function used in calculations.

Value axis   Also known as the y-axis in a 2-dimensional chart, this area often contains numerical values that help you interpret the size of chart elements.

View   A set of display or print settings that you can name and save for access at another time. You can save multiple views of a worksheet.

Virus   Destructive software that can damage your computer files.

Visual Basic Editor   A program that lets you display and edit macro code.

Visual Basic for Applications (VBA)   A programming language used to create macros in Excel.

Web discussion   Comments attached to an Excel worksheet that you will save as an HTML document, allowing people viewing your worksheet on the Web to review and reply to your comments.

What-if analysis   A decision-making feature in which data is changed and formulas based on it are automatically recalculated.

Wildcard   A special symbol you use in defining search criteria in the data form or Replace dialog box. The most common types of wildcards are the question mark (?), which stands for any single character, and the asterisk (*), which represents any group of characters.

Window   A rectangular area of a screen where you view and work on the open file.

Workbook   A collection of related worksheets contained within a single file.

Worksheet   An electronic spreadsheet containing 256 columns by 65,536 rows.

Worksheet tab   *See* Sheet tab.

Worksheet window   Includes the tools that enable you to create and work with worksheets.

Workspace   An Excel file with an .xlw extension containing information about the identity, view, and placement of a set of open workbooks. Instead of opening each workbook individually, you can open the workspace file instead.

X-axis   The horizontal axis in a chart; because it often shows data categories, such as months, it is also called the category axis.

X-axis label   A label describing a chart's x-axis.

XY (scatter) chart   Compares trends over uneven time or measurement intervals; used in scientific and engineering disciplines for trend spotting and extrapolation.

Y-axis   The vertical axis in a chart; because it often shows numerical values in a 2-dimensional chart, it is also called the value axis.

Y-axis label   A label describing the y-axis of a chart.

Zoom   A feature that enables you to focus on a larger or smaller part of the worksheet in Print Preview.

Some of the exercises in this book require that you begin by opening a Data File. Follow one of the procedures below to obtain a copy of the Data Files you need.

Instructors

■ A copy of the Data Files is on the Instructor Resources CD under the category Data Files for Students, which you can copy to your school's network for student use.

■ Download the Data Files via the World Wide Web by following the instructions below.

■ Contact us via e-mail at reply@course.com.

■ Call Course Technology's Customer Service Department for fast and efficient delivery of the Data Files if you do not have access to a CD-ROM drive.

Students

■ Check with your instructor to determine the best way to obtain a copy of the Data Files.

■ Download the Data Files via the World Wide Web by following the instructions below.

Instructions for Downloading the Data Files from the World Wide Web

1. Start your browser and enter the URL www.course.com.

2. When the course.com Web site opens, click Student Downloads, and then search for your text by title or ISBN.

3. If necessary, from the Search results page, select the title of the text you are using.

4. When the textbook page opens, click the Download Student Files link, and then click the link of the compressed files you want to download.

5. If the File Download dialog box opens, make sure the Save this program to disk option button is selected, and then click the OK button. (NOTE: If the Save As dialog box opens, select a folder on your hard disk to download the file to. Write down the folder name listed in the Save in box and the filename listed in the File name box.)

6. The filename of the compressed file appears in the Save As dialog box (e.g., 3500-8.exe, 0361-1d.exe).

7. Click either the OK button or the Save button, whichever choice your browser gives you.

8. When a dialog box opens indicating the download is complete, click the OK button (or the Close button, depending on which operating system you are using). Close your browser.

9. Open Windows Explorer and display the contents of the folder to which you downloaded the file. Double-click the downloaded filename on the right side of the Windows Explorer window.

10. In the WinZip Self-Extractor window, specify the appropriate drive and a folder name to unzip the files to. Click Unzip.

11. When the WinZip Self-Extractor displays the number of files unzipped, click the OK button. Click the Close button in the WinZip Self-Extractor dialog box. Close Windows Explorer.

12. Refer to the Read This Before You Begin page(s) in this book for more details on the Data Files for your text. You are now ready to open the required files.

Macintosh users should use a program to expand WinZip or PKZip archives. Students, ask your instructors or lab coordinators for assistance.

Keep Your Skills Fresh with Quick Reference CourseCards!

Thomson Course Technology CourseCards allow you to easily learn the basics of new applications or quickly access tips and tricks long after your class is complete.

Each highly visual, four-color, six-sided CourseCard features:

- **Basic Topics** enable users to effectively utilize key content.

- **Tips and Solutions** reinforce key subject matter and provide solutions to common situations.

- **Menu Quick References** help users navigate through the most important menu tools using a simple table of contents model.

- **Keyboard Shortcuts** improve productivity and save time.

- **Screen Shots** effectively show what users see on their monitors.

- **Advanced Topics** provide advanced users with a clear reference guide to more challenging content.

Over 75 CourseCards are available on a variety of topics! To order, please visit *www.courseilt.com/ilt_cards.cfm*